Ethics into Action

Ethics into Action

Learning from a Tube of Toothpaste

Peter Singer

ROWMAN & LITTLEFIELD
Lanham • Boulder • New York • London

Published by Rowman & Littlefield
An imprint of The Rowman & Littlefield Publishing Group, Inc.
4501 Forbes Boulevard, Suite 200, Lanham, Maryland 20706
www.rowman.com

6 Tinworth Street, London SE11 5AL

British Library Cataloguing in Publication Information Available

Library of Congress Cataloging-in-Publication Data

Singer, Peter.
    Ethics into action : Learning from a tube of toothpaste/ Peter Singer.
       p. cm.
    Includes bibliographical references and index.
    ISBN 978-1-5381-2389-8 (alk. paper)
    ISBN 978-1-5381-2390-4 (electronic)
    1. Spira, Henry, 1927-. 2. Animal rights activists—United States—Biography.
3. Animal rights movement—United States—History. I. Title.
HV4764.S69S55 1998
179'.3'092—dc21
    [B]   98-6157
                                                                      CIP

♾™ The paper used in this publication meets the minimum requirements of
American National Standard for Information Sciences—Permanence of Paper
for Printed Library Materials, ANSI/NISO Z39.48-1992.

Printed in the United States of America

"If you see something that's wrong, you've got to do something about it."

HENRY SPIRA

Contents

Preface

On April 15, 1980, the *New York Times* ran a startling full-page advertisement. In the middle of the page was a picture of a white rabbit with bandages over both eyes, next to two glass laboratory flasks. Across the top of the page three lines of heavy black type asked a single question: "How many rabbits does Revlon blind for beauty's sake?" The text began under the picture:

> Imagine someone placing your head in a stock. As you stare helplessly ahead, unable to defend yourself, your head is pulled back. Your lower eyelid is pulled away from your eyeball. Then chemicals are poured into the eye. There is pain. You scream and writhe hopelessly. There is no escape. This is the Draize Test. The test which measures the harmfulness of chemicals by the damage inflicted on the unprotected eyes of conscious rabbits. The test that Revlon and other cosmetic firms force on thousands of rabbits to test their products.

The advertisement gave precise figures for the number of rabbits Revlon used. It quoted scientists who said that the test was unreliable and that alternatives to it that did not use animals could be developed. Then it asked readers to write to Revlon's president and report that they would not use Revlon products until Revlon funded a crash program to develop nonanimal eye irritancy tests.

Roger Shelley was Revlon's vice president for investor relations on the day the advertisement appeared. Later he said,

> I knew the stock was going down that day, but more importantly I knew the company had a very significant problem that could affect not just one day's stock price trading, but could cut to the core of the company. In fact if it weren't really well handled, it would have such a deleterious effect that

it could theoretically wipe Revlon off the face of the counter in drugstores and department stores.

Shelley was soon put in charge of the unenviable task of handling the problem. A smooth-voiced, immaculately groomed, and elegantly dressed representative of a corporation that prides itself on its refined image, he soon found himself talking to Henry Spira, a bushy-haired New York high school teacher who spoke with a broad accent that came from years spent on ships as a sailor in the merchant marine and on the General Motors assembly line in New Jersey. Shelley saw that Henry's clothes were crumpled, that he rarely wore a tie, and that when he did, he seemed incapable of getting it to meet his collar. But that wasn't all that Shelley noticed: "There was not one ounce of product on his body that was produced by an animal, and that included his belt, that included shoes, that included everything. Here was a man who did what he said he would do."

Does living according to your beliefs help you to win a battle with a billion-dollar corporate giant? Could there be a more unequal contest than this one, which pitted a high school teacher working out of his own apartment against the flagship of the cosmetics industry? Those who had studied Henry's past record, however, would not have dismissed his prospects of success. They would have known that he had already tackled FBI director J. Edgar Hoover, corrupt union bosses buttressed by hired thugs, the august American Museum of Natural History in New York City, and the New York state legislature. If he had not always got what he wanted, his record was improving. So it was to prove in this case. Before the year was over, Revlon agreed to donate $750,000 to Rockefeller University for a three-year research project aimed at finding nonanimal alternatives to testing cosmetics on the eyes of rabbits. It was the first step toward putting the words "Not tested on animals" on cosmetic products.

For more than a century, antivivisection societies had been campaigning against animal experiments without having the slightest impact. They were dismissed as cranks. While they put out their strongly worded leaflets condemning animal experimentation, the number of animals used in research grew from a few hundred a year to an estimated 20 million. Yet in his very first campaign, Henry brought to an end a series of experiments that involved examining the sexual behavior of mutilated cats. From there he went on to tackle such organizations as Revlon, Avon, Bristol-Myers, the Food and Drug Administration, and Procter & Gamble. Turning then to the even more intractable problem of the suffering of animals used for food, he targeted the chicken producer Frank Perdue, several major slaughtering companies, the U.S. Department of Agriculture, and McDonald's. In twenty years, his unique campaigning methods have done more to reduce animal suffering than anything done in the previous fifty years by vastly larger organizations with millions of dollars at their disposal.

Indirectly, I played a role in these events. It was my article "Animal Liberation," published in the *New York Review of Books* in 1973, that made Henry think seriously of animals as a group in need of someone to act on its behalf. More effectively than anyone else, he has taken my ideas and forged them into a weapon for reducing the pain and suffering that animals must endure. I have written this book to show how he has done it. An account of Henry's life as a campaigner can serve as a handbook for activists, not just in the animal movement, but for many other ethical causes as well. But that is not the only reason why I find the story of Henry's life worth telling. It serves as a counterexample to two pervasive and dispiriting assumptions about what we can do with our lives.

The first of these assumptions is that society has become too big and too complex for an individual to make a difference unless, perhaps, that individual has extraordinary wealth or the good fortune to rise to the top of a major organization. After all, our societies consist of tens or hundreds of millions of people. Our governments are tied down in bureaucracy and fear doing anything that could lose them votes. Multinational corporations, with annual profits running into billions of dollars and advertising budgets to match, wield such formidable power over public opinion that the biggest organizations of consumers cannot hope to match them. How, then, could an individual possibly bring about any significant change?

Henry's victory over Revlon did not require wealth or the leadership of a large organization. It came from applying insights gained over four decades spent working on the side of the weak and exploited, learning from others what strategies are likely to succeed and trying them out. Knowledge of that kind is empowering. It can be passed on to others who will use it in the same way, adding to it and adapting it to the circumstances they face.

The second dispiriting but pervasive assumption to which Henry's life is a counterexample is that our lives are essentially meaningless. With religious belief widely regarded as irrelevant, all that seems to be left for us is to take our values from the assumptions of the culture around us. Since ours is a culture based on pursuing endless opportunities for more and more consumption and spending, we assume that the pursuit of self-interest is the only reasonable goal for anyone, and we understand self-interest in narrowly materialist terms. In this quest for material wealth, some succeed and some fail. Those who fail and find their lives lacking in fulfillment assume (naturally enough) that they are unhappy because they are not rich; but the remarkable thing is that those who succeed in acquiring wealth are often equally unfulfilled.

Henry is not religious and he lacks many of the material possessions that most of us take for granted, but he finds life fulfilling and enjoyable. Over the years, when I have stayed with him in his rent-controlled New York apartment, I have never found him bored, depressed, or at loose ends. Unlike many New Yorkers I know, he has never been to a psychoanalyst or any other kind of psychotherapist. I didn't realize just how remarkable this was until, in researching this book, I learned that his mother was mentally ill for much of her life, and in his nuclear family of five, there were three attempted suicides, two of them successful.

Henry's life can serve, therefore, as an example of a way of finding meaning in one's life by living in accordance with one's own values. In an age in which the people we admire are models, sports stars, self-made multi-millionaires, and movie stars, we need some alternative role models. Henry is one.

But that is not all. Henry's work can teach us how to make our ethical views become more than words—how to put them into action, so that they have an impact on the world. It is hard to imagine anything more important than that.

Preface to the 2019 Edition

*H*enry Spira achieved something that no one else had ever done. Starting with a handful of individuals meeting in his apartment, he built a movement that could take on giant corporations and persuade or pressure them to stop inflicting vast amounts of unnecessary suffering on animals. He started with a small target because he needed to prove that he could achieve a real success, but after that he was continually raising his sights, seeking larger targets where success would be more difficult, but would achieve more.

Henry's methods were drawn from a lifetime of working for the powerless and the exploited. As a young man, he thought about exploited people, and sought to help them, whether they were African Americans denied their civil rights in the South; his fellow merchant seamen, sold out by the corrupt boss of the National Maritime Union; or disadvantaged kids struggling to get a decent education in New York City schools. Only when Henry was approaching fifty did he realize that nonhuman animals are the most powerless of all, and the most ruthlessly exploited. He then applied what he had learned from his struggles for exploited people to the cause of reducing animal suffering.

Henry had strong feelings about those who oppressed either humans or animals, but he never let his feelings override his judgment of how best to end that oppression. He knew that attacking his adversaries for the sake of venting one's feelings and making a lot of noise accomplishes nothing and can be counterproductive. He spent a lot of time in thinking through his plans, explaining them to trusted advisers and inviting them to find flaws. When he was ready to start a campaign against a corporation or other institution, he was always courteous to his adversaries, trying to convince them that it was also in their interests to do what is right.

Toward the end of his life, Henry became concerned that the lessons he had learned about how to help the weak and exploited should not die with him, but be passed on to new generations of activists. He lived long enough to see the first edition of this book and to know that those lessons would not be lost.

In the United States, Henry's methods have been used to great effect, in large part because animal activists who knew and admired him rose to prominence in the animal movement. They observed the successes Henry's campaigns achieved, and they adapted his tactics to their own situations. Campaigns drawing on those methods continue to lead to major successes, including a 2015 commitment by McDonald's to phase out the use of eggs from caged hens. That is, as Henry would have said, "no small item." McDonald's uses 2 billion eggs a year. In Henry's time, virtually all U.S. laying hens were in cages, and such a change, though obviously desirable, was out of reach. Henry knew that once McDonald's moved to improve animal welfare, many other corporations would follow. That happened, and is continuing to happen, with many fast food outlets, supermarket chains, and catering corporations now pledged to phase out their use or sale of eggs from caged hens.

Similar campaigns have had success throughout the English-speaking world and in some European countries as well. What would have surprised—and pleased—Henry is the major impact that his ideas have had in France. In a country where *pâté de foie gras* is regarded as one of the nation's prized cultural achievements, to be concerned about the welfare of animals who end up being part of gastronomy is to risk being seen as unpatriotic. Yet France is changing. The catalyst for these changes has been a French organization named L214 Éthique et Animaux. The name L214 refers to the article in the French rural code that lays down that animals are sentient beings who should be treated with respect. In just a few years L214 has grown into the largest and most vocal French advocate for animals. Its campaigns have succeeded in persuading dozens of French supermarket chains to phase out the sale of eggs from caged hens.

The founders of L214, Brigitte Gothière and Sébastien Arsac acknowledge that their inspiration came from Henry Spira, who they learned about through this book. "For many years, France was rather backwards in terms of its thinking of animals," Arsac told the *New York Times* in 2018, "but L214 has made a lot of progress based on the methods of Spira, who showed the animal movement that it was possible to win against big corporations and revered institutions."

Gothière and Arsac were so convinced of the value of this book, not only for animal activists but for activists working for people or for the environment, that they persuaded Goutte d'Or, a small French publisher, to bring the book out in a French translation. Their intriguing title —*Théorie du tube de dentifrice*, which translates as *Theory of the tube of toothpaste*— caters to, even if it smiles at, the French love of "theory" and refers to Henry's comparison between trying to change a corporation's behavior and getting toothpaste out of a blocked tube. In each case, success will depend on how bad the blockage is, and how much pressure you can exert. *Théorie du tube de dentifrice* was an instant hit in the French media. Not only did it sell very well, it also won the Fondation de 30 millions d'amis 2018 prize for the best nonfiction work relating animals.

At a time when many progressives are despairing about political developments and asking themselves what they can do, I believe that the next generation of activists can draw hope from the life and work of a remarkable man. During the Occupy movement that began in New York's Zuccotti Park in 2011, I could not help compare its vague rhetoric, amorphous targets, and lack of any focused strategies with Henry's careful selection of achievable goals and precise planning to achieve those goals. I was not surprised that, despite the far larger number of people who were active in the Occupy movement than in anything Henry ever did, the movement eventually dissipated without achieving any of its aims.

To bring about change, we need to have victories, to encourage activists to get involved and bring about further successes. That is true whether we are concerned with economic inequality, or climate change, or factory farming. Henry's methods are applicable to all these causes, as long as the target is one that can be achieved by a series of discrete steps. So, for example, Henry would not have campaigned simply to "Stop Climate Change," desirable as that goal would be, but for a specific step that would reduce greenhouse gas emissions. He might have started a campaign against a corporation that is using or promoting the use of fossil fuels in an especially egregious manner, failing to use renewable energy where it can. Ideally, the target corporation would be associated with a leading consumer brand. Henry would then contact the corporation, asking to meet with executives to discuss their energy policy. As an incentive, he might have sent them some drafts of ads he had prepared exposing the company's large contributions to global warming and linking that to the brand in a manner that would damage its image. He would have urged the executives to set an example by reducing their use or promotion of fossil fuels, and increasing their use of renewables. If the corporation did not respond adequately, the next step would have been a campaign to publicize the harm they are doing to our planet and all who will live in it, and to link that to their brand.

If you are an activist on the side of the weak and powerless, you have in your hands a tool to become more effective. Make good use of it.

Peter Singer
Princeton, New Jersey

Acknowledgments

$\mathcal{W}$ithout the enthusiastic cooperation of its principal subject, this book would never have been written. So thanks, Henry, for the many days we spent talking about your life, the way you planned and carried out your campaigns, and your view of the world—and for providing me with access to your extraordinary collection of files containing your correspondence and other material on each issue you have taken up. Nor should I forget the more personal items you passed on to me, such as the long letter your mother wrote to you in 1954, which gave her view of your character and of the circumstances in which you left home at the age of sixteen. Thanks, too, for putting me in touch with your sister Renee and many other people who have known you at different times in your life.

For their willingness to be interviewed, either in person or by phone, and in some cases more than once, I am grateful to Renee Bloch, Berta Green Langston, Gaston Firmon-Guyon, Mary Wilbert, Dolores McCullough, Renee Landau, Nicholas Wade, Susan Fowler, Elinor Molbegott, Barnaby Feder, Mark Graham, Myron Mehlman, Andrew Rowan, Helaine Lerner, Barbara Clapp, Roger Shelley, and Temple Grandin. Some of these interviews were recorded on videotape by Julie Akeret or John Swindells, and transcribed by Susan Wein. I thank them for their assistance. Thanks also to Chaiya Amir, John Black, Sue Leary, Nachum Meyers, Jerry Silverman, and Robin Walker for corresponding with me about Henry.

Mark Graham, Elinor Molbegott, Andrew Rowan, and Renata Singer read over the manuscript and provided me with helpful comments. Henry Spira also checked it and was always ready to provide me with further documents to fill any gaps I had in my account of events. Katherine Stitzel of Procter

& Gamble provided me with detailed information on that corporation's policies and activities regarding alternatives to the use of animals in testing and research.

A chance meeting at an environmental ethics conference with James Sterba led me to Rowman & Littlefield, for which he is a series editor. For that fortunate suggestion I am most grateful. The enthusiasm of Maureen MacGrogan, as editor, and Robin Adler as assistant editor has been wonderful, and Dorothy Bradley and Cindy B. Nixon have done sterling work as production editor and copyeditor, respectively.

I am grateful to Helga Kuhse, director of the Centre for Human Bioethics, and Marian Quartly, Dean of Arts at Monash University, for supporting my request to switch to a part-time position, without which I would still be trying to find the time to write this book.

The Buildup

It is like collecting material for a big work. But the work has to follow, otherwise the preliminary experience is lost. Up to now it was a rich life but it was like the first act of a play, the buildup.

Margit Spira, Letter to Henry Spira, 1954

EUROPEAN ROOTS

Henry Spira was born in Antwerp, Belgium, in June 1927, the first child of Maurice and Margit. The family was Jewish, and Henry's grandfathers were both rabbinical scholars. In addition to his French name (spelled "Henri"), he was given a Hebrew name, Noah, after a great-grandfather. His parents later had two daughters: Renee was five years younger than Henry, and Susan was fourteen years younger.

Maurice Spira was born in Belgium to immigrant parents who had arrived near the end of the nineteenth century. Maurice's father came from Poland and his mother from Hungary. The oldest of ten children, Maurice worked with his father in the diamond trade. Henry describes his father's own views as "cynical, somewhat nihilist." His mother later said that what Henry's father taught him was that "nothing is worthwhile, nobody is good. The only positive values are success and money."[1] Henry sees his father differently: as an independent spirit, so crushed by circumstances and traditions that he was able to get little pleasure out of life.

Henry's mother was born in Hungary. When she was still a small child, the family moved to Germany, where her father, Samuel Spitzer, became chief

1

rabbi of Hamburg. She trained to be a schoolteacher and did some student teaching, but at the age of twenty she married Maurice Spira, moved to Belgium, and did not work again. The marriage, in accordance with traditional Jewish practice, was arranged through a matchmaker. Margit's view of the world contrasted with that of Maurice. In a long letter she wrote to Henry in 1954, she said: "I still believe in the good in men. Maybe it is naif as Daddy tells me; maybe he is more realistic." The letter goes on to suggest to Henry that he got his belief in the possibility of people changing for the better from her. Henry, however, is anything but naive. The outlook he was to develop is a surprisingly successful blend of his father's cynicism and his mother's belief in a latent goodness in human beings that can be brought out in the right circumstances.

The family was, at first, financially comfortable. Henry had a nanny and was educated at a French-speaking *lycée*. Summer holidays were spent at a Belgian beach resort. Of this period in Belgium, Henry remembers more about his nanny than about his mother. Margit found Henry an easy child to bring up. In her 1954 letter, she expressed puzzlement at the "hate of authority" that she saw in her adult son considering his past:

> As a child I had never trouble with you abiding by authority or law. . . .
> [Problems were solved] not by force, but by working them out in mutual
> confidence. I was often astonished how few conflicts arose. You got along

Henry at the age of two, at the Belgian seaside with his parents.

perfectly well with all your teachers, with group leaders . . . with Uncle Eli, Uncle Alex, me and Daddy up to that time. We never had a problem concerning obedience. Do you remember ever having been punished or scolded or even being seriously disapproved of?

Henry may have got along well with everyone, but the family was not close. He recalls: "There was never any hugging, or any of that sort of stuff . . . it just wasn't part of the scenery." Margit wrote that she "always had the fear of attaching myself too much to my children," and for that reason, "I must have suppressed any outward signs of love toward you and Renee."

Margit spent long periods in institutions suffering from severe depression and episodes of irrationality. When she was lucid, she suffered greatly from being aware of the times when she was not. She attempted suicide on several occasions. During one of her stays in a mental hospital, in 1937, Henry was sent away for a year to live with his uncle Eli—a rabbi—and aunt in London. While he was in London, his father abruptly left Belgium for Central America. Why he did so is unclear. There are stories that he was in some kind of trouble, either with a bank or with the law. One version is that he had been the victim of a con artist and was in financial difficulty. Henry thinks that he may just have been trying to make his fortune in the New World.[2] In any case, from 1937–1938, while Maurice was in Central America preparing for his family to join him, Margit took Henry's sister Renee, then about five years old, to Hamburg, where her family was still living, and arranged for Henry to be sent to her there. In Hamburg, Margit and her children waited for Maurice to send word that they should set sail for the New World. Though Germany under the Nazis was hardly a good place for Jews to be at the time, they tried to live a normal Jewish life. Henry began to learn Hebrew and became part of a Jewish youth group where he learned carpentry, a skill that he never forgot. The family was still in Hamburg on *Kristallnacht,* November 9, 1938, the night on which synagogues were burned, Jewish shops and residences had their windows smashed, and many Jews were beaten, rounded up, and sent to concentration camps.

Soon afterward, Maurice wrote saying that the family should come to Panama. Margit and her two children booked passage on a ship and joined Maurice, now established as a small trader. Henry, who had spoken French and German at home and picked up English in London, went to a Catholic school run by nuns and learned Spanish, too. If this sounds like a difficult childhood, Henry's recollection is different:

I adjusted well to the varieties of circumstances. I had an independent spirit, and I didn't question how come or why, I just figured I was here, I got to make the best of it, and I think I did. I had to depend on developing my own value system because the various ones I encountered—one was super-religious, one was atheist—were mutually exclusive.

PANAMA

Maurice had a store in Panama that sold cheap clothing and rings to sailors passing through the Panama Canal. Henry helped with the business and made a little extra money selling the stamps that he had collected for several years before coming to Panama. The store's takings fluctuated. Once, when the business was doing badly, the family moved into a basement room in a mansion that was the home of a wealthy landlord Maurice knew. This led to an incident that made an indelible impression on the twelve-year-old Henry:

> I got talking to people in the mansion, and then this guy invited me to go with him when he went collecting rents. And here we were living in this enormous mansion, taking up a whole city block, and there were these people living in pitiful slums, and these two guys come up there with pistols, collecting the rent. And basically, that's how the landlord enriched himself, and I sort of felt that this wasn't right, this wasn't the way it should be. There wasn't a whole lot I could do about it. But I think it was a turning point in my life. I identified with those who get pushed around.

According to his sister, though, it was their own family life that led Henry to identify with those who got pushed around. Renee, Henry, and Margit had been apart from Maurice for a long time. Now Renee found him an unbearable tyrant: "My father was big and strong and loud, and it was endless. My mother was pathetic and couldn't defend herself against him. It was like a soap opera . . . it was just a nightmare." Renee looked up to Henry as her protector and remembers him as a wonderful older brother. She hated the Catholic school they both went to, but this ceased to be a problem when Maurice's business went badly, because after that, he could not afford to pay the fees. For almost a year, the children did not attend school. Instead, Henry worked in his father's store and spent time talking to the seamen who came in there.

AMERICA

When Henry was thirteen, Maurice succeeded in getting a U.S. visa, and in December 1940, the family sailed for New York via Havana on the SS *Copiapo*. Margit later described her feelings:

When we arrived with the boat, all the refugees coming from Havana, though mostly younger than I, were much depressed. They were afraid of starting a new life without money. The future seemed to have very little or no hope. I was astonished that I was so hopeful. What did I have to fear? I had my husband, my children. I was used to getting along with the bare necessities. Naturally, I would like to have a little more. Maybe we would have a chance to live comfortably as we did before. What luck to be in America where you have all the opportunities.

The family moved into an apartment on West 104th Street, and Henry went to the local public school, PS-165. In the first few weeks after their arrival, Margit's hopes seemed to have been fulfilled:

Daddy earned a living. We went Saturdays shopping with all the money he had made—the whole family together. We bought furniture, a piano, a sewing machine, a desk for you [Henry]. What luxuries! It was fun exploring New York, Broadway, Times Square, auction sales, ferry rides, visits to former friends where I could show off my children.

That year, Henry had his bar-mitzvah and, from the perspective of Jewish law, became a man. He had learned Hebrew in Germany and kept up the study in Panama, finding a teacher himself. In America, he continued to study Hebrew and observe Jewish religious law, wearing the yarmulke, or skullcap. His father objected, fearing, as Margit later explained to Henry, that "you would become too religious and lose respect for him." Nevertheless, Henry continued the Hebrew lessons, paying for them himself with money he had earned during the summer vacation.

Maurice moved into the industrial diamond trade and here found the financial success that had so long eluded him. But success also changed him. Margit wrote later:

He was a different man with the power of building up a business, of making quite a lot of money. It meant concentrating on this one purpose, sometimes 24 hours. When I asked: is it worthwhile? Wouldn't we be happier with a little less? I made him unhappy. I didn't appreciate him . . . To him, money meant more than to other people. It redeemed him in the eyes of the others for past failures.

This led to more conflict in the family. Maurice wanted Henry to take up his lifestyle—to wear a jacket and tie and have friends in the social and economic bracket in which he wanted to move. Henry had very different ideas. Around the end of 1943, while attending Stuyvesant High School, he became involved with a left-wing Jewish youth movement called Hashomer Hatzair. HH, as the movement was known, was Zionist but not religious. It promoted a form of humanistic socialism based on the collective settlements, or kibbutzim, that were being established in Palestine. The movement saw its role as preparing young Jews for lives dedicated to building a socialist community in the harsh environment of Palestine. It demanded dedication and idealism from its members. They had to shed their bourgeois habits and prepare for a life close to nature, in which all were equal and would share the physical labor needed to become self-sufficient. Women did not wear makeup, and men did not wear suits and ties. HH groups went hiking in the country and attended summer camps at which they were taught how to farm. They were strongly antimaterialistic and independently minded, almost—but not quite—to the point of anarchism. Although Henry did not fully accept the Zionism of HH and never saw himself as emigrating to Palestine, the antimaterialism and independence of mind that HH encouraged were to remain with him all his life.

Given Henry's involvement in HH, it is not surprising that he didn't like his father's taste in clothes or friends. When Henry tried to discuss his newfound beliefs with his father, Maurice called him a communist and refused to discuss it further. From this period, Renee recalls "just one scene after another" between Henry and his father. According to Margit, Henry tried hard to resolve the problem:

> You and Renee took all my suggestions for appeasing, making new approaches to have Daddy see things as you saw them. Unfortunately there was no common ground to start and often enough these attempts ended in arguments that Daddy took for an offense against his authority. . . . Instead of making things better, they increased the tension.

Henry was open with his mother and talked freely to her, but that was a problem in itself, because Maurice then accused her of letting Henry do what he wanted without criticizing him in order to hold on to her friendship with him. Margit had believed that parents should show "a united front" in the best interests of the children, but now she found that excusing Maurice's faults meant condemning her son in situations where she did not believe he was wrong. Instead, she took Henry's side:

> I didn't see any wrong in the way you chose your friends and it was no difference if they lived on Riverside Drive or on the Lower East Side. If you did or did not wear a tie or even a jaquet didn't seem to be worth a quarrel. . . . I thought if you were left alone, you would come to your senses and find out yourself that it was stupid to freeze while a good coat hangs in the closet.

But this was not enough for Maurice. The differences in ideas were being played out against a background of changing attitudes to the authority of the father. Maurice was, in Henry's words, "an autocratic patriarch of the Old World," and Henry had shifted to more modern ways of thinking. Margit wrote:

> He asked for 100% subordination. That were his rights in exchange for being such a good provider. You proposed a family group discussion for grievances once a week. Something you had read about in *Parent's Magazine*. He wouldn't have understood the meaning of it even if he would have agreed. There he was expected to treat children as equals, a position he could not accept.

Today, Henry paints a more sympathetic picture, seeing his father as "a man who took total responsibility for what he considered the welfare of his family. He worked very hard, gave up much of his freedom. . . . His independent spirit was largely crushed by circumstances and traditions."

But at sixteen, Henry did not see it that way. To resolve the constant quarreling, Margit suggested seeking professional advice from a Jewish family counseling service. Henry was willing to take part, but Maurice rejected the idea, saying, "Who are they? They do it for the money?" Margit began to hate herself for her weakness: "I could only make objections in a meek voice." She thought of leaving, with her three children. Henry offered to work to support the rest of the family if she left, an offer that Margit said "I would have loved to accept if that could have worked out as easily as you imagined with your good will and your youthful enthusiasm." But she couldn't do it:

> There were women who could earn a living, care for their children if there was the need and what is most important, being emotionally able to do it. Maybe it is an excuse that I was in a strange city, a strange country, had a baby [Susan had been born in 1941] and though I had reason to have grudges against Daddy, was nevertheless emotionally not finished with him.

Since Margit would not leave, Henry told her that he was thinking of leaving on his own. Though he was still in high school, she did not try to dissuade him. Ten years later, she told him how she had felt at the time:

> Maybe no home is better than this home? I was not sure. I had to take a chance. With the responsibility all my own in advising you. I knew I would miss you. You were a great moral support to me, if you knew it or not. Daddy was right that my children were my only friends and my best friends. I think I made an unselfish decision when I agreed to your leaving home. . . . But I didn't see any other way out. I only would pray that the good influences and experiences that shaped your earlier happier life had built your character and strengthened it enough to withstand the bad influences. That you would not fall prey to criminals, alcohol, dope and what else a hostile world had to offer a boy that was not even 17.

Henry took lodgings in a rooming house and found an afternoon job in a machine shop. In the morning, he went to Stuyvesant High School, where classes were taught in two streams, morning and afternoon, and students went to either the morning or afternoon sessions. Maurice threatened to get the police to bring him back, but as Henry was sixteen, it was a threat he could not act on.

From that time on, Henry saw his parents only when he chose to visit them, which wasn't all that often. Renee remembers reminding him to call on their mother's birthday. She understood, however, that he needed to separate himself from his father. The family, minus Henry, subsequently moved out of New York to the more affluent suburbs of Mount Vernon and, later, Bronxville.

INDEPENDENCE

The universal aspirations of socialism are not easy to reconcile with Zionism. Some of Henry's friends in Hashomer Hatzair became interested in other forms of socialism. The highly authoritarian culture of the Communist Party had no appeal for those who had breathed the much freer atmosphere of HH, but the ideas of Leon Trotsky, then Joseph Stalin's foremost communist critic, were more attractive. Henry went with his friends to classes in socialism organized by Trotskyists. He began reading Trotsky and V. I. Lenin, as well as the early Russian Marxist, G. V. Plekhanov. Linking what he read with what he had seen in Panama, he began to see injustice not as a matter of the greed or sadism of particular individuals, but as something more systematic. If you wanted to do something about it, you would have to change the system. He became a socialist, sharing Trotsky's view that Stalin had derailed the idea of a real socialist revolution. As part of this change in his views, he ceased to observe Jewish religious law and stopped wearing a yarmulke.

In HH, people called one another by their Hebrew names, so Henry was known as Noah. Here he is, at seventeen, as recalled by Nachum Meyers, a fellow member of the West Bronx branch of HH:

> Noah was tough. . . . Dealing with him was like chewing a heavy duty rubber band instead of chewing gum; there was little satisfaction in the endeavor. . . . I recall his intense vehemence in defense of whatever point of view he held on any subject under discussion at the moment. . . . The movement provided him, possibly for the first time in his young life, with sharp doctrinaire thinkers and polemicists worthy of his mettle. Here he found opponents who could argue talmudically on the merits of Stalinist

Renee, Susan, and Henry in New York.

socialism against Noah's brilliant adamant Trotskyist analyses. But when the intellectual battle was in question, Noah brought his other weapons into play. His arguments were tidal waves of high intelligence, some knowledge, huge amounts of scorn and often brilliant swordsmanship. . . . Noah would skewer the most doughty defender of Stalin . . . with dripping sarcastic derision and leave them, unconvinced but panting in exasperation and exhaustion. And then he would smile and lick his chops and look for girls.[3]

For a time Henry shared an apartment on Manhattan's Upper West Side with Meyers and another friend, Mordy Sprinsock. Meyers recollects trying, often without success, to get Henry to pay his share of the rent. The trio split up in 1944 when Henry became a supporter of the Socialist Workers Party (SWP), the leading Trotskyist political organization. Through the SWP, he met John Black. Black had grown up in Germany and there joined a German Trotskyist organization. When the Nazis came to power, he fled to England, moving on in 1940 to the United States, where he mixed mostly with other young, left-wing immigrants from Europe. Henry fitted into this category, and Black and Henry hit it off right away. Henry moved into a furnished room next door to Black, at 26 West Eighteenth Street, in Manhattan. Black found Henry willing to work hard, and together they went recruiting for SWP members in the high schools of New York. The results, Black recalls, were "amazing." They ran well-attended weekly meetings of young, left-leaning people. Some of the students went on to be active in the SWP for many years. This work came to an end early in 1945, when Henry became a seaman on merchant ships.

THE MERCHANT MARINE

The merchant marine was a center of militant union activism in America, and there were a lot of Trotskyists in the union, so it was a natural place for an enthusiastic young Trotskyist to go. "At that point we all thought that the trade union movement would help create a new society," Henry said later. But enlisting others in the struggle for a new society didn't prove easy. Meyers recalls Henry after he joined the merchant marine:

> Every so often I would see Noah, wearing a sailor's pea jacket, looking for the girls of HH, telling tales of being beaten up by sailors whose lot he was trying to improve but whose patriotism in wartime led them to believe that unions were undermining the war effort.[4]

Henry is sure that the last part of this is an exaggeration: Even if the sailors didn't all agree with him, they didn't beat him up.

The merchant marine offered other advantages: unlimited travel and exemption from the draft. Not that Henry was avoiding danger entirely. On the Atlantic crossing, many merchant ships had been sunk by German submarines. But Henry was lucky. By the time he got to sea, the Nazis were well on the road to defeat. He saw no military action, and the convoys on which he sailed did not lose any ships.

Once the war was over, Henry worked mostly on ships sailing around the Americas, although he also traveled to Europe and to Africa. His earnings were relatively high, and since he was getting his food and board on ship, he had all the money he needed. He liked walking around in the ports he visited, but he also took pleasure in being at sea. He would get up early and watch the sun rise or walk around the deck. He enjoyed the camaraderie but found that his shipmates also respected his privacy. If he preferred going ashore alone, rather than with a bunch of other sailors who went ashore to get drunk, that was his business. "It was a little bit like the foreign legion. You just do your own thing and don't ask a lot of questions." Under these circumstances, Henry found himself relaxed and at peace with the world. He had plenty of time to read and, during this period, got to know the work of the Russian anarchist Peter Kropotkin, as well as that of such American leftists as Lincoln Steffens and John Reed. He was also an active participant in onboard union meetings.[5]

Apart from his reading, Henry's thinking was most deeply affected by the revelations of the Nazi genocide. His close family, including the relatives he had known in Hamburg, had all left Europe before war broke out, so the impact was not personal but political and ethical. He was troubled by the thought that so many people had stood by and done nothing to stop innocent people from being murdered; and while he had already ceased to be religious before the war ended, after the Holocaust, he thought that for Jews to believe in God "just totally defied common sense."

In 1948, Henry stayed ashore long enough to complete his high school education at Washington Irving Evening High School. Two years later, he began studying for a B.A. at Brooklyn College, but his attendance was intermittent, and he did not complete his degree until 1958. Between voyages, Henry lived at the Seamen's House, at 550 West Twentieth Street. Since he preferred to keep his distance from his parents, he did not leave his belongings with them but stored them in a couple of duffel bags at the Seamen's House. He lived this way until 1958, when he took an apartment at 188 Avenue B, on Manhattan's Lower East Side. The fact that for thirteen years Henry had no permanent place to live meant that he never got into the habit of accumulating possessions. Later, when he had his own apartment, everything in it was always there to serve a purpose. Even the larger three-room apartment on the Upper West Side, where he has lived since 1970, is entirely functional. There are beds, a sofa that converts into a spare bed, a kitchen table that seats two (there is nowhere else to eat: Henry doesn't do any entertaining), and a large dead branch for his cat to climb on. There are some gray metal filing cabinets, but most of Henry's comprehensive filing system is held on shelves made of unpainted planks that cover, from floor to ceiling, the walls of most of the rooms.

Most seamen in the merchant marine belonged to the National Maritime Union (NMU). During the war, it had been dominated by communists who followed Stalin's line—whenever Russian foreign policy changed, their policy changed, too. Henry was among the minority of union members who belonged to the Socialist Workers Party. After the cold war began and Senator Joseph McCarthy started his campaign against communist influence, the communists were thrown out of their leadership positions in the National Maritime Union and a right-wing group took over. The right-wingers joined with the U.S. government to blacklist anyone who had been associated with radical or left-wing politics. There was a routine procedure, before ships sailed, that involved an official of the Coast Guard coming on board every ship to check the seamen's papers and sign the crew on to the ship's articles. In March 1952, when he was about to sail on another ship, Henry gave his seaman's papers to the official as usual, but instead of having them returned, he was handed a sheet of paper that said that his continued presence on an American merchant vessel was "inimical to the security of the U.S. government." He could no longer work on ships. Whereas many of those who were blacklisted took the decision very hard, Henry was philosophical about it: "I just figured it was part of the game: Fight the system and they get even with you."

By a strange bureaucratic quirk, the fact that Henry could no longer work on merchant ships meant that he was liable to be drafted into the army. Henry suggested to his draft board that since his presence on merchant ships was considered inimical to the security of the United States, the nation would be in even more serious trouble if it had him in its army. The board told him that different branches of government had different standards and drafted him anyway.

THE ARMY

Henry became a member of the United States Army in October 1952. He soon found himself out of step, literally, with the rest of his world. Marching and drilling seemed useless to him, and he never quite got it right. This may well have been deliberate, because he had a clear sense of what the drilling was really for:

> We were drilled from "left shoulder arms" to "right shoulder arms." We were marched and counter marched: "Double to rear by the left flank march!" Automatic, instantaneous response to orders was the goal: "Yours is not to question why, yours is but to do and die." The army did not attempt to inspire us. They struggled to make human robots. . . . A draftee was given a toothbrush to clean out the orderly room. Everyone concerned knew it was senseless, but it was meant to tell the new soldier that he does what he is told. . . . There were countless inspections. Everything had to be uniform and in a precise place. Even the soles of boots had to be polished. Like a zombie, the soldier was to be permitted neither consciousness nor spontaneity.[6]

Henry may not have learned to march in step, but he did see the power of an organization to change people:

> The trainees who were being drilled all wondered at the sadism displayed by the drill masters. The question on everyone's lips was: "Where on earth did the army find such bastards?" After basic training was complete, they found out. The army took a number of them, put them through leadership school, showed them a big fist coming out of a star that said "We lead, others follow," and after a few weeks the same people who couldn't imagine anyone being as sadistic as the drill masters they had had were doing exactly the same thing to the new trainees.

When basic training was over, Henry was given an IQ test and did well on it. As a result, when he was sent to Berlin, he was assigned to Troop Information and Education. Essentially, he was there to indoctrinate the troops. He said that a job like that wasn't really his bag, but he was told that it was his, regardless of whether it was his bag or not. He found it the softest job he ever had. For an hour a week, he spoke about news and current affairs to an audience of about two hundred soldiers and discussed some topical issue with them. The rest of the time, he told his superiors, he was unable to do any marching or drilling because he had to prepare for the next talk.

In Berlin, on American army pay, Henry had plenty of money in his pocket. Though the city was divided among the former Allied powers, this was before the Berlin Wall had been built; so during his off-duty hours, he could visit the French sector, the British sector, or the Russian sector. Fluent in English, French, and German, Henry could talk to people everywhere he went. The contrast among sectors was immense. He arrived a few months after the East German uprising of June 1953, when the workers of East Berlin

This photo appeared in The Berlin Observer, *the newspaper of the Berlin Command, December 4, 1953, under the heading "Army Education Chief Praises Program Here." The caption read: "Pvt. Henry Spira . . . briefs Col. Edward R. Ott in the company I&E [Information and Education] Room."*

laid down their tools and took to the streets, only to be crushed a few days later by Soviet tanks. While the demonstrators wanted free elections and the reunification of Germany, the uprising had also been fueled by a shortage of food and consumer goods. Refugees from East Germany were pouring into West Berlin, and Henry went to talk to them at the Tempelhof camp, where they were held until they could be interviewed and assigned refugee status. East German workers told him that the Nazis and communists were all alike—you had to join to keep from getting into trouble—and it was always the officials who benefited, never the guy at the bottom who didn't really know what it was all about.

In October 1954, after two mostly enjoyable years in the army, Henry was given an undesirable discharge for "subversive and disloyal activities" because of his support for left-wing organizations. He protested that the army had known that he was a security risk before they drafted him. With the help of the Workers Defense League, he eventually succeeded in getting the discharge changed to an honorable one. Nevertheless, he left the army as he had entered it, a private.

ON THE ASSEMBLY LINE

Back from the army, and still banned from working on ships, Henry had to decide what he would do next. His mother, writing to him when he was coming to the end of his army service, had suggested that his life up to that point, with its varied experiences and contacts with people from all walks of life, had been "like collecting material for a big work," but "the work has to follow, otherwise the preliminary experience is lost." She thought that on coming out of the army, he should choose a profession, and she mentioned some that she thought matched his abilities. His proficiency with words and his attraction to "sensational happenings" would make him a good news reporter. He could also do well in labor relations because of his "strong sense of justice and fairness" and the fact that "you get well along with people, no matter of [what] rank or economical status." Margit also suggested taking a higher position on a ship, like that of electrical engineer, or becoming a teacher. Less plausibly, perhaps, she saw Henry's capacity for leadership and his "psychological insight" as suiting him for a role as a prison director. What was clearly troubling Margit, however, was a sense that Henry lacked purpose and did not want to succeed in any profession. She traced this attitude to the break with his father:

> It is not the theoretic question if life has any purpose. It is the practical question which purpose do we put into life. It is understandable that life lost its purpose for you at that moment. The picture that you had made of your father through the years had failed. Your family could not mean much to you. You had to find some substitute—Greenwich Village after you left [Ha]Shomer Hatzair, the Merchant Marine, also the Army though you didn't choose it yourself.

Margit was unable to persuade Henry to embark on a career path of the kind she had in mind; but she was wrong if she thought that he was without purpose in his choice of field of work. He was seeking another field in which he could become involved with politically active workers. The workplace that typified the modem industrial age was the automobile assembly line. Henry got a job at the General Motors auto assembly plant in Linden, New Jersey, across the river from New York, and found that it lived up to its reputation:

> I was working on an auto assembly line installing the rear bumper, harness clips, generator wires and nuts. Every minute and a quarter another car came by. At union meetings there were angry demands that something be done about the speedup, since we didn't have time to get a drink from the water fountain ten feet away. The men were filing overwork grievances and getting reprimands for "not showing sufficient effort" in return.[7]

In this situation, the union was not a lot of use. Henry learned that there were ways of righting wrongs that did not involve the established institutions:

> There was this Hungarian fellow who was working on quarter panels down there. He was a superb worker, he really was into cars, there wasn't any job he couldn't do, and he was able to shut down the whole plant by himself. If there was a grievance he would get his little area to stop working and that would just close down the whole plant. This fellow didn't even attend union meetings. He just figured unions were, like from nowhere, and if [the workers] had a grievance they would take it up themselves and just deal with it right on the spot, on the floor. That gave me the idea that sometimes you can have power without being part of the organization.

Henry worked on the assembly line from early 1955 until mid-1956. He found that assembly line work tended to burn him out, but it was still easier for him to take than for most of the workers. Without a mortgage and family responsibilities, he didn't need to earn the kind of money he was making. He was there largely for the experience and the education he was getting, and when he really felt he needed a break or wanted to do something else, he got a note from a doctor and took time off without pay. But after about eighteen months at General Motors, Henry decided that having a university degree would give him a bit more flexibility in looking for work. He went back to Brooklyn College and completed the degree he had begun in 1950. But he made no immediate use of it. He worked for a time at night at Bellevue Hospital as an assistant for a research project on premature infants, and then in 1959 he took a job as a social investigator for the New York City Department of Welfare. Around this time civil liberties groups succeeded in lawsuits against the blacklisting of merchant seamen, and he went back to work on ships.

THE CIVIL RIGHTS MOVEMENT

Throughout this period, Henry continued to be involved with the Socialist Workers Party, though he found branch meetings largely pointless and avoided them. His major activity was writing for the party's weekly newspaper, *The Militant*. In October 1955, on one of his breaks from the General Motors assembly line, he went to New Castle, Indiana, to cover a strike that led to the governor of Indiana calling up the National Guard and declaring martial law. *The Militant* ran his article as its front-page lead, under the byline Henry Gitano—"Gitano" being Spanish for "gypsy"—because Henry thought it prudent not to be widely known to be a member of the SWP.[8]

In December 1955, Rosa Parks, a middle-aged African American seam-stress from Montgomery, Alabama, refused to obey a bus driver's order to move to seats reserved for blacks at the back of the bus. When she was charged with an offense, Montgomery blacks boycotted the buses. Five months later, blacks in Tallahassee, Florida, also boycotted their segregated bus service after two young black women were arrested for demanding a refund of their fare rather than vacate their seats to whites as segregation laws required.

In June 1956, Henry went to Montgomery and Tallahassee to see for himself what was happening. Arriving in Tallahassee a few days after the boycott began, Henry attended a mass meeting. He saw and felt more than a thousand people shake the walls of the hall with applause in favor of the motion that "When you pay your fare, you can sit anywhere you want." At a similar meeting in Montgomery, he heard the president of the Montgomery Improvement Association, a young minister named Dr. Martin Luther King Jr., tell another enthusiastic audience, "We've got a long, long way to go to get our first-class citizenship. Nothing will stop us." A thousand voices responded, "Nothing, Lord, nothing."[9] King told Henry: "The idea of the Montgomery Improvement Association will spread, for the Negro has proven that he can unite and organize to gain his self-respect."

When Henry had returned to New York after covering the New Castle strike, someone at *The Militant* asked him, "What did the people say?" That comment made him realize that the task of a good journalist isn't just to pass on the official statements that both sides put out, but to listen to the people involved in what was happening, to find out what makes them do what they are doing, why they do it, and how they feel about it. Now he put that lesson into practice. In Tallahassee, he talked with the Reverend C. K. Steele, president of the Inter-Civic Council, which had been set up to coordinate the protest. Steele told him that some of those whom whites considered the black leaders of the protest had in fact been hesitant to demand the end of segregation on the buses, but the mass meetings had insisted that nothing less be demanded. Henry wanted to get these people to say in their own words how they felt about what was happening and what they were doing. In an article written in December 1956, when the black people of Tallahassee had been boycotting buses for seven months, he quoted a domestic servant who, after finishing for the day, had a two-hour walk home: "I walk steady along. My hardest trouble is the hill after the depot. I got a little song in my heart and I just keep walking."

Another heavy-built woman said: "The first day when I got to work, my feet was big as my body, I was so tired. My ankles have been swollen ever since I started walking. I'm gonna walk until things get better. . . . I'm doing very well walking. I haven't been on a bus since the 28th of May."[10]

Henry was moved by the spirit of something new happening to people who had been at the bottom of the heap all their lives. People who had never spoken publicly stood up at church meetings, shared their stories with others, and felt empowered just by the fact that people listened to them. African Americans of all ages came to literacy classes, eager for new opportunities. It had never occurred to them before that anything they learned could make a difference. Now they had enormous hope that things could change.

The Montgomery bus boycott received national attention and was supported financially by opponents of segregation all over the country, but the Tallahassee boycott was not such big news and its organizers had little money. Henry went back to New York to see what he could do to help. With him he took a letter from Reverend Steele stating that he was "a friend of the Inter-Civic Council" and "authorized to tell you and your organization of the efforts of the Negro people of Tallahassee to secure equal rights in city bus transportation." The letter also authorized Henry to seek financial help for the council but asked that contributions be mailed directly to the group in Florida. Using this letter as an introduction, in May 1957, Henry spoke at the Freedom Fund Dinner sponsored by the Labor and Industry Committee of the Brooklyn branch of the National Association for the Advancement of Colored People (NAACP), the purpose of which was to establish a closer relationship between the trade union movement and the NAACP. By this time, the struggle to desegregate the buses had been won, as a result of a federal court ruling that barred segregation on public carriers. But the bus boycott had been only the spark for a broader fight for equal rights for African Americans in every area of life, and Henry spoke as a representative of the Tallahassee Inter-Civic Council about that struggle. With him on the platform were leaders of the United Auto Workers and other major unions. Henry persuaded union officials and civil rights organizations to send some money to Tallahassee and worked to encourage the union movement to give more support generally for the movement against segregation. Most of his articles on the Tallahassee boycott ended with an address to which donations could be sent.

In the South, state police stood by while white racists terrorized blacks who stood up for their rights. Civil rights leaders called for the federal government to step in and enforce the law. When the Eisenhower administration took no action, the civil rights movement decided on a "Prayer Pilgrimage" to Washington. Through articles in *The Militant,* Henry helped rally unionists to support this first mass demonstration in Washington against racism in the South. On May 17, 1957, an estimated 27,000 people from all over the United States gathered to hear Martin Luther King speak, together with A. Philip Randolph, president of the Brotherhood of Sleeping Car Porters, and

Roy Wilkins, the veteran leader of the NAACP. Henry traveled down from New York on a "freedom train" chartered by various unions.

> There was a joyous mood. Singing, from spirituals to calypso to Mexican love songs, filled the coaches. I asked a District 65 [a New York section of the Retail, Wholesale, and Department Store Union] member about the spirited atmosphere: "Everyone is happy doing what they are doing. They are doing it with their heart. This should have been done a long time ago. It's the same fight all over the USA."[11]

Over the next few years, while Henry was involved in many other activities, he kept up his links with the civil rights struggle. In 1963, he went to Mississippi to report on the movement to register African-American voters. By now, the scene had changed. Local African Americans were no longer on their own. There was something known only as "the Movement." It consisted of young activists, both white and black, from groups like the Congress of Racial Equality and the Student Non-Violent Coordinating Committee (SNCC), who would go where they were needed to work for racial equality. In Canton, Mississippi, Henry spoke to one of these activists at a voter registration center:

> A young lady, Miss Barbara Tompkins, whose very eyes flash with determination and courage, said: "I'll tell you how to start your story: This was formerly a pool hall. As long as the Negroes used this place to play, it was safe. As soon as we started using it as a voter registration place it was wrecked."
>   In Madison County, where there are 29,630 Negroes and 9,267 whites but only about 300 registered Negroes, the police vigorously defend what they consider Dixie's most precious constitutional right—the humiliation and terrorizing of Negroes who comprise 76 percent of the community.[12]

In another article, Henry chronicles the reign of terror inflicted by Southern whites on blacks in Leflore County, Mississippi. He describes beatings of blacks by whites that are ignored by police and beatings of blacks by local police that are ignored by FBI agents. He quotes a sharecropper who, with his fourteen children, was evicted from the plantation he had farmed on for thirteen years because he refused to take his name off the register of voters. And he describes how, as he headed for the black part of town, he was himself stopped by police:

> The police asked for my identification. When and how did I get into town? Was I with Snick [the SNCC] . . . or the NAACP?
>   I explained that I was a reporter. Was I going to write for a white or a Negro publication? Where was I staying? and then, what room? I thought

there must be some mistake and I innocently repeated "What room?" The police replied laconically: "Yes—just in case something happens to you."[13]

This article ends by describing a youth workshop at which some people said they had learned more in one week than during years of attending public school:

> In discussions, the youth utilize all their intellectual resources, and when they sing, it's from deep in the heart. The students sang an old Negro spiritual, "Oh oh freedom, Oh oh freedom over me, And before I'd be a slave, I'll be buried in my grave, And go home to my Lord and be free." Then, as we clasped our neighbors' hands, the meeting ended with, "Oh deep in my heart, I do believe, We shall overcome some day."[14]

In the summer of 1964, Henry went to St. Augustine, a Florida beach resort where African Americans were attempting to integrate restaurants, motels, and beaches. They were subjected to a reign of terror from the Ku Klux Klan, with police connivance. Henry's first experience of St. Augustine was not encouraging:

> Getting off the bus, I asked a friendly looking white youth the way to the center of town. At the sight of a stranger, he scowled and replied ominously: "What you all going to do down there? You're Jewish, ain't you? If you are, you might never make it to the Plaza."[15]

Henry talked to African Americans taking part in direct action and to white freedom fighters who had traveled from all over the United States to support them. He also spoke to one of the white defenders of the status quo, the manager of a segregated motel, who blamed all the troubles on "outside agitators" who had disturbed the "harmonious relations" that had previously existed between the races. Then Henry watched civil rights marchers being greeted with cries like "Kill the black apes" and saw police standing by while marchers were assaulted:

> Acid was hurled in the face of a 14-year-old Negro girl and a number of marchers were beaten. . . . A racist attempted to yank a white marcher from the line and a Negro march captain blocked the attempt by placing his own body between them. The Negro was arrested.[16]

THE FBI

In the 1950s, the Federal Bureau of Investigation seemed an unchallengeable pillar of American society. To criticize the FBI, especially its director, J. Edgar Hoover, was to immediately make one's own loyalty suspect, to such an extent that the *New York Post* was moved to state in an editorial: "The issue is whether public criticism of FBI director Hoover is to be considered evidence of treason."[17]

The FBI had its tentacles everywhere. It infiltrated all leftist groups; a joke that made the rounds among SWP members was: "How can you pick which member of the party is the FBI agent?" "He's the one who stays awake at meetings." Since the FBI was checking up on everyone else, Henry decided to do some checking on Hoover and the FBI—and to write a series of articles for *The Militant* on the topic. With a thoroughness that was to become one of his trademarks, he spent about six months gathering materials before he started writing. He read widely, and he talked to anyone he could find who had had a negative experience with the FBI. He went to see black organization leaders who had been struggling for civil rights and had compiled dossiers on how the FBI had helped racists by denying blacks their rights.

The Militant launched the FBI series on December 8, 1958, with an article headed "J. Edgar Hoover, Chief of Thought-Police." The theme of the series is set out in the opening paragraph of the first article:

> The FBI's highly publicized "gang-busting" activity serves as a facade for its primary function: the political policing, through stoolpigeons, perjurers, frame-ups and dossiers by the millions, of all thought which could be dangerous to a crisis-ridden social order. The true role of the FBI is to engineer the witch-hunt.

The article then supports this thesis by analyzing Hoover's own writings and tracing his career back to 1919, when he was made head of the newly established General Intelligence Division, an organization formed to investigate radicals.

The series eventually ran to twelve articles, ending in June 1959. The second article describes the vast system of files that the FBI keeps on Americans who are not involved in any criminal activity. The third shows that FBI informers reach even into the White House and points to the absurdity of some of their allegations (e.g., one informer claimed that there were 126 communists employed on the Sunday section of the *New York Times,* although the entire Sunday section staff consisted of only 90 people). The fourth article documents the vilification of the few people who had the temerity to criticize the FBI—a risk that Henry knew he was running himself.

The fifth article in the series was based on a novel investigative technique: In January 1959, Henry went on a guided tour of FBI headquarters. Together with a group of other tourists, he was shown various FBI "souvenirs," including the cigar that John Dillinger was smoking on the night he was cornered and shot by FBI agents in Chicago. The tour also included the laboratories where bloodstains are examined and the six-story Identification Building, which covers an entire block and contained 150,965,472 fingerprint cards at the time. The group was given a pamphlet called "The Story of the FBI," which focused on the heroism of its agents:

> Mortally wounded in a gun battle with a notorious criminal . . . the Agent regained consciousness on the operating table. . . . Told that the criminal had been killed on the spot, the Agent murmured with his dying breath, "May God have mercy on his soul."

When the time came for questions, however, Henry was more interested in what he had seen of the FBI in the South than in the courage of its agents. There are two accounts of the questions Henry asked on that day. The first, briefer one comes from Henry's subsequent article in *The Militant*:

> I decided to ask our guide about the FBI record in the South where crime against Negroes is rampant. "How come the FBI can't catch kidnappers, arsonists and bombers in the South?"
>
> The guide seemed prepared for questions like that. "Maybe they're not federal cases."
>
> I argued with him. "A man's constitutional freedoms, which are federal, are seriously infringed, aren't they, when he is murdered for voting or defending his human dignity?"
>
> This flustered the FBI spokesman. "Maybe," he answered, "the FBI is working on it but is not giving away its hand."
>
> (The truth is, of course, in view of the years of terror in Dixie, that the FBI is either completely incompetent or else it doesn't give a damn. Or else its real job, as more and more people are beginning to understand, is to serve American big business as a political police.)[18]

The second account comes from Henry's FBI file, which he later obtained under freedom of information legislation. This four-page report, written on the day of the tour, summarizes the question-and-answer session between Henry and a special agent whose name has been blanked out. Henry began by asking why the FBI was not conducting investigations in connection with the bombings and kidnappings in the South. The special agent asked Henry who he was, and "[Spira] stated that he is on a confidential assignment and that he is a 'leg man' for someone." The agent pressed Henry on this, but "he would not reveal for whom he was working and he was, therefore, dealt with most circumspectly." Henry did say one thing, however, that interested the Bureau:

> As [name deleted] was escorting Spira to the Crime Records Section, Spira said in effect, "I have got one suggestion for Hoover. His people congre-

gate in the cafeteria downstairs and in the restaurant across the street, the 'Hi-Boy' and they discuss their business." Spira told [name deleted] that he was at the "Hi-Boy" this morning.

There is a handwritten note on the report at this point: "We ought to discreetly check this"; then, in a different hand, "Yes. H." A subsequent memo confirms that the approval came from Hoover. The report concludes with a brief summary of information on Henry, which shows that he was already on the Security Index as a member of the Socialist Workers Party and, under the pen name Henry Gitano, was the author of the series of articles about the FBI appearing in *The Militant*. At the end of the report, there is another handwritten comment:

> I think it is a waste of time and lowers FBI prestige to answer such questions propounded in such a manner even though we don't know the background of the individual. It would have been sufficient to refer him to the "FBI Story" in a curt manner to indicate we haven't the time to spend listening to such dribble. H.[19]

Although *The Militant* had only a small readership—according to an FBI internal memo it had 785 subscribers[20]—the fact that it dared to attack Hoover and the FBI outraged Walter Winchell, a nationally syndicated columnist. In *Columbia,* the monthly magazine of the Knights of Columbus that proudly proclaimed itself on its masthead as "The Largest Catholic Magazine in the World," James Conniff asked, "What's Behind the Smear on the FBI?" Describing the "G-men" and Hoover as "keystones of human decency and sound democracy," he said that over the past year they "have been zeroed in on with unprecedented malice. Dazed and angered, the average loyal American has only one question: *Why?* Make no mistake, there is only one answer: *Moscow wants it that way.*"[21] Conniff's article was read into the *Congressional Record* by Senator Karl Mundt of North Dakota.[22]

One result of the attention that Henry's series attracted was that the *New York Post* picked up a lot of the material that he had brought to light and used it as a basis for a series of its own. Henry didn't mind that his work was being used by someone else—he was delighted to have had an impact beyond the narrow circles of the Socialist Workers Party and its supporters.

Another consequence of the series was that Henry's FBI file grew. In one of the memos in this file, dated December 17, 1958, an unknown source reports the appearance of the second article in the series, which was about the FBI's files. Without showing any sense of irony, the memo quotes the article's opening paragraph:

> The FBI's most powerful weapon and its major activity revolves around the compiling and filing of information, mostly defamatory and unverified,

about persons against whom no crime has been charged. Most of the FBI's work is done by stoolpigeons, anonymous letter writers and filing clerks. Secret files are the raw material needed to impose thought control on the American people through blackmail, intimidation and victimization.

The file also contains reports like the following:

OFFICE MEMO:

Date: 11 Feb 1959
To: Director, FBI
From: SAC [Special Agent in Charge], New York

In an effort to determine subject's activities and employment status, physical surveillances, at various times during the day, were maintained at subject's residence on January 16, 19, 20, 31 and February 5, 1959 by SA [Special Agent] [name deleted] and SA [name deleted]. The subject was observed by SA [name deleted] on 1/16/59, shopping in the immediate area of his residence at approximately 12:15 p.m. and returning to his residence at approximately 12:45 p.m. The subject was not observed at all on the other days that surveillances were maintained.

On 2/6/59 at approximately 8:35 a.m., SA [name deleted] and SA [name deleted] observed subject leave his residence and run at great speed to a crosstown bus, located at 14th Street and Avenue B, NYC. Subject boarded the bus, as did the agents. At 14th Street, Union Square, NYC, the subject stepped from the bus and again with great speed darted to the nearby subway entrance and went to the platform of the uptown station, at which time he was lost from view in the milling throngs of people alighting from the subway trains.

Although this reads as if Henry were deliberately trying to lose the agents, at the time he had no idea that he was being followed, and the "great speed" was just his usual hurried state.

On February 20, 1959, a memo from the FBI's New York office refers to Henry's articles on the FBI as "defamatory" and states that "the Bureau has requested that investigation in this case be intensified." On March 2, the New York office reports that it has considered the feasibility of "developing an anonymous source at subject's residence, 188 Avenue B, NYC, New York." (The term "anonymous source" covers both someone who would report on Henry's movements and the planting of a listening device.) The FBI decided that "the disadvantages in connection with the development of such a source, outweighed the expectancy of any productive information."

Researching and writing about the FBI taught Henry that careful research can often turn up internal contradictions in what a large organization says and does. He was to put that lesson to good use on many other occasions.

CUBA

In 1959, Fidel Castro and his followers ousted the corrupt Cuban dictator Fulgencio Batista. At first, most observers saw Castro's victory as just one Latin American dictator replacing another. Too many self-styled "revolutionaries" had made sweeping promises of land reform and redistribution of wealth—and then when they succeeded in gaining power, redistributed the wealth only to themselves. Even the American left was slow to realize that the changes Castro was bringing about amounted to a real social revolution. Berta Green, a member of the SWP at the time, recalls that "a lot of people in the Socialist Workers Party thought that this was just an adventurous kind of thing, some academics were doing something, and it wasn't really going to help very much."[23]

From the little he had heard about Cuba in the first few months after Castro's victory, Henry thought something interesting was happening. As soon as he had saved enough money from his work as a seaman to support himself there for a few weeks, he bought a plane ticket to Havana. Arriving in November 1959, he went to the offices of the National Institute for Agrarian Reform and told them he wanted to see what land reforms were taking place. The institute was pleased to find a supportive American who spoke Spanish and put him to work drafting some standard responses in English to letters they were receiving from abroad. When the work was done, they offered to pay him, but he said he'd rather they just give him a letter stating that he should be allowed to travel freely and observe the process of agrarian reform. They wrote out a letter saying that he was a person in good standing and should be made welcome and stamped it lots of times to make it look impressive. He was able to travel where he wished, and in districts where there were no hotels, he stayed in army barracks or in the local offices of the institute.

For the next seven weeks, Henry found himself in the middle of an enormous and exciting release of hopes and energies that had been suppressed for decades. The articles Henry wrote reflected the exhilarating early days of the revolution, before American hostility had pushed Castro into the arms of the Soviet Union and led him to repress opposition. In *Young Socialist,* under the headline I SAW A CUBA WHERE THE PEOPLE ARE RUNNING THE SHOW!, he wrote of agricultural laborers, local peasant farmers, tractor drivers, and government experts working together to run plantations on which the laborers had previously been told what to do by foreign bosses. He also told of soldiers who built roads and schools, of an army that did not salute because it did not want people to act as puppets, of fortresses that were being turned into schools, of new housing projects, of reduced rates for housing and electricity, and of a free press under the control of newspaper workers. There was not even a cult of the leader: "In today's Revolutionary Cuba, statues to living leaders are prohibited and their photographs are not permitted in public buildings."[24]

In "First Year of the Cuban Revolution," published in the *International Socialist Review,* Henry was scathing about the Cuban Communist Party, which he said was discredited because it had supported the Batista regime and now was irrelevant to the mass movements of the workers and peasants. He quoted Che Guevara, just appointed president of the National Bank (and still so obscure a figure that Henry felt it necessary to inform his readers that Guevara was "part of the top leadership"), saying that "the revolutionary government has cut its colonial links, both economically and politically." The article describes the rapid progress of land reform, the government takeover of the oil industry, and other revolutionary decrees that "have given American millionaires the creeping jitters."[25]

Henry's articles helped to awaken the American left to the fact that a real revolution was taking place on its doorstep.[26] But it wasn't only the left that was becoming aware of the fact that Castro was no ordinary Latin American dictator. Newly elected President John F. Kennedy was keen to show that he was tough on communism, and overthrowing the new regime in Cuba would be an easy way to do it. As the flood of propaganda against the Cuban government grew, Henry became involved in the Fair Play for Cuba Committee, writing for its newsletter and helping in its New York office. Originally set up by liberals, rather than those on the left, Fair Play's aim was to tell Americans the truth about what was happening in Cuba and to win over liberal opinion to the view that it would be unfair for America to invade Cuba and destroy a government supported by the Cuban people. Fair Play grew slowly at first, because it had no links with established political organizations. The Socialist Workers Party took an interest in it, and Berta Green became a member of the steering committee of Fair Play's New York chapter. She proved herself a more efficient organizer than other members and, eventually, with the blessing of the founders of Fair Play, threw the entire SWP into organizing Fair Play nationally. Within six months, Fair Play had 7,000 members, with 27 "adult chapters" spread across every major American city and 40 affiliated student councils.

Henry was nominated by Cuban supporters of the revolution for an executive position with Fair Play, but he refused to accept the nomination. Instead, he did odd jobs around the office when he was ashore, and he wrote for the committee's newsletter. On April 1, 1961, in an article titled "Blueprint for Aggression: How the CIA Plots Against Cuba," Henry reported that Cubans in exile were being trained, armed, and sponsored in Guatemala by the CIA and that an invasion would take place with American air support. The plan was for rebel troops to secure an area of land, declare themselves a provisional government, and invite anti-Castro governments to help them fight Castro. But Henry also pointed out that to succeed, such tactics require that the army have the sympathy of the people; the popularity of Castro and his chief lieutenant, Guevara, meant that anti-Castro rebels had no chance of gaining this support.

Just over two weeks later, anti-Castro rebels trained by the CIA in Guatemala landed at the Bay of Pigs with air and naval support organized and financed by the American government. Henry immediately wrote a one-page leaflet asking people to join protests against the invasion and to support the right of the Cuban people to determine their own future; but the need for protest was short-lived. The invaders were soon captured or killed by Cuban forces loyal to Castro.

For the next year or two, Henry continued to write in opposition to American foreign policy regarding Cuba,[27] but as Castro began to follow the Soviet model and become more of an authoritarian ruler, Henry's involvement in supporting the Cuban revolution dwindled and eventually ceased.

MORE SURVEILLANCE

Berta Green became the acting national secretary of the Fair Play for Cuba Committee, as well as its New York office manager. In that capacity, she was responsible for an incident that drew the renewed attention of the FBI to Henry:

> At one time, after the Bay of Pigs invasion, somebody called and said they had $10,000 for a full-page ad in the *New York Times*. Sure enough, they came up to the office, with $10,000 in a shopping bag. I looked around the office, and Henry was the only one I knew that I could completely trust to go to the bank with the money, and he did.[28]

The bank reported the unusually large cash transaction to the FBI. There were stories going around at the time of "Cuban gold" being used to pay for pro-Castro propaganda, and the FBI suspected—without any evidence—that the money had come from the Cuban government. If that had been the case, its acceptance would have been a violation of the Registration Act prohibiting such donations. On May 19, 1961, Hoover wrote to the New York SAC in the following terms:

> Although it is recognized that Spira, who has been active participant in SWP affairs since 1946, is not likely to cooperate, Bureau feels that we should not overlook possibility he might make damaging admissions or

reveal significant information under pressure of a forceful interview. . . .
Your office is already aware of subject's prior criticism of Bureau and Director as exemplified in three articles he wrote for *The Militant* during December, 1958. . . . For your additional information, the subject on 1/2/59
took part in a guided public tour of Bureau facilities at which time he
provoked an argument with the tour leader regarding various FBI policies
and displayed a most hostile attitude toward the Bureau. He subsequently
wrote an article in the 1/12/59 issue of *The Militant* in which he attempted
to ridicule our tours and in which he made numerous misleading and false
statements.

You are instructed to arrange for an interview of Spira by two experienced Agents who are thoroughly familiar with his background.

Shortly afterward, Henry came home to find two FBI agents waiting to
interview him. He refused to let them into his apartment and told them to put
their request in writing. On the staircase, they attempted to intimidate him by
saying that they had information that he had violated the Registration Act, but
Henry knew that this was a bluff and told them he had nothing to say. The
agents gave up, and no charges were ever filed.

Meanwhile, the Naval Investigative Service was watching Henry at sea.
Between August 1962 and May 1964, the District Intelligence Office of the
Third Naval District sent four reports to the FBI, describing Henry's voyages
as a merchant seaman. The first report, for example, states that he worked as
a relief electrician aboard the SS *Argentina,* which left New York on July 18,
1962, and called at Reykjavik, Hammerfest, North Cape, Tromsjll, Bergen,
Oslo, Gdynia, Stockholm, Helsinki, Leningrad, Copenhagen, and Southamp-
ton before returning to New York on August 21, 1962. Two sources noted
that Henry did not leave the ship at Reykjavik, Hammerfest, North Cape, or
Tromsjll, but for the other ports, the report gives the time at which he went
ashore, the time at which he returned, and such other details as that "he was
not observed to take anything ashore or bring anything back to the ship" and
"was not known to have been accompanied by anyone." The report also provides the following description of Henry on board the ship:

Subject was described as a "loner" who did not fraternize with anyone on
the ship, not even his roommate. He spent very little time in the crew mess
where most crew members congregate in their spare time. He preferred
his room. He was a satisfactory seaman who did his job well and with
minimum supervision. It was the opinion of one source that subject was
very quick-witted. This opinion was based on the fact that subject seemed
to learn his job, which incidentally was new to him, very rapidly. This
source was certain that subject had the capability to get an endorsement
for a higher job. Subject was never seen to smoke or drink. He gave no

indication of having partaken of any alcoholic beverage when he returned to the ship after shore leave.

Subsequent reports describe other voyages Henry made and include some more general observations:

> He was quiet, kept to himself, had no special friends but was generally liked by the crew, did an excellent job and was preferred by his associate electricians to the crew member for whom he was a replacement. The source had occasion to be in subject's room and did not recall seeing any books or other reading material. The source stated that he found copies of some Russian propaganda material, which was brought aboard when the ship was last in Leningrad, in both the electrician's shop and the public address system room. The source displayed two such books, one a hard cover volume, the other a paperback book, both of which were authored by N. S. Jruschov [Kruschchev] but were printed in Spanish. Subject has occasion to be in both rooms but there was nothing to connect him with these books.

The other reports were equally unsuccessful in finding evidence of subversive activities.

GUINEA

In 1965, Henry heard about a vacancy on the hospital ship SS *Hope,* which was spending several months docked in Conakry, the capital of Guinea, in West Africa. Given that he spoke French, the second language of the former French colony, Henry thought it would be interesting to spend some time there. The personnel officer of the shipping company was hardly encouraging. "Let me tell you about Guinea," Henry recalls him saying. "If you were going to give the world an enema, you'd put the needle in Guinea." But Henry was undeterred and flew out to join the ship. He found a country with only 2,000 whites, so he was immediately treated as a member of an elite group. He could mix with the various enclaves of foreigners—British, Americans, Russians, Czechs, Israelis, and French—who lived there, and at the end of a day's work, he would sometimes be collected by a driver in a limousine to attend a party at one of the embassies. There would be drinks on the terrace with a view of the sun setting over the sea, or a movie would be shown. He was also free, on his days off, to travel into the spectacular tropical rain forests or to venture inland up one of the rivers. It was a lifestyle with which he had not come into contact before, and he didn't find it hard to enjoy.

The SS *Hope* was supported by an American charity and visited developing countries in order to train the local medical community in the latest American medical procedures. These local health care professionals would then train others in the country, so that the project would have a ripple effect. That, at least, was the ostensible purpose of the project, but Henry rapidly became cynical about what it was achieving. The medical staff did not speak French. The doctors used sophisticated X-ray machines that were not going to be much use in the jungle, where the power supply was erratic and spare parts would be unobtainable. The drugs used, donated by pharmaceutical companies that could claim tax write-offs for them, were so out of date that the medical staff dumped them over the side by the bucketful. Doctors flew over for a couple of weeks, saw the country, flirted with the nurses, and left. Whenever the staff treated African children, however, a United States Information Agency photographer would be there to record the scene.

Guinea had been the first of the French colonies to break away and become an independent nation. Under Sékou Touré, who had led the country to independence, the government had pronounced its adherence to lofty egalitarian ideals. The country had a new flag and a new national anthem, and instead of the French colonial service it had its own bureaucrats, who seemed obsessed with putting rubber stamps on papers. Guinea had received aid from many nations trying to find favor with its regime. But the contrast with the Cuba that Henry had seen five years earlier could not have been greater. Apart from the rubber stamps, nothing worked. The capital had buildings with elevators, but people used the stairs because the elevators were always breaking down. Modem refrigeration systems had been installed, but they did not keep anything cold. The Guineans had obtained independence, but the people at the bottom of the heap, Henry thought, were no better off than they had been before.

Henry's experience on the SS *Hope* did have one significant effect on the future course of his life. He mixed with American and European teachers who spent time in different African countries, getting to know the culture and lifestyle of the places in which they were living while they taught in the schools. They seemed interesting people, and Henry found the idea of that kind of life attractive. That led him to consider becoming a teacher and doing the same thing himself.

A LONER?

The spy on board the SS *Argentina* was right to describe Henry as a loner. While he had good and friendly relationships with many people, he was reluctant to get closely involved with others. With women, too, he preferred to keep himself independent. His most serious relationship, lasting twenty-five years, was with Myra Tanner Weiss, a prominent figure in the Socialist Workers Party and its vice presidential candidate in the elections of 1952, 1956, and 1960. Born in Salt Lake City, her grandfather had left the Mormon Church when it discontinued polygamy, and her father, a highly successful insurance salesman, later moved to Los Angeles. Myra dropped out of college to work at unionizing agriculture and cannery workers, then helped to establish the SWP in Los Angeles, running for mayor of that city in 1945. She met Henry when his ship called into Los Angeles and he contacted the local Trotskyists. He was seventeen, and she was twenty-seven and already married to Murray Weiss, another party organizer. The marriage was an open one, with neither accepting restrictions on ties to others, and Murray knew of his wife's relationship with Henry.

At first, Henry saw Myra only when he was on a ship that docked in Los Angeles, but in 1949, she and Murray came to New York, where they both worked on *The Militant,* he as editor and she as a staff writer. According to the *New York Times,* Myra "cut a stylish figure in leftist circles—a small, attractive woman who was always immaculately turned out, gene rally in a well-cut suit of lush material run up by her husband's tailoring family."[29] Her forays into federal politics—sharing a ticket with Teamsters Union founder Farrell Dobbs—never gathered more than 40,000 votes. Myra and Murray Weiss withdrew from the SWP in the 1960s because they felt it was no longer following the democratic ideals for which it had been formed, but she remained involved in radical politics. Henry's relationship with Myra faded in the early 1970s, as their interests drifted apart. She remained absorbed with leftist splinter groups to an extent that Henry found pointless, and she did not share his growing interest in campaigning for animals. She eventually moved back to California, where she died in September 1997.

Henry's mother raised the question of his relationship with Myra in the long letter she wrote to him when he was in the army:

> There are many girls that would be right for you. I don't say this one is wrong. I am sure, she is a very fine sincere woman who did you a lot of good. But it is not a perfect relationship though there is none that is perfect. Here everything is against commonsense (or is it against my conventional outlook?). I am willing to give up my outlook if you could convince me, it is the right thing for you. She is married. Married to a man whose exceptionally fine character you admire. He knows about it. Everything, you say, works out well though you have sometimes doubts yourself if it works. Can that be a relationship that excludes any other, the main relationship in your life?
>
> You asked me if I had the wish to see you married. I have the wish.

Perhaps the arrangement suited Henry well because it was a relationship that could not become all-encompassing. In any case, he never came near to fulfilling his mother's wish to see him married. When a lover Henry had met in the South told him that she was going to come and live in New York, he started having anxiety attacks and ended the relationship. On another occasion, he had an affair with a woman on a ship, and when they got into New York, she moved in with him. "I sort of began to feel trapped and figured this really wasn't going to be the thing for me. . . . So I shipped out." He came to accept that while he could have lovers and lasting friendships with women, he couldn't live with a woman. Nor did he want to have children. He told his mother that they were too much of a responsibility.

The same fear of getting tied down may have deterred Henry from getting too closely involved with the Socialist Workers Party. As Berta Green described him: "He was very undisciplined. He didn't attend meetings. He did pretty much as he liked, without making much fuss about it. He shouldn't have, according to the rules of the organization."[30] Eventually, both Henry and the party's leadership decided that he might as well continue his work outside the party.

Henry once told Berta that the main reason he was in the party was to have an outlet for his writing. An important factor in Henry's departure was a clash with the editorial board of *The Militant*. The trigger was a change the editors made to an article Henry wrote about the Reverend Fred Shuttlesworth, a black civil rights leader whom he had seen in action in the struggle to integrate St. Augustine, Florida:

> He was part of the black movement, and the guy just continuously made anti-Semitic remarks all the time we were together. So I threw very lightly one sentence in there about it, and they ran the article taking it out. I wouldn't have cared if they'd said, "Look, it either goes out or it doesn't run," which was sort of their privilege. But for me to break my ass to do an article, and have my journalistic integrity violated . . . it was something I really couldn't handle.

Henry was ready to leave the party for other reasons, too:

> One of the things that Trotsky wrote about was the idea of "the permanent revolution." That meant that you had to have your feet on the ground and you had to figure out what's possible today, and what's possible tomorrow. It was a permanent struggle, not one big leap, and it had to be based on what's actually happening. All the various campaigns are linked with one another. You move forward a step, then you see further ahead, and you can move forward another step.

While the Trotskyists were selling *The Permanent Revolution* and urging people to read it, they themselves were totally out of synch with everything. Even the language they were using—if you weren't a Trotskyist you would hardly know what they were talking about. It was totally unimaginative, totally uncreative. The most important thing for those people was if they would make it on to the political committee of the organization in their own lifetime, or even the national committee. That became the life force of the organization, like the organization was almost substituting itself for the real world.

It was very dispiriting because a lot of things needed to be done. One of the things that happened was, if you had a good rank-and-file activist in a trade union situation, they would make them an offer to become part of the staff—at which point the person was totally lost to the campaign where they were a catalyst and became part of an apparatus that was basically going nowhere. The odd thing is, despite *The Permanent Revolution* being on the bookshelves, they would explain everything by going back and finding a quote from Trotsky or from Lenin in order to explain things, as opposed to explaining how things were in the real world. . . . They were basically just living in their own universe as opposed to making real life connections.

CALLING FOR DEMOCRACY IN THE NMU

When the National Maritime Union was founded in the 1930s, it was democratic and so egalitarian that the salaries of its officials were tied to those of its union members. By the 1960s, however, it had degenerated into a racket run for the personal enrichment and greater glory of its first and only president, Joseph Curran. Curran was president of the union for thirty-six years. He and his cronies broke the relationship between their own salaries and those of their members so thoroughly that in 1969, when a working seaman might earn around $6,000 a year, Curran was paying himself $102,637, in addition to a rent-free luxury New York apartment and a chauffeur-driven limousine.[31] A *New York Times* labor specialist described Curran's offices as "one of New York's most sumptuous executive suites. . . . No shipping tycoon can boast a more impressive penthouse, from the verdant plants and flowers that grow out of an indoor stream to the pebbled terrace outside the glass walls of the executive suite."[32] This penthouse suite was situated at the top of the Joseph Curran Building, built with money raised from the dues of NMU members. The original union hall was renamed the Joseph Curran Annex. The new building cost over $13 million, which was taken out of the pension and welfare funds of the union. The ordinary seamen who had paid for the building and wanted to visit their own union headquarters were forced to use the back door.[33]

Nor did the union do its job for its members. For five years before the reform struggle in which Henry took part, the seamen received no wage increases. The union had locked them into long-term sweetheart contracts, without putting the deal to its members for a vote. These contracts also delivered to the shipowners reductions in manning requirements that so far exceeded those agreed to by other unions that the *New York Times* reported: "Some industry executives privately concede that Mr. Curran has been 'given a snow job.'"[34]

The arrogance with which Curran and his men exploited the hapless seamen aroused Henry's ire. In the books of Lincoln Steffens, he had read about labor bosses who take the faith and loyalty of the people and then betray them for their own personal advantage; now in Curran he had a real-life example.[35]

Henry first took aim at Curran in 1964, when an article in the *Village Voice* praised the then-new Joseph Curran Building and failed to ask any critical questions about the way in which the NMU was run. Henry wrote a long letter that was published in the *Voice,* pointing out that Curran's luxurious offices made a stark contrast to the total lack of facilities in the building for ordinary seamen. The unsigned letter concluded: "The NMU bosses show no mercy toward those who do not partake of the Curran mystique. . . . Thus, since I earn my living by the sea, I must perforce remain anonymous."[36]

There was no exaggeration in that. The system of allocating work through the union-run hiring hall enabled the union leadership to favor its supporters by holding back some positions for its friends, rather than putting them up for open competition in accordance with the rules of the hiring hall.[37] Moreover, when shipowners wanted seamen, the union sent the seamens' files to the shipowners and could attach its own notes regarding their work record. And when the threat of loss of work did not suffice to stifle opposition, the Curran machine had other methods.

In 1966, James Morrissey stood for the office of secretary-treasurer on a reform ticket, against the Curran slate of candidates. As he was handing out his reform group's newspaper on New York's Seventh Avenue, within half a block of the Joseph Curran Building, three men sprang at him wielding lead pipes. They attacked him with such ferocity that he suffered a severely fractured skull and was placed on the hospital's critical list. The attackers were never found. The union was quoted on television as suggesting that Morrissey may have organized the attack on himself in order to embarrass the union. The American Civil Liberties Union (ACLU) said that this suggestion "flies in the face of common sense" and called on Curran to condemn the assault and provide information on other allegations of intimidation of those seeking to exercise their democratic rights as union members. Curran neither condemned the assault nor replied to the ACLU.[38]

Shortly after the attack on Morrissey, Henry joined a reform group called the Committee for NMU Democracy. The committee's aims were to return control of the union to its membership, give the members the right to vote on their contracts, and tie the salaries of union officials to those of the most skilled seamen on the ships. In the days after the attack on Morrissey, tempers were high and some members of the group wanted to retaliate in kind. Gaston Firmin-Guyon, one of Morrissey's key supporters, had himself been beaten up by hired goons inside the union hall. He remembers Henry's response to the idea of the committee copying the union's methods:

> He said, "What are we going to prove by breaking their leg or breaking their head? We are probably going to wind up in hospital, we'll have to pay the dentist. Where are we going to get the money? . . . Emotion is good, but we've got to think before we act. . . . We might have a confrontation, and we might hurt them, but then we look bad. Don't be what they are. If you've got the backing of the membership, you don't have to be a goon."[39]

Henry's cool head prevailed, but if the committee was not going to use violence, it had to find a way to stop the other side from using it. Henry recalls:

> We had somebody pass a message to the union officials that if anything happened to any one of us, the same thing would happen to them. And the message was passed by somebody who they knew would have the where-withal to follow through on it. That made it possible to function. There was no more trouble.

Henry's recollection that there was "no more trouble" is a little on the rosy side. Firmin-Guyon had his apartment broken into and ransacked, and when he and Morrissey went to Panama to campaign for the election, they were told that if they didn't get out of the country, they would be found floating in the canal.[40] Henry himself didn't feel entirely safe. One friend recalls that during that time, he kept his place of residence secret and was very fearful that he would be attacked in some way.[41]

Henry edited, and largely wrote, the group's newspaper, *The Call for Union Democracy*. *The Call* was a four- or eight-page tabloid that appeared irregularly. It graphically described the ways in which Curran and his cronies were ripping off the membership. Curran was so well entrenched, organizationally, that he seemed impregnable, but Henry thought that he was vulnerable, because he treated the seamen as if they were stupid, doing things like raising the dues paid by pensioned-off seamen at the same time as he increased the fringe benefits of union officials. Henry spent a lot of time talking to seamen, on ships and in the cafeteria they used in port, and he spoke and wrote

Henry wrote extensively for left-wing publications, and edited—and largely wrote—the newspaper of the Committee for NMU Democracy.

their language. He knew that they were not stupid. He believed that if they understood the way in which they were being ripped off, they would demand change. The articles he wrote for *The Call* showed that West Coast sailors, who were represented by a different union, were making 36 percent more than NMU members were for doing the same work. He attacked the union's failure to halt the loss of jobs in the industry. Photos showed disgruntled members standing in front of an empty shipping board, where jobs should have been listed. *The Call* also poked fun at Curran's cult of personality, reprinting a column from the *New York Post* in which columnist James Wechsler reported that Curran's picture appeared no less than twenty-three times in a single issue of the NMU's house journal, *The Pilot,* and that NMU chefs won a prize in an international culinary contest for a cake topped with a bust of Curran.[42]

Henry wrote the leaflets that the committee handed out to union members, and he did the research that gave them ammunition to use against Curran. From public documents available from the government's labor office, he learned the details of the salaries that Curran paid himself and his cronies and showed that Curran was at the time the highest paid labor leader in the country.

The Committee for NMU Democracy never succeeded in defeating Curran, but it did make life much more difficult for him. After an electoral defeat in 1966, it took its complaints about several electoral irregularities to the Department of Labor. The election was declared invalid because the rule that only those who had held salaried office within the union were eligible to run for office effectively disenfranchised the membership. The committee then ran a strong campaign in the 1969 election. Morrissey received 54 percent of the vote in New York, where the committee was able to scrutinize the ballots as they were counted; but this was heavily outweighed by one-sided results in regions such as the Panama Canal Zone, where there was no independent surveillance, and the official tally gave 98 percent of the vote to the Curran slate. Subsequently, the reform group forced the Curran machine to withdraw the increases in fringe benefits for NMU officials that were to have been paid for by an annual levy of $100 on the pensions of retired seamen.[43] The Curran machine could no longer ride quite so blatantly over the interests of union members.

The activities of the Committee for NMU Democracy had a ripple effect, encouraging the formation of similar insurgent groups in other corrupt unions. Some of these were more successful. For example, the United Mine Workers ousted Tony Boyle, its long-standing boss, and slashed his annual pension by two-thirds. After this, Curran decided it was time to quit while his $1 million lump sum pension payout was still there for the taking.

TEACHING

When Curran quit, Henry was still a member of the NMU and active in the Committee for NMU Democracy, but he no longer worked regularly as a seaman. Life on the ships had lost its attraction for him. With cargo now packed

On the ships: Henry in June 1966.

in containers, the ships spent much less time in port, and when they were in port, instead of being in the center of the town, they were likely to be out at some new container station in the middle of nowhere. As the job became more factory-like, the labor force also changed. People were no longer sailors because they loved the sea and the way of life of a sailor, but because it was a job and they needed one. Then supertankers, containerization, and the decline of the passenger fleet meant that employment in the merchant marine nosedived. Henry no longer found it an exciting place to be working.

In 1966, New York City was short of teachers. Henry already had a degree, so he needed only to take a short crash course to get his teaching license. His plan—sparked by his visit to Guinea—was to get some teaching experience in New York and then go to Africa. He started his first teaching job in 1966, but in 1968, his father died suddenly. Although the medical certificate did not say so, Maurice had committed suicide. Maurice was under financial pressure, partly because of the expense of paying for institutional care, not only for Margit, but also for his youngest daughter, Susan, a very bright but tormented young woman who was often depressed. Henry said:

> At the end, when his luck was down, he took out a high-premium life insurance policy for which he had to borrow to pay up, and when he had no more access to payments, he committed suicide and arranged very methodically that it be covered up. He literally gave up his life for my mother and sister.

Henry stayed in New York to look after both his mother and his younger sister. He brought his mother back from Bronxville to New York so that he could be closer to her. In 1977, during a period of depression, Susan committed suicide. Henry continued to care for his mother, often visiting her in her own apartment as long as she could live alone, and afterward finding her a place in a home where she was looked after until her death in 1994. By this time, Henry had long ago abandoned his plans to continue his teaching career in Africa.

Henry taught English, both literature and reading and writing, mostly at Haaren High School, a public school on Tenth Avenue, on New York's Upper West Side. The students at Haaren were largely from the ghettoes, black and Hispanic, and for much of the time that Henry taught there, the school took only boys. Comments made by a student in a class newspaper suggest some of the problems that the school had:

> First, there are racial problems: Black versus Spanish. There should be only one school, not one school divided into two different parts. Secondly, there is a lack of discipline due to the fear that teachers have of students, also you have the ones who don't care what's going on around them. Thirdly, all the things I have said have made this school what it is today: nothing but a dump where they bring rejects from other schools. This is the last stop for education and this is wrong.[44]

Yet Henry didn't see his students as unteachable or his job as difficult:

> The key to not having trouble with your students is to never let them lose face. The kids don't like to lose face, don't like to be shoved or pushed around. They don't like to be sat upon, and I think once you get over that it's not a power struggle between you and them but, rather, "let's work together" and figure out areas where there's a commonality, . . . after that, you don't really have problems.

Another way of enhancing the students' self-esteem, Henry found, was to publish their writing:

> You start a sentence, like "From my window I see . . . ," and then you
> have them finish the sentence, and then you take this material and Xerox
> it up and pass it 'round to the class and it becomes the class newspaper,
> with "From my window I see . . ." and the kid's name underneath it. It's
> something they can take home and show around. And then I took this stuff
> and sent it to a publisher who was doing a book about ghetto kids, and
> some of the stuff was published in there, and so the kids saw, "my stuff is in
> print," and it gives kids a certain amount of self-confidence. It takes damn
> little to make kids feel good about themselves. I used to do this newspaper
> routinely. . . . Kids would do poetry, essays, finish a sentence. Everybody
> would see their name in print. It made it easier for me, easier for them,
> and it worked well.

In addition to occasionally producing a class newspaper, Henry coordi-
nated the school newspaper, which regularly won a certificate of merit from
the *New York Times* in the annual High School Press competition. He used
the newspaper to get students to think about values. One issue starts off with a
report that a Haaren student has been arrested for assaulting an elderly person
at a nearby subway station. The incident led to class discussions, and some of
the comments made are reprinted in that and the next issue of the newspaper.
Many of the comments condemn the action as taking advantage of the weak,
or ask those who do such things how they would like it if it were their own
father who was assaulted. But not all of the comments make negative moral
judgments:

> They're bored, they want to make a carnival out of the train station. They
> want to show off how tough they can be—beating up on an old woman
> or man. It's a way of entertaining your friends so they won't say you're a
> drag, he isn't cool, he's boring to be with. It's done without thinking of the
> consequences. We're getting even, paying him back for his color. That's
> the way life is, the strong messing over the weak.[45]

Henry got on well with his students but not with all of his fellow teachers. Dolores McCullough, who taught at Haaren when Henry was there, put
it like this:

> It broke down to whether or not his colleagues remembered why they
> were there, which was to educate. If they were in that category, he was
> very comfortable with them, and they with him; but if not I think they felt
> exposed in front of him [because of the possibility that] he would let go
> with one of his satirical remarks. He had little patience for a person who—

how did Henry put it?—would use his students as fodder, or raw material to achieve their own professional goals.[46]

While Henry liked teaching, it never absorbed all his energies. For the first seven years after he became a teacher, he was still working with the Committee for NMU Democracy. For the next seven years, he combined teaching with his campaigning for animals. Gradually, this took over his life to such an extent that in June 1982, the month in which he turned fifty-five, he took early retirement and became a full-time activist. McCullough wondered at his decision: "I asked him once why he left teaching, and he said that he felt that human beings had a mind, they had freedom in this country, they could help themselves, and animals simply could not, they needed the help."[47]

· 2 ·

Animal Liberation

If we have learned anything from the liberation movements, we should have learned how difficult it is to be aware of the ways in which we discriminate until they are forcefully pointed out to us. A liberation movement demands an expansion of our moral horizons, so that practices that were previously regarded as natural and inevitable are now seen as intolerable.

Peter Singer, "Animal Liberation"

THE LOGICAL EXTENSION

At forty-five years of age, Henry scarcely thought about animals. He had never had a cat or a dog. He ate meat without asking where it came from. But in 1973, two events coincided in a way that changed all that. First, Henry acquired a cat:

> Somebody going to Europe had dumped a cat on me. I wasn't even the first choice for this cat, just the backup or emergency if something went wrong with someone else who had agreed to take her. But then that person couldn't take the cat, and I got dumped with her. I sort of figured I had more important things to do than to play with this cat, but the cat seduced me in a matter of a few minutes, and I've stayed seduced with cats ever since.

Soon after, Henry picked up a leftist American newspaper, *The Guardian,* and in a column by Irwin Silber read the following:

"I sort of figured I had more important things to do than to play with this cat, but the cat seduced me in a matter of a few minutes . . ." Henry with Savage, the seducer who was dumped on him by a friend going to Europe.

ANIMAL LIBERATION

Readers of the *New York Review of Books* may well have thought that the lead article in a recent issue of that intellectually prestigious journal was a giant put-on. Certainly it starts that way by proclaiming itself "a manifesto for an Animal Liberation movement."

Indeed, the author, Peter Singer, indicates that he is aware of the problem. "Animal Liberation," he concedes, "sounds more like a parody of liberation movements than a serious objective."

But what is clear some four pages and several thousand words later is that Singer is not only serious, he is positively passionate in his opposition *to* the second-class treatment that he feels all human societies accord the denizens of the animal kingdom. The argument, as you might expect, is essentially a moral one. Predictably, Singer invokes the analogy with the oppression of blacks and women to issue "a challenge to every human to recognise his [*sic*] attitudes to nonhumans as a form of prejudice no less objectionable than racism or sexism."

Singer calls this prejudice "speciesism."

His program is simple and straight-forward: vegetarianism; an end to scientific experiments using animals; elimination of all clothing and products taken from animal hides; abolition of such "sports" as deerhunting and duck-shooting; the outlawing of fishing; etc. . . .

Well, what shall we make of all this? The temptation, of course, is simply to note the fact that the social collapse of capitalism gives rise to a certain collapse of the intellect among some sectors of the bourgeois intelligentsia, and let it go at that.

But this cultural curiosity may prove somewhat instructive in other respects. For what it does is lay bare the ultimate moral and intellectual bankruptcy of that brand of liberalism which bases itself on abstract principles of "justice" or "truth," rather than on the historically evolved real world we live in.[1]

The object of Silber's scorn was my first published work on the ethics of our relations with animals.[2] The essay was built around a review of *Animals, Men and Morals,* a book of essays edited by Stan and Roslind Godlovitch and John Harris. I had met Stan, Ros, and John in Oxford, where I was then studying for a postgraduate degree in philosophy. They were part of a small group of ethical vegetarians who challenged me to think critically about the way we treat animals. I was working in ethics and political philosophy, and like everyone else, I took it for granted that all human beings were equal, but I hadn't thought very hard about what this meant. It had never occurred to me that when we say that all humans are equal, we do more than include all human beings within the sphere of moral equality: We also exclude nonhuman animals from that sphere, thereby granting every member of our own species—psychopaths, infants, and the profoundly intellectually disabled included a moral status superior to that of dogs, pigs, chimpanzees, and dolphins. Why, my friends challenged me to explain, should this be? Why was it that it was all right to eat, or experiment on, nonhuman animals, when we would never think of doing the same to human beings?

As a diligent philosophy student, I responded to this challenge by searching for answers in the works of older and wiser philosophers. I found none that were at all persuasive. Many philosophers just ignored the question. They happily pronounced all humans equal and never asked why animals should not also be equal. They did this even if the grounds that they gave for human equality—for example, that all humans have interests that can go well or badly—manifestly applied also to many nonhuman animals. That animals were so invisible was itself significant. Others philosophers who at least asked why animals were so inferior in status answered the question by appealing to lofty ideas that themselves cried out for further examination. They would say that all humans have "dignity" or "intrinsic worth," which animals lack, but they would then go on to the next topic without pausing to explain why every human being, no matter how morally monstrous or lacking in capacity for thought or feeling, should possess a dignity or worth that was out of reach for every nonhuman animal. Another group of philosophers appealed to something more specific—like the capacity to reason, or self-consciousness and the ability to plan one's own life, or the possession of a moral sense—without ever addressing the obvious fact that some human beings do not have these capacities or senses. Did this mean that we could eat them or experiment upon them in the way we do with animals? Here was another question that went unanswered.

The only thinkers who seemed to have a coherent account of why animals are excluded from the sphere of moral protection were those who said that humans had a special status because they alone were made in the image of God and possess an immortal soul. Since I did not believe in God or immortal souls, I couldn't accept that answer either, but at least it made sense. I began to think that our assumptions about the superior moral status of human beings were the obsolete legacy of an era when a religious outlook on the world was the background to almost everyone's thought.

In the end, I could not meet my friends' challenge. There was no ethical justification for granting all humans a moral status superior to that of all nonhuman animals. Instead, I came to the conclusion that the interests of all beings should be given the same weight, insofar as rough comparisons can be made among different beings, irrespective of the race, sex, or species of the beings in question. This theoretical conclusion had practical consequences. Animals reared under modem intensive farming techniques cannot move around, stretch their limbs, or socialize with others of their species. Their most fundamental interests are ignored. Hence we ought to stop supporting this system of farming. The most direct way in which we support it is by eating its products. Since I knew that I could nourish myself perfectly well without eating meat at all, I became a vegetarian.

Animals, Men and Morals was published in Britain in 1971. My friends and I hoped it would trigger widespread public debate on these issues. Instead, it was ignored. Not a single major newspaper reviewed it. They probably saw it as just another book on animal welfare, a topic of interest only to spinsters living with cats. By 1973, my friends' book was heading for the remainder shelves in Britain. The only spark of hope was that an American edition was about to appear. To try to prevent it from meeting the fate of the British edition, I wrote to the most widely read intellectual journal of the day, the *New York Review of Books,* and offered them a review essay of the book.

"Animal Liberation" appeared in the *New York Review of Books* on April 5, 1973. In it, I summed up the ethical position for which I was arguing as follows: "If a being suffers, there can be no moral justification for refusing to take that suffering into consideration, and indeed, to count it equally with the like suffering (if rough comparisons can be made) of any other being." Drawing on the essays in *Animals, Men and Morals,* I then showed just how far from this position our practices of animal experimentation and factory farming are.

Silber's column was the first published reaction to the article. It was hardly encouraging, but it proved better to be ridiculed than ignored. Silber presented just enough of my argument for Henry to think that it might not be as absurd as Silber himself clearly thought. He got a copy of the *New York Review* and read it. Later, he wrote about the time when he began living with a cat:

> I still had no inkling of animal welfare as a political issue, although . . . I soon began to wonder about the appropriateness of cuddling one animal while sticking a knife and fork into others.
>
> It was then that I came across Peter Singer's essay . . . . Singer described a universe of more than 4 billion animals being killed each year in the USA alone. Their suffering is intense, widespread, expanding, systematic and socially sanctioned. And the victims are unable to organise in defence of their own interests. I felt that animal liberation was the logical extension of what my life was all about—identifying with the powerless and the vulnerable, the victims, dominated and oppressed.[3]

Of Henry's thoughts about my essay, I then knew nothing; but our paths were converging. By this time, I was a lecturer at University College, Oxford, holding a temporary position that would end in June 1973. My next job was at New York University, where the Department of Philosophy had invited me to take up a visiting position. So in September, together with my wife and our first child, I moved to New York. In addition to the courses I was teaching for the department, the School of Continuing Education asked if I would be willing to teach an evening course for adults. I agreed, in part because I was then developing my ideas on animal liberation into a book, and the classes offered an opportunity to get some feedback on an early draft. So in 1974, New York University advertised that Peter Singer would teach a continuing education course titled "Animal Liberation," consisting of one two-hour evening seminar a week over the span of six weeks. The topics covered included the ethics of animal liberation, a short history of speciesism, factory farming, animal experimentation, arguments for ethical vegetarianism, and objections to animal liberation. Each of these topics became a chapter in my book *Animal Liberation*.[4]

The course attracted about twenty students, most of them already involved in working for animals in some way. The format allowed plenty of time for discussion, so we all got to know one another rather well. One man stood out from the others. He certainly wasn't a typical "animal person." His whole appearance was different: His voice had too much of the accent of the New York working class. The way he put things was so blunt and earthy that at times I thought I was listening to a character from a gangster movie. His clothes were crumpled, his hair tousled. In general, he struck me as an unlikely type of person to enroll in an adult education course about animal liberation. But he was there, and I couldn't help liking the direct way he had of saying what was on his mind. His name was Henry Spira.

If I liked Henry's approach, he also liked mine:

> Singer made an enormous impression on me because his concern for other animals was rational and defensible in public debate. It did not depend on sentimentality, on the cuteness of the animals in question or their popularity as pets. To me he was saying simply that it is wrong to harm others, and as a matter of consistency we don't limit who the others are; if they can tell the difference between pain and pleasure, then they have the fundamental right not to be harmed.[5]

Another person who attended the course was to be crucial to Henry's future work. Dr. Leonard Rack was a psychiatrist with a science background and ethical concerns about animal experimentation. Rack, who had graduated

"The closest thing I'd seen to a genius" was how Henry described Leonard Rack, here seen with Henry at a typical strategy planning session. Rack, a psychiatrist with a science background, provided the biomedical expertise for Henry's early campaigns. He died in January 1990.

from college at the age of sixteen, struck Henry as "the closest thing I'd seen to a genius. . . . He could see twenty facets to an issue that nobody else could see." Rack was to immerse himself in Henry's early campaigns, providing the biomedical expertise that Henry lacked.

For Henry, the course helped to confirm his view that animals are at the bottom of the heap, as far as oppression and exploitation are concerned, and that they therefore most need our help. "During that semester, between classroom and conversations, it all began to gell."[6] Gradually during the course he became a vegetarian, first giving up red meat, then chicken, and then fish. He had resolved his personal discomfort at cuddling one animal and eating another. But he wasn't going to leave it at that:

> I guess most people think knowledge is a good thing just to have in your head for its own sake. The way I see things, if you see some thing that's wrong, you got to do something about it, and at the last session of the course, I just asked people if they wanted to continue to meet, not in order to discuss more philosophy, but to see if there was something they wanted to do about it.

About eight people took up Henry's invitation to meet in his apartment, on the corner of Central Park West and Eighty-fifth Street, to see what they could do to put the ideas of animal liberation into practice.

Designed twenty years after Henry became a vegetarian, this ad sums up the feeling that led him to stop "cuddling one animal and sticking a knife and fork into another."

THE STRATEGY

A few of us met and planned what we could do. We did not want to build a tax-exempt charity to raise money in order to be able to raise more money. We wanted to adapt to the animal movement the traditions of struggle which had proven effective in the civil rights movement, the union movement and the women's movement. We knew that we were surrounded by systems of oppression, all related and reinforcing each other, but in order to influence the course of even ts we knew that we must focus sharply on a single significant injustice, on one clearly limited goal. Moreover that goal must be achievable. The animal movement had been starved of victories. It desperately needed a success which could then be used as a stepping stone toward still larger struggles and more significant victories.[7]

It seems safe to assume that most of the small group of people who turned up at Henry's apartment for that first meeting would have wondered if they really had any hope of achieving anything. Without much debate, they decided to start with the issue of experiments on animals; but they knew that they could look back on a century of antivivisection activity in Britain, the United States, and many European countries that had had absolutely no impact on animal experiments.

Henry was aware of this background, but he was not daunted by it. He had read the newsletters put out by the traditional antivivisection organizations and didn't wonder at their abysmal record of achievement:

It didn't make any sense to me, to put out a publication, to tell people about atrocities, and ask them to send money so we can tell you next month about more atrocities. Meanwhile, the atrocities keep increasing, the treasuries of the antivivisection groups keep increasing, and it doesn't help one solitary animal.

It just defies common sense to me why people would be doing that. What's the point in giving people an ulcer, getting people upset, getting them frustrated, and telling them, what we're going to do is frustrate you next month, isn't that nice?

Henry's experience of campaigning for human rights led him to a different approach:

Certainly, self-righteous anti-vivisection societies had been hollering, "Abolition! All or Nothing!" But that didn't help the laboratory animals, since while the anti-vivisection groups had been hollering, the number of animals used in United States laboratories had zoomed from a few thousand to over 70 million. That was a pitiful track record, and it seemed a good idea to rethink strategies which have a century-long record of failure.[8]

There was a difference between the way I had presented the issues in the classes and the way Henry was thinking about them: "In selecting material for his course and his book, Singer based his priorities on the number of the victims and the intensity of their suffering. In one way this was obviously right, but my personal concern was rather: what can we do about it."[9] That thought, and Henry's awareness of the animal movement's desperate need for some kind of victory, set the group its first task: to find one concrete experiment that would make a good target. In my course, I had given examples of experiments on animals that were carried out, not in a quest for a cure for cancer or some other major disease, but for more trivial, and sometimes quite bizarre, purposes. Often these experiments inflicted severe pain on animals. The group wanted experiments of this kind as a target for its work, but it wanted experiments taking place in New York City, where public support would be readily available and the media could be counted upon to cover the protests.

THE TARGET

Henry started gathering information about animal experiments at institutions in New York City. In the summer of 1975, he saw a report about sex research on animals published by United Action for Animals, an antivivisection organization. Included in the experiments described in the report were some conducted on cats at the American Museum of Natural History. The museum, one of New York's major public attractions, was on Central Park West just five blocks south of where Henry lived. He had walked past it hundreds of times, but—like the crowds of visitors who passed through its doors to look at its dinosaur skeletons and geological specimens—he had had no idea that up on the fifth floor, experiments were being conducted on animals.

The fact that the experimental subjects were cats was significant. Ethically, in Henry's view, it does not make any difference whether an experiment is done on a cat, a hamster, or a rat: They are all sensitive creatures, capable of feeling pain. But he knew that it would be easier to arouse members of the public to protest against experiments on animals to which they could easily relate. Since dogs and cats are by far the most commonly kept companion animals, experiments on them made an ideal target.

Better still, from the point of view of Henry's plans, was the fact that these experiments were about the sexual behavior of the cats. No claim could be made that the experiments would lead to a cure for some fatal disease. The experimenters would have a hard time explaining why their research on the sexual behavior of cats would be of any great value to the community.

Next, the experiments were funded by the National Institute of Child Health and Human Development—a member of the National Institutes of Health (NIH), the principal government funding agency for medical research. In other words, the experiments were being paid for from revenue raised by taxation. The link between the experiments and the purposes for which the institute was established was tenuous at best. Since no one wants public tax money wasted or misused, that made the experiments particularly vulnerable. Even more vital was the fact that as a government agency, the NIH would have to comply with the Freedom of Information Act and provide documents relating to its funding of the experiments.

Finally, the experiments were clearly distressing for the cats. They were being mutilated in various ways so experimenters could observe the effects that removal of their senses had on their sexual behavior. A description of the mutilations would be easy for the public to understand and could be counted on to arouse their sympathy for the cats. Henry started describing the experiments to people he knew who had no connection with the animal movement, to see what reactions they elicited. They were shocked.[10]

This looked like an ideal target; but to make sure that he had not just a good target, but the best possible target, Henry did a computer search of experiments on animals being carried out in New York City. After reviewing all the experiments thrown up by the computer, the group considered that a campaign against the experiments at the museum was the most likely to succeed:

> We wanted an issue which we merely had to describe in order to put our opponents on the defensive. Here we had just such an issue: "Do you want your tax monies spent to deliberately mutilate cats in order to observe the sexual performance of crippled felines?"[11]

THE OPENING

The NIH issues a free publication listing all its research grants. In this publication, Henry found a grant to Dr. Lester Aronson at the American Museum of Natural History. On August 13, 1975, he submitted a request under the Freedom of Information Act for all project proposals, evaluations, progress reports, and other papers relating to this grant and asked that fees be waived on the grounds that this request was in the public interest. The National Institutes of Health granted the request and waived the fees. Soon Henry found himself with a stack of papers on the museum's cat experiments.

The papers chronicled fifteen years of experiments in which Aronson, chairman and curator of the Department of Animal Behavior at the museum, had, together with his assistant, Madeline Cooper, mutilated cats in order to observe the effects of particular mutilations on their sexual behavior. These experiments were themselves based on similar earlier studies by other experimenters who had mutilated monkeys, hamsters, rats, and mice, often with "contradictory conclusions." At the museum, cats had their sense of smell destroyed, their sense of touch deadened by cutting nerves in their sex organs, and parts of their brains removed. The mutilated animals were then scored on their sexual performance in various situations. For example, in a paper titled "Olfactory Deprivation and Mating Behavior," Aronson had published tables, complete with standard deviations, for "mean frequency of mounts" for cats who had had their sense of smell destroyed by surgery. In grant applications, the experimenters proposed blinding and deafening cats as well, although these experiments had not yet been carried out. After the experiments the cats were killed and their brains studied.

In 1974 alone, the experimenters had used seventy-four cats. Each set of taxpayer-funded experiments had led to the conclusion that further experiments were needed, and the researchers had been funded to mutilate more cats. Leonard Rack sifted through the papers, summarizing them and providing an evaluation of the findings. He noticed that after the most recent grant application, the amount of money given had been reduced—a sign that the granting body itself did not see the research as vitally significant or particularly brilliant work. Rack's own view was that even if the researchers succeeded in answering the questions they had posed, those answers would be of no use to anyone.

In February 1976, while Henry was still laying the groundwork for the campaign, he read in the *New York Times* that the city of New York had cut its contribution to the museum's budget and that the museum was therefore considering cuts in its expenditure. Among the museum programs that were discussed were those that the *Times* described as "not of any obvious practical value." Included in this category was a reference to Aronson's project on "the sexual behavior of surgically disturbed cats." What particularly caught Henry's eye was the way in which the museum's director, Thomas Nicholson, defended the museum's research program: "If anything has distinguished this Museum, it has been its freedom to study whatever it chooses, without regard to its demonstrable practical value. We intend to maintain this freedom."[12] Nicholson had neatly framed the issue that Henry wanted to contest. Should researchers have the freedom to study, at public expense, whatever they choose, without regard to its demonstrable value? Should they have that freedom even if their research inflicts suffering on nonhuman animals? The campaign, Henry resolved, would not be about the abolition of animal experimentation, but about "How much pain for how much gain?"

THE CAMPAIGN

The preparation for the campaign had taken nearly a full year, but by June 1976, the group was ready to take the first step. This was not a public one. Instead, Henry sent a letter to officials at the museum, telling them what he had learned as a result of his freedom of information request and suggesting a meeting to discuss the future of the experiments. From the group's point of view, this was a strategy with no downside. The goal was not to have a big public campaign for its own sake, but to stop the experiments. Perhaps the easiest way to get the museum to do that was to allow it to cease the research without losing face. Confronted with the prospect of a damaging campaign exposing the kind of experiments it was doing, the museum could have said that it had found out everything it needed to know, and hence there was no need for the experiments to continue. If that happened, then the group would have achieved its goal and could move on to another target. If, on the other hand, the museum refused to end the experiments, then the group would be able to say that they had tried to start a dialogue with the museum but that the door had been shut in their faces.

There was no response to the letter. Phone calls were equally unavailing. Henry even signed up for a course at the museum, hoping to get an opportunity to discuss the problem with one of its scientists, but to no avail. When he learned that Lester Aronson was to give a lecture at the museum, he went to that too, but Aronson refused to talk about his cat research with a mere layperson.

Henry's next step was to go to the *New York Times,* hoping that it would pick up the story. It did nothing with it. He turned to less authoritative, but more sympathetic, media. Pegeen and Ed Fitzgerald hosted a popular daily talk show on a New York radio station. They were long-standing antivivisectionists and needed little prompting to describe the experiments and stir their listeners to protest them. This led to the museum receiving, in June, 400 letters of protest about the experiments.

The campaign gained further invaluable publicity when *Our Town,* a free Manhattan weekly, published a long article by Henry giving full details of the experiments and of the museum's failure to respond to the objections to them.[13] Henry also circulated his materials to other animal organizations, inviting them to make use of them and to join him in protesting the experiments.

The first demonstration outside the museum, supported by such organizations as the Society for Animal Rights and Friends of Animals, took place in July. The demonstrators carried placards and gave out leaflets describing the experiments. They did not ask people to refuse to go into the museum. That would have put most visitors in a difficult situation, since the visitors had come there, often with their children, looking forward to seeing the museum's displays. Instead, the demonstrators made use of the fact that the museum had no fixed admission charge. Admission was by donation, but the museum suggested a donation of $3.00. The picketers gave visitors a penny and suggested that they use it as their donation. In that way, the visitors could show in a tangible way their opposition to the experiments, save themselves some money, and still see the museum.

Gradually, the mainstream media began to take an interest. Their attitude showed the wisdom of selecting a target that could be seen to be objectionable even by those who were not against all animal experiments. In Chicago, for

Henry addresses protestors at the American Museum of Natural History, summer 1976. Photo by Dan Brinzac.

example, the *Sun-Times* published an article called "Cutting Up Cats to Study Sex—What Fun!" in which the writer, Roger Simon, took aim at the museum director's defense—which Henry had ensured was widely publicized—of the freedom to conduct research without regard to its "demonstrable practical value":

> I am not against the cutting up of animals if it might do some good to somebody some day. But before I blinded cats for 14 years, I would like somebody to tell me that there might be some "demonstrable practical value" somewhere down the road.[14]

The demonstrations continued every weekend for more than a year. The demonstrators included such stalwarts as Sonia Cortis, a retired cabaret singer, then in her sixties, who protested outside the museum with a bullhorn every weekend for the entire duration of the campaign. At the height of the demonstrations, a thousand people took part and briefly blocked the entrance in a symbolic protest. On another occasion, a petition against the experiments, with thousands of signatures, was used to make a scroll that was unrolled across the front of the museum. At other times there may have been only a handful of demonstrators, but there was no letting up. The idea was to send a message to the museum that they weren't going away until the experiments were stopped and the labs dismantled.

When people carried their placards into the museum, officials said that they would have anyone who came into the museum with a sign arrested. The campaigners then had T-shirts printed with pictures of cats and slogans calling on the museum to stop its experiments. Protesters wore the shirts into the museum, which could hardly ask them to remove them.

At the end of each demonstration, the demonstrators went across the road to Central Park, and Henry told them what had been happening in the campaign, so that they would feel that they weren't going to be demonstrating at the museum forever. A bullhorn was passed around, and the demonstrators were invited to say what they had heard, thought, or done about the campaign during the past week.

The campaign took care not to present itself as opposed to scientific research as such. It said that it supported science, but that experiments of this sort gave science a bad name. To inspire young people to take up science as a career, the campaigners argued, it was necessary to stop experiments that were brutalizing and basically meaningless.

Meanwhile, Henry and his supporters were working on other fronts as well. In its publications, the museum regularly thanked its many benefactors, including the state of New York, the city of New York, public foundations, major corporations, wealthy individuals, and artists who donated their films and their skills to the museum. All of these were contacted and asked not to support the museum while it continued the cat experiments. The editors of *Discover America,* a travel magazine that had in the past publicized exhibitions at the museum, wrote to the museum's director saying that they would not mention the museum again while the experiments continued. Campaign supporters who owned stock in corporations that gave money to the museum were asked to move a shareholders' resolution to stop further donations until the experiments were ended. Everyone was asked to contact their elected federal, state, and city representatives and ask them to stop the waste of tax monies on meaningless research that was creating more victims and helping no one.

The group developed model newspaper advertisements about the cat sex experiments and offered them to animal organizations and sympathetic individuals with the suggestion that they might like to run the ad in a newspaper, with their own name on the bottom. Some did, and advertisements appeared in a number of newspapers. Gradually, the publicity spread. In July, 650 letters of protest arrived at the museum. In August, there were 1,500. On September 8, the museum's director received a memo from one of his staff showing that in the past five weeks, 350 of the museum's members had canceled their memberships. The memo noted that the numbers "don't appear catastrophic, except that one can only guess at how many people had a negative-but-silent reaction to our direct mail and renewal promotion."[15]

The recipient of most of these letters was the museum's director, Thomas Nicholson. Afterward, in the museum's 1977 *Annual Report,* he described the situation from the center of an institution under siege:

> A broad segment of the public—by no means limited to anti-vivisectionists—became involved in questioning the research. More than 8,000 letters were received and an uncounted number of telephone calls were taken. While we provided answers and information that were satisfactory to many who inquired, the core of anti-vivisectionists who initiated the campaign in the spring of 1976 kept it alive throughout the year through a well-executed campaign. Advertisements were taken out in the media, attacks were written in humane society publications, letters and telephone calls of harassment (some threatening) were directed at employees and Trustees, demonstrators picketed the Museum on most weekends, inflammatory handbills were distributed, the granting agencies that supported the research were attacked, political intervention was sought and contributors to the Museum (particularly corporations and private foundations) were pressured in various ways.[16]

The museum responded to the campaign by setting in motion a review by its own animal welfare committee. The review found that the project was in compliance with federal guidelines for the use of laboratory animals. The

*In the name of sanity,
is this where you want your tax dollars to go?*

Stop the cat-torture at The Museum of Natural History.

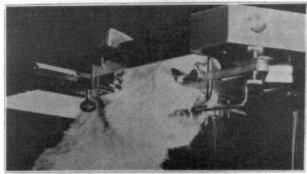

This stereotaxic machine was bought with your dollars. It is used on kittens and cats in the live-animal "research" quarters of The Museum of Natural History. For 17 years — supported by your taxes — they have been surgically mutilating these cats, then "testing" them for their sexual performance. It's an issue that goes beyond inhumane treatment that demeans the human race. Nearly *one half million dollars* have been squandered on this, while real priority needs go begging. *It's useless, nonproductive, repetitive torture that gives science a bad name and adds nothing whatever of value to the sum of human knowledge.*

Behind locked doors, in sound-proof labs, hidden from an unknowing public passing in the Museum corridors, these experiments have been going on and on. Unknown, until an investigative reporter invoked the Freedom of Information Act. (You can do it, too—and should—simply by writing The National Institutes of Health (H.E.W.) Bethesda, Maryland, 20014.) By so doing, you get the complete files and learn that the Museum originally applied for funds to do the following (and more) to the cats:

Blind them by enucleation (removal of eye sockets). Deafen them by destruction of the cochlea (which permits hearing). Deprive them of their sense of smell. Destroy the nerves of the penis of kittens. Injure certain brain centers to "replicate" human injuries. Ironically, the objective is to study the sex behavior of these crippled cats in order to understand perverted sexual behavior in human beings.

They're not telling the truth

When the project was first exposed a year ago, the Museum refused to comment. Under the glare of publicity they finally issued statements to the effect that they abandoned the blinding-procedure. They claimed treatment of

the cats was "humane" (whatever that means in this context). And they identified all opposition to their project as "emotional" and "anti-science". This, despite the fact that eminent, respected writers in the scientific community have questioned the ethics and/or validity of so-called "pure behavioral research" which seeks parallels to human behavior from cats who spend their lives in cramped cages in an artificial environment of alternating boredom and terror. The experiments were probed and questioned in such publications as SCIENCE, the prestigious journal of the American Association for the Advancement of Science. And in the recently published book by Dallas Pratt, M.D. Finally, when the tide of letters and protests rose to flood proportions, they publicly announced that the experiments would terminate in August, 1977, when the funds lapsed and the supervising PH.D., Dr. Lester Aronson, retired. But they weren't telling the truth. And now they are asking the N.I.H. for more funds to continue the cat-sex projects.

Moreover, in a self-incriminating letter, the not-so-retiring Aronson asks his colleagues for help in perpetuating the experiments, and he portrays all those opposed as people who are dangerous to the future of science. You be the judge of who is really dragging science down.

Here's how you can stop this ripoff now!
1. *WRITE YOUR CONGRESSMAN AND CONGRESSWOMAN* . . . your senators and representatives. Ask them to stop this misappropriation of funds. Ask for meaningful legislation against existing laws that permit and encourage such mindless slaughter of laboratory

animals by virtually anyone with a PH.D., a scalpel, a pack of stray cats and dogs, and a greed for public funds. Ask them to prod the H.E.W. and N.I.H. and reject the "canned" explanations that the Museum project has been investigated and found O.K. They did their own investigating. (That's like the F.B.I. investigating itself). Somebody other than the functionaries, the research cronies, the lobbyists and the professional apologists for the booming billion-dollar lab-animal business has to answer for this.

2. *WRITE YOUR BOROUGH PRESIDENT AND CONTROLLER GOLDIN* and ask them to withhold the $5 million subsidy the Museum wants until the live-animal labs shut down. (Never mind writing the Mayor. He's on the record as just not caring!)

3. *JOIN THE WEEKLY PROTEST DEMONSTRATIONS* in front of the Museum of Natural History (Central Park West at 79th Street Saturdays from 1 PM to 3.) Meet the people from all walks of life, with varying ideas and philosophies, all joined together in this fight. Be there this coming Saturday to help us get these questions answered. Why should the remaining cats be tortured even one more day? Why cannot the Museum spend the remaining months of their funded period evaluating their 17 years and then explaining to the scientific community and the public at large exactly what has been accomplished in those 17 years with that half million dollars in your tax money?

The Museum has been notified that we, the undersigned, will adopt the surviving cats, blinded or not.

This advertisement is a cry for help for the helpless . . . voiced by a tax-deductible organization.

The Millennium Guild

Pegeen Fitzgerald, President
40 Central Park South — New York, New York 10019 (212 PL 2-5829)

This full-page advertisement, the first Henry organized, was paid for by Pegeen Fitzgerald's Millennium Guild, and appeared in the New York Times, May 3, 1977.

favorable finding was not surprising, because the review was carried out by a committee of three: Lester Aronson; his assistant, Madeline Cooper; and the consulting veterinarian to the project.

In November, the campaign targeted Robert Goelet, the president of the museum's Board of Trustees. Under the headline "This Man Can Free This Doomed Cat," a newspaper advertisement featured a photograph of Goelet and one of a cat in the museum's laboratory. On November 20, a "Motorcade of Protest" with hundreds of cars, motorcycles, and bicycles traveled from the museum to Goelet's home in New York's exclusive Sutton Place, and from there to Gracie Mansion, the residence of the mayor of New York. Flyers were also distributed to Goelet's neighbors, giving them details of the cat sex experiments over which he presided. When one of his neighbors wanted to know more about the campaign, a meeting was held in the neighbor's elegant apartment, and a lively discussion of the experiments followed.

BREAKING THROUGH

With such pressure on the museum, and such an indefensible program of experiments as a target, one might expect that the museum would crumble very quickly. That expectation neglects three aspects of the climate of opinion at the time that made it very hard for any campaign on behalf of animals to succeed. The first of these was the refusal of leading politicians, opinion makers, and the most influential newspapers and television news services to treat issues regarding animals as if they raised any serious concerns. That, no doubt, lay behind the initial refusal of the *New York Times* to make use of the documents that Henry had presented. The second aspect was the total contempt that scientists had for those who objected to experiments on animals. To most scientists, these people were ignorant antiscience fanatics, usually motivated by some weird religious or mystical beliefs, and there was no reason to listen to them, much less give in to them. After all, the antivivisection movement had been in existence for more than a century without ever stopping a single experiment. The third aspect was the high prestige that science still retained, coupled with the reluctance of politicians and many members of the general public to question the idea that the scientists themselves know best. Typical of this attitude was the following statement by Congressman Thomas Foley, chairman of the House Committee on Agriculture, which is responsible for the legislation relating to animals in research:

> We do not feel that there is any substitute for the continuation of experimentation with live animals and that the authority of laboratories must be

given a great deal of attention and regard in order not to interfere with the
necessary advancement of medical science.[17]

One congressman, however, was open-minded enough—and received
enough letters from his constituents—to go and take a look. At the time, Ed
Koch, later to be mayor of New York, was a relatively junior congressman
from Manhattan. He later told Congress about his visit to the museum:

> I asked them to tell me what it is they were actually doing, and they asked
> me if I would like to go in and see the cats in their cages. I said yes, and I
> went in there, and there were about thirty-five cats. They appeared well-
> treated, in the sense that they were in clean cages and they did not seem to
> be in any pain. So I said to the doctor who was explaining what was hap-
> pening: "What do you do here? What is the purpose of this experiment?"
> And she said, "Well, the purpose is to look at the effect of hyper- and
> hypo-sexuality in cats. We find," said she, "that if you take a normal male
> cat and you place that cat in a room with a female cat that is in heat, the
> male cat would mount the female cat."
> I said, "That sounds very reasonable to me."
> Then she said, "Now if you take a cat, a male cat, and you put lesions
> in its brain—"
> I interrupted and asked, "What are lesions?"
> She said, "Well you destroy part of the brain cells." I asked, "What hap-
> pens then?"
> She said, "Well, if you take that male cat that has lesions in its brain and
> you place it in a room with a female cat and a female rabbit, the cat will
> mount the rabbit."
> I said to her, "How does that rabbit feel about all this?" There was no
> response.
> Then I said to this professor, "Now, tell me, after you have taken a
> deranged male cat with brain lesions and you place it in a room and you
> find that it is going to mount a rabbit instead of a female cat, what have
> you got?"
> There was no response.
> . . . I said, "How much has this cost the government?" She said,
> "$435,000."[18]

Members of Congress found this hilarious, but they also thought it ridiculous
that so much government money had been spent for this kind of nonsense.
Koch wrote to the National Institutes of Health asking why it was continuing
to fund the experiments, and 120 other members of Congress wrote letters to
the NIH about the experiments as well.[19] Since the entire NIH budget was
ultimately dependent on Congress, it was not something that the NIH could
ignore.

Congressman Ed Koch visits the American Museum of Natural History to see the laboratories in which the cat sex experiments were being conducted. From left to right: Koch; Thomas D. Nicholson, Director of the Museum; Henry Spira; unknown journalist; Jerome G. Rosen, Director of Research; Madeline L. Cooper, cat vivisector.

Letters from the public had also been arriving at the National Institutes of Health in large numbers. The *New York Times* reported Dr. William Sadler, head of the branch of the NIH that had funded the experiments, saying that a deluge of complaints from the public and inquiries from Congress had brought the operation of his office to a standstill. After initially approving the findings of the museum's animal welfare committee, the NIH subsequently decided that a review by the experimenters themselves was not good enough. Saying that "anybody intimately involved with the project should have excused themselves from the review," Dr. Sadler stated that the NIH would conduct its own review, but it would "center only on care and maintenance of animals."[20] In other words, it would not question the value of the research itself or try to balance that against the suffering experienced by the animals while being experimented upon. An NIH official was sent to New York to inspect the laboratory. He reported: "I couldn't find anything wrong. As far as we can determine, the animals are treated humanely and spared unnecessary suffering."

But on what basis was the suffering of the cats deemed "necessary"? The NIH did not answer that question directly, but it said, through Dr. Roy Kinnard, the animal welfare officer at the NIH's Office for Protection from Research Risks, that the museum had complied with federal regulations regarding animal experimentation.[21] To the campaigners, that merely showed the inadequacy of the regulations.

Koch's visit and its aftermath were the first major breakthroughs for the campaign. The next came from an unexpected direction. In October 1976, *Science,* the weekly organ of the American Association for the Advancement of Science (AAAS) and the most prestigious of American science journals, published a four-page article by staff writer Nicholas Wade titled "Animal Rights: NIH Cat Sex Study Brings Grief to New York Museum." The article opened with a striking image: "A public relations disaster has settled like a poisonous fog over the American Museum of Natural History in New York and seems to grow thicker with every attempt to dispel it."[22]

Given the nature of the journal and the unbreachable solidarity that scientists had always shown in the face of criticism from antivivisectionists, readers might have expected the article that followed to laud Lester Aronson as a martyr in the quest for knowledge and to denounce his critics as misguided bigots. Instead, it was the animal rights side of the issue that emerged as having some fresh approaches, which Wade linked with recent work on animal rights by "people outside the mainstream animal lovers, such as philosophers." Describing *Animal Liberation* as "the new testament of the animal rights movement," he quoted Henry as saying that the book "has helped create a new seriousness about animal welfare." In contrast, Wade pictured the museum's response as the usual knee-jerk reaction to criticism.

Henry himself was portrayed in the article as quite a reasonable person:

> Spira is not an all-the-way anti-vivisectionist, like many in the animal rights movement, but he believes that for the purposes of many experiments the scientist can use alternatives to live animals, and that the killing of live animals in school room demonstrations is brutalizing and unnecessary.[23]

Wade clearly liked Henry as a person. Looking back on the campaign many years later, he said:

> I think he was effective because he was such a friendly, outgoing, moderate sort of person. He wasn't strident. He didn't expect you necessarily to agree with everything he said. But he was very bubbly and full of ideas, and just interesting to listen to. So I found him an engaging character to cover. I thought he had lots of good points, so I was ready to run with them and bounce them off his adversaries.[24]

Wade did reject some of the claims that Henry and the animal rights groups supporting the campaign had made against the experiments. He accepted the museum's statement that the "sound retarded" testing room described in the grant applications was in fact intended to insulate the experiment from outside noises, rather than—as Henry had suggested—to muffle the screams of the cats. He wrote that there was no evidence to suggest that the cats were poorly housed, fed, or cared for, or that any of the surgery was done without anesthesia. He said that the allegation that the experimenters took a sadistic pleasure in the experiments was "an obvious absurdity." But when he came to the charge of cruelty in the conduct of the experiments themselves, Wade's comments were delicately double-edged. After describing the experiments in scientific terms, he went on:

> In plainer language, of course, this means that the experimenters planned to deafen the cats, blind them, destroy their sense of smell, remove parts of the brain, sever the nerves in the penis, and cut off their testicles. . . . To those not inured to the practices of experimental psychology, it sounds like no picnic. . . . [T]he public outcry about the experiments stems from the difference between what the experimental psychologist and the ordinary person would instinctively regard as cruel.[25]

Remarkably, given the nature of the journal in which the article was appearing, there was no attempt to whitewash the scientists. Wade was critical of the fact that the "review" carried out by the museum was anything but independent, and he was also severe on the museum's response to its critics:

> The museum's few public statements have been couched in general terms, in contrast to the detail-laden accusations of the animal rights groups, and it has also shifted its main defense of the project from arguing that all basic research is important to contending that the cat study "relates closely to human problems."

Wade's view was that the museum's original suggestion—that the experiments should be judged as basic research—was closer to the truth.

Wade added something of his own to the debate. He checked the Science Citation Index, which lists for each article published in a scientific journal the number of times it has been cited in the scientific literature:

> Of the 21 articles that Aronson and his colleagues had published on the cat study since 1962, 14 have never been cited in the scientific literature between 1965, when the Science Citation Index starts, and March 1976. Because of the short citation half-life of scientific papers, it is unlikely that

they ever will be cited. The seven other papers have an average 5.6 citations each over the same 11-year period.

If a paper is never cited—as indeed is the fate of about half the scientific articles published—it is hard to make the case that it has contributed in any important respect to the advance of knowledge.[26]

For the readers of *Science,* most of them scientists who knew all about the Science Citation Index, this was damning stuff. Reading it, Henry saw the first crack in what had hitherto been such a solid wall.

Another reader also recognized the significance of the *Science* article. Aronson commented on it in a letter to the chairman of the Board of Scientific Affairs of the American Psychological Association:

> The AAAS, which should have come to my support as a long-standing member and fellow, and as a service to all scientists, first remained silent and then in the *Science* article by Wade and in their selection of letters to the editor they clearly showed that their sympathies lay with the growing movement aimed at the reduction and eventual abolition of all animal experimentation. . . . Assuming that the editorial position of *Science* reflects that of the AAAS leadership, I find their behavior very distressing.[27]

While it is certainly not true that either the AAAS or the editor of *Science* had joined the antivivisection movement, Wade's article marked the first time a major science publication had published a piece that treated opponents of animal experimentation respectfully and seriously, in a way that challenged scientists who carried out experiments on animals.

Was it possible that instead of rallying around Aronson, the science establishment was getting ready to cut him adrift? Aronson clearly thought so: "We also believe that the National Academy of Sciences should be concerned about the problem because it represents an attack on science, but I have good reason to believe that they are trying very hard to evade the issue at this time."[28]

Many years later, Nicholas Wade offered one explanation for why the National Academy of Sciences may have been less supportive of Aronson than the researcher believed it should have been. Aronson had been in the habit of naming the mutilated cats whose sexual behavior he was observing after leading figures in the American science establishment. This news had gotten around, including the fact that one of the cats had been named after the president of the National Academy of Sciences.[29]

The mainstream media gradually took notice of the new phenomenon of animal rights. The *New York Times, Chicago Tribune, Christian Science Monitor, Newsweek,* and NBC TV's news service were among those to cover its most dramatic manifestation, the museum protests. The NIH had responded to the 121 members of Congress by establishing a review of the funding of the cat experiments and of its general funding guidelines regarding animal experimentation; but it showed no urgency in bringing the review to a conclusion.

THE VICTORY

The weekly demonstrations continued through the winter of 1976-1977 and all of the following spring. So, too, did the experiments. But, meanwhile, developments were taking place that would bring them to an end. In February, Aronson wrote to Donald Clark, chief of the Office of Grants and Contracts at the National Institute of Child Health and Human Development, which had been funding his research, saying that he would not seek renewal of his grant when it terminated on August 31. He gave two reasons for this. The first was that he would retire in July. (He was going to be sixty-six in April.) The second was that "in view of the recent attacks by the antivivisectionist groups, I believe that the museum is not the most suitable place for this research since we are much more vulnerable and have weaker defenses against such attacks than a number of other types of institutions."[30] Aronson did, however, request that the existing grant be extended for one year in order "to terminate the project in an orderly manner." Clark replied seeking further information, which Aronson provided in a letter outlining four experiments that he wanted to complete during the period of the extension. In most cases, the completion involved analyzing data already obtained, rather than further experimentation on living cats; but one of the proposed experiments included additional "behavioral observations." Despite this request, the museum began to tell protesters that the experiments would end in August, when the grant terminated and Aronson retired.

Since Henry had continued to use freedom of information legislation to obtain NIH documents, he knew that while the museum was telling the public that the experiments would end in August, Aronson's request for an extension envisaged some experimentation beyond August. So the demonstrations continued. In May 1977, a full-page advertisement appeared in the *New York Times,* asking, "In the name of sanity, is this where you want your tax dollars to go? Stop the cat-torture at the Museum of Natural History." The advertisement, paid for by radio host Pegeen Fitzgerald, featured a large photograph of the head of a cat held in a stereotaxic machine, of the kind used in the cat experiments. The text below referred to the museum's announcement that the experiments would end in August and then said: *"But they weren't telling the truth. And now they are asking the NIH for more funds to continue the cat-sex projects."* The advertisement asked readers to write to their

congressional representatives and to officials of the city of New York, asking them to withhold "the $5 million subsidy the museum wants" until the
experiments were stopped.[31]

Aronson's request for an extension had said that the experiments would
be nearly complete by the end of August 1977. The NIH decided that they
would have to stop altogether at that point. On May 6, Clark notified Aronson that his grant had been extended for only three months, until November
30, 1977; furthermore, "Research efforts during this extension shall be limited
to the analysis of data already collected as of August 31, 1977, on the projects
described in the 16th year continuation application and the preparation of the
terminal progress report."[32]

In theory, Aronson could have obtained financial support from the museum to complete his "behavioral observations." But the museum itself was
under too much pressure for this to be a real option. During the annual budget
discussions of the New York City Council, Paul O'Dwyer, president of the
council, asked the budget director to contact the museum to elicit a promise
to discontinue the experiments—and said that he wanted the promise before
the budget was passed. On June 1, 1977, O'Dwyer wrote to a supporter of the
campaign against the museum telling him that the museum had agreed to stop
the experiments after August 1977. On August 22 an NIH official confirmed,
in a letter to Henry, that Aronson's grant would end on August 31, except
for the three-month extension to analyze data collected prior to that date, and
that there were no grant applications "in the pipeline" from the Department
of Animal Behavior of the American Museum of Natural History.[33]

Meanwhile, and quite independently of the group with which he had
been working on the campaign against the museum, Henry had encouraged
an activist to go ahead with a different form of attack. In August, people in
Hillsdale, New Jersey, where Aronson lived, received an anonymous mailing:

DO YOU KNOW THIS MAN ?

Lester R. Aronson is your neighbor! He lives at 47 Cedar Street in your
town of Hillsdale. His telephone number is (201) 666-0175.

For more than forty years Lester R. Aronson has been earning his living
performing animal sex experiments. Attached is a more detailed description of his work and a partial bibliography of his publications. While this
partial bibliography is concerned only with experiments on cats, Lester R.
Aronson has done the same type of experiments on numerous species of
fish, on the leopard frog, and on hamsters.

After you have read the enclosed information why don't you telephone
Lester Aronson and tell him what you really think of him and of Madeline
Cooper.

Attached to the letter was one of the campaign's flyers, describing the experiments, and a list of twenty-one publications by Aronson and Cooper, with such titles as "Genital Deprivation and Sexual Behavior in Male Cats" and "Persistence of High Levels of Sexual Behavior in Male Cats Following Ablation of the Olfactory Bulbs." A similar mailing was sent to people living near Madeline Cooper, except that this included an extract from the museum's own grant proposal justifying Cooper's salary. The extract refers to establishing the following groups of animals for experimentation:

1. Blinded—enucleation of both orbits
   A. Experienced adults
   B. Kittens blinded at three months
2. Anosmic—olfactory bulbs of the brain destroyed
   A. Experienced adults
   B. Kittens made anosmic at three months

The extract also included a section headed "Significance of the Research," which stated that "this research offers a new approach to the study of factors influencing the decline of sexual behavior after castration."

Henry calls such a strategy "Dada tactics." Just as the Dada artist Marcel Duchamp had made us look at a urinal in a different way by exhibiting it in an art gallery, so Henry wanted us to look differently at a scientist's publications and grant proposals by taking them outside the context of the laboratory and the university. In doing it at this time, when he knew that the campaign against the cat sex experiments had been won, he was looking ahead to a broader goal: to change the culture of science, in which such work was taken as normal. The real target of the mailings was not Aronson and Cooper—although if they found their neighbors less friendly than they had been, Henry was not going to shed tears over that. The objective was to have an impact on other scientists, especially those at an early stage of their career, who might be thinking about areas of research to pursue. To reach that target, Henry sent—again anonymously—copies of the mailings to the National Society for Medical Research, a Washington-based lobby group that sees the defense of animal experimentation against its critics as one of its major activities. The National Society for Medical Research put a story about the mailings on the front page of its monthly *Bulletin,* which was exactly what Henry had hoped it would do with it. Thousands of scientists were led to think about the possibility that their neighbors, too, might one day receive extracts from their grant proposals.[34]

When the end of the cat sex experiments became official, Aronson and the museum tried to deny the protesters victory by saying that the experiments had been completed anyway. While Aronson certainly was at the age at which many people retire, he had himself requested a full year's extension for work that included some behavioral observations. This made it difficult for him to maintain that the experiments were stopping because all the work had been done.

In December, the protesters were allowed to visit the area where the labs had been. By then, they had been dismantled. In the museum's *Annual Report,* the director said that, in the future, the museum's research would put "greater emphasis on natural populations of animals and on field research, as opposed to physiologically-oriented laboratory research with domesticated or laboratory-bred animals."[35] The victory was complete.

How had a complete newcomer to the cause of animals been able to achieve the kind of victory that had eluded so many of his predecessors? Asked what he thought crucial to the success of his campaign against the museum, Henry refused to single out any one element:

> I think it was just absolutely necessary to do the full-page ad. It was abso-
> lutely necessary to have demonstrations every weekend. It was absolutely
> necessary to get these companies and legislators to pressurize NIH. It was
> absolutely necessary to put pressure on city and state legislators and all the
> benefactors and donors. At one point, the museum just figured, it ain't
> worth it to continue this. I think the other crucial thing is for them to
> realize we're not going away. We're not going after a week to dump on
> somebody else. We're staying till it's finished, over, all over, till it's closed
> down, till it's basically "finished with engines."

While all of these moves may have been necessary, the crucial decision had been made right at the beginning of the campaign: to choose the most vulnerable target. Today that strategy may seem self-evident, but in a movement that had a platform of demanding the total abolition of animal experimentation (and in which those who asked for anything less were often denounced as traitors to the cause) it was an innovation. Granted, Henry was fortunate to find such an ideal target, but the cat experiments were not the only winnable target that his computer search revealed. The ready availability of such indefensible targets was an accurate reflection of the nature of animal experimentation in the 1970s.

While the museum campaign can be seen as a march down a route that Henry had mapped out, it would be wrong to portray the marchers as a happy band, always united in their common goal. The campaign was fraught with bitter disagreements that might have derailed it entirely. On this, too, Nicholas Wade was perceptive:

> Whether the animal rights groups have the power to change the system is
> open to doubt. Most of them are essentially one-person organizations, each
> bitterly jealous of the other. Even the crowd-drawing campaign against the

museum has been marked by a feud between the Society for Animal Rights and a loose coalition of 11 other groups. The Society for Animal Rights held its meetings on different dates and has now ceased to demonstrate altogether because more aggressively minded groups prevented its demonstrations from being orderly. About the only unifying factor among the various groups is their dislike for Representative Koch, who has introduced legislation in Congress to set up a commission on the humane treatment of animals. The animal groups accuse him of using the museum affair to gain publicity for himself. They make similar accusations of each other. For example, the Society for Animal Rights, whose expenses last year exceeded its revenues by $136,000, has been criticized for attacking the museum and soliciting donations in the same advertisement.[36]

The criticism of Koch did not come from Henry. His view is that you take people as they are, and if what they are doing is helping you achieve some good, then you don't attack their motivation. That was a lesson Henry had learned from his work with the Committee for NMU Democracy. In that campaign, Henry had found that some of the people with whom he was working were against the Curran machine only because it was in office and they were out. He was still willing to work with them to give seamen a voice in their own union. Perhaps Koch *was* using the museum campaign to help his own career, but so what? The essential point is that he was also helping the museum campaign in a very substantial way, and his attention seeking—if that is what it was—did not do the campaign any harm. There should be more people who believe that promoting the cause of the weak and defenseless will advance their own careers.

Wade was right about the suspicion with which members of the animal movement regarded one another. To some extent, Henry's position as a newcomer to the movement, unburdened by any old enmities, gave him an advantage. But he was still regarded with suspicion, especially by the more conservative organizations. Elinor Molbegott, a lawyer, was appointed general counsel to the American Society for the Prevention of Cruelty to Animals (ASPCA) in 1977. She soon saw one of the more striking manifestations of the way in which Henry was regarded:

> One day the executive director of the ASPCA told me that there was a troublemaker coming, and he wanted me to attend a meeting, just as a witness to a meeting with Henry Spira, as he was a person not to trust. . . . When I arrived, the executive director sat at his desk, Henry sat down, and the executive director then proceeded to take his gun, place it on his desk in front of him, and said: "We are now ready to start the meeting." I took it as his way to try to intimidate Henry. I felt obviously uncomfortable that I was at a meeting with a gun, and hoped to come out alive, but Henry

didn't even blink an eye; it was as if nothing happened. Henry proceeded with the meeting and took notes the entire time, which I think was troubling to the executive director.[37]

That executive director did not last long at the ASPCA, and Henry eventually formed a close working relationship with John Kuhlberg, his successor.

Henry's attitude was not quite so calm when it came to groups that used the campaign as a means of raising funds for their own—unrelated—financial needs. Such groups were effectively siphoning off money that members of the public thought was being donated to the campaign but that was actually being allocated to pay staff salaries and office rentals. Precisely because he did without paid staff and rented office space, Henry was always riled by this form of rip-off. When it happened for the first time during the museum campaign, he became so disgusted that he went to the airport, told someone at the ticket sales counter that he needed to go off somewhere to relax, and found himself on an island in the Caribbean. After a few days, he got restless and went back to New York and the campaign. (Though he had another twenty years in the animal movement ahead of him, that was to be the last vacation he ever took.)

The victory at the American Museum of Natural History had ramifications that went far beyond the sixty or seventy cats that were saved from mutilation and painful experimentation every year. It was the victory for which Henry and his colleagues had been planning, and both the animal movement and the scientific world took note. Dr. Stephen Toulmin, a distinguished University of Chicago philosopher of science and a member of the National Commission for the Protection of Human Subjects, wrote of his fear that

the same climate that has been unfavorable to biomedical research involving human subjects is also unfavorable toward biomedical research involving animals. The recent shindig at the Museum of Natural History in New York may be, in this respect, an indication of a difficult phase that animal research workers are going to have to live through in the years ahead.[38]

Henry put it more positively: "We may well be entering the decade of animal rights."[39]

The Dream of Beauty and the
Nightmare of the Rabbit

*Looking at the thing strategically, if you do a campaign like this on
the Museum of Natural History, the next person you go to, you send
them a letter, a phone call, a fax, they pay a lot more attention to you
because [they see that] you've got a track record . . . that when you start
something, you finish it, and that you're looking to win. You're not
just looking to campaign, you're not just looking to make a lot of noise,
you're looking to win.*

Henry Spira

A CEREBRAL CAMPAIGN

*W*hen victory in the campaign against the American Museum of Natural
History was in sight, Henry began thinking hard about who was going to be
the next person who would receive a letter, a phone call, or a fax from him.
On October 11, 1977, the decision was made for him by a newspaper headline
reporting that Amnesty International had won the Nobel Peace Prize for its
fight against the imprisonment and torture of prisoners of conscience. Henry
already knew, from information circulated by the British-based International
Association Against Painful Experiments on Animals, that Amnesty International had sponsored a Danish group of researchers to burn pigs with hot
metal rods and give them electric shocks, with the aim of finding out whether
torture could be conducted without leaving visible traces. Henry had no desire
to tarnish the image of Amnesty International. He admired its efforts to assist the victims of ruthless governments and secret police forces. Yet precisely
because Amnesty had such high moral standing—now enhanced by its Nobel

71

Prize—its support for the Danish research was legitimizing the routine use of animals as laboratory tools and so could not be allowed to pass unchallenged.

Henry sent a memo to Amnesty pointing out that the experiments made no sense because torturers who didn't want to leave evidence of what they had done would be able to use Amnesty's own findings to ensure that they left no traces. Moreover, he added, the experiments were at odds with Amnesty's tradition and values. Following the memo, he met with staff from Amnesty's New York office. When they seemed to treat the issue as a mere public relations problem, he was left with no alternative but to go public. He turned again to *Our Town* and wrote an article that accused Amnesty of betraying its own principles. First he described the experiments that Amnesty was funding, then he quoted Amnesty's own literature about the dehumanizing effect of torture, and finally he asked: "When it comes to suffering, what relevant difference is there between us and other animals?" Even more ironically, he found a passage in an Amnesty leaflet that said, "Torturers in various countries insist on being addressed as 'doctor' . . . instead of as sadistic criminals" and then put this together with an internal memo from Amnesty's head office that said, in reference to the experimenters it was sponsoring, "The doctors wish to make it clear that they are not torturing pigs." Henry's article was scrupulous in quoting Amnesty's claim that the pigs did not suffer because they were anesthetized; yet readers could infer that he had no confidence in this claim. Animals who are burned or shocked under anesthesia may still suffer on recovery. The article concluded by warning that unless Amnesty declared a halt to the experiments, the people who had come together to stop the experiments at the American Museum of Natural History would mount demonstrations against Amnesty.[1]

Amnesty International's U.S. director responded by defending the experiments as "carried out in accordance with the highest legal and ethical standards," but also by recognizing that many people, including many within Amnesty, are opposed to any experiments involving live animals. The issue had therefore been referred to Amnesty's International Executive Committee, and Henry was asked to postpone any protest until after that committee met at the end of November.[2]

This turned out to be the first in a series of exchanges, each of which would begin with Amnesty asking Henry not to take action until a meeting had been held. Henry would agree to this. Then he would receive a reply saying that the meeting had been unable to resolve the issue and requesting that he please be patient until after the next meeting. Thus the November 1977 deadline became a March 1978 deadline, and when that meeting failed to reach a decision, the deadline was pushed back to September 1978. Meanwhile, Henry and Leonard Rack sent Amnesty a memo giving several reasons why the experiments were pointless and urging Amnesty to direct its energies toward assisting victims of torture, rather than creating more victims.

When Amnesty seemed to be doing nothing more than bouncing the issue from one committee to the next, Henry again told the group that it was forcing him to make the experiments a public issue. He began to plan a large demonstration outside the organization's New York headquarters. He told his media contacts about his plans and suggested that they call Amnesty for a comment. Amnesty officials complained to Henry that he was doing the same thing to them as they were doing to torturers in Latin America. He replied: "Exactly, you are playing the same role as they do."

While Henry was working on Amnesty's American office, the International Association Against Painful Experiments on Animals was putting pressure on Amnesty's leaders in London to end their support of animal experimentation. Animal groups in Sweden and Germany were taking part, too, and a number of Amnesty members and supporters had contacted the organization opposing the experiments. In September 1978, Amnesty's International Council decided that the organization would not sponsor further medical experimentation on animals.

This was, as Henry subsequently described it, "a short campaign, a cerebral campaign." The victory had been won without the public demonstrations that would have damaged Amnesty's reputation. Once Amnesty had changed its policy on animal experimentation, he wrote a letter and enclosed a check, asking the group to sign him up as a member. He briefly reported this second victory to the supportive readers of *Our Town* and left it at that. Putting pressure on a humanitarian organization was something he would rather not have had to do, and having done it, he wanted to move on.

GETTING INTO POLITICS

In 1953, the state legislature of New York had passed a law that infuriated the animal protection community. Section 505 of the New York Public Health Law, known as the Metcalf-Hatch Act, provided for "pound seizure"—that is, it gave researchers the right to take unclaimed dogs and cats from animal shelters or pounds that received any public money and use those dogs and cats in experiments. The law meant that researchers could get a dog for $5.00 when dogs specially bred for research cost at least $200. All they had to do was submit a formal request to the shelter, and the shelter had to give up the animals or else lose all public funds—something that most of them could not afford to do.

The research community argued that pounds across the state were killing thousands of unclaimed dogs and cats every year. If scientists were able to learn something from them before they died, why not put to use a valuable resource that would otherwise be wasted? To animal welfare groups, on the other hand, the law was an insult. Many shelters had been set up by people concerned about the welfare of stray animals. They tried to find homes for them, and when they failed to do so, they at least ensured that they did not suffer any longer. The last thing they wanted to do was hand their dogs and cats over to researchers.

For twenty-six years, animal welfare organizations in New York had been trying to bring about the repeal of the Metcalf-Hatch Act. Repeal bills had been introduced into the state assembly on many occasions, and in 1977 and 1978, they had actually been passed; but they had failed even to get onto the agenda of the Senate Health Committee, and without that, they could not pass through that committee to be voted on by the state senate. The National Society for Medical Research boasted of its success in stifling the repeal of the act.[3]

During the museum campaign, one of Henry's co-workers referred to the Metcalf-Hatch Act as the supreme symbol of the impotence of the animal welfare movement. Henry had more pressing things to do at the time, but he did not forget the remark. Thinking, as always, of what the ordinary citizen might feel about the issue, he could sense a winnable campaign:

> I just figured the average person in the street didn't want to see animals taken out of a shelter, which by definition is a place of refuge, to go to a lab. It just defies common sense that the average guy in the street would say, "Hey, that's a real neat thing to do."

Henry was also well aware that it didn't help the animal movement to have a symbol of impotence hanging over it. Early in 1979, he set out to see if that symbol could be reversed.

As with the museum campaign, the first step in the campaign against Metcalf-Hatch was a search under freedom of information laws. This revealed that New York's Department of Health estimated that more than 2,000 dogs and cats had been seized by half a dozen laboratories in 1978. Other sources suggested that the figure was closer to 10,000. The next step was to find out why the animal movement had been unable to get the law repealed. In the eyes of the animal welfare movement, the villain was the powerful Republican chair of the Senate Health Committee, Senator Tarky Lombardi. Angry animal groups published abusive articles about him, even accusing him of being paid off by the pharmaceutical industry for keeping the Metcalf-Hatch Act in place.

Henry decided to start with an open mind and discover for himself what the problem was. As a part-time journalist, a natural place for him to begin the investigation was the press room of the state legislature in Albany, the state capital. There he asked for the name of someone on the staff of the legislature who could tell him how the place really operated. He was given a name and went to see the staffer:

> I said: "Look, I went to the press room and asked who knows how this place really operates, and they pointed to you. So let me tell you what I'm down here about. I'm here about the Metcalf-Hatch Act, and I'm not looking for your support, but we've got a right to a fair shake, and the only way to a fair shake is to know how things work. . . . If you were us, what would you do?" . . . And he said: "If I were you, I would call up Lombardi and say I want to talk with you. Lombardi's got a reputation for being a fair shooter. Just tell him you want to talk to him. Go to his assistant and say you want to have a meeting with Lombardi."

Henry took this advice, and Lombardi's staff made an appointment for him to see the senator. Then serendipity—and a policy of using whatever circumstances might help—worked in his favor. To kill time before the meeting, he went to a local bar where he got into a conversation with a woman who happened to be the nurse in charge of the intensive care unit of a hospital that was in Lombardi's electorate. She asked Henry what he was doing in Albany, and when he told her about pound seizure, she showed interest in the issue. So he invited her to come along to the meeting with Lombardi, and she did. Henry felt that the fact that he was there with a senior health care professional from Lombardi's district may well have helped his cause with the chair of the Senate Health Committee.

Henry told Lombardi that he had heard that he was a fair shooter, yet the issue of pound seizure had never even been debated in the Senate Health Committee. As a result, there was enormous frustration among people concerned about animals. He added that he wasn't asking for Lombardi's personal support for repeal, just a chance to have the issue debated and voted on, on its own merits. Lombardi replied that if Henry could show him that there was a lot of interest in the issue, he would have it debated.

To show Lombardi how much interest there was in the repeal of the Metcalf-Hatch Act, Henry needed to get organized. He contacted every animal group he could find in the state of New York and formed the Coalition to Abolish Metcalf-Hatch. According to its letterhead, the coalition had a steering committee consisting of himself; New York radio personality Pegeen Fitzgerald; *Our Town* editors Ed and Arlene Kayatt; the chief executive of the

New York-based ASPCA, John Kuhlberg; and Regina Frankenberg, a director of Friends of Animals, who had personally paid for advertisements for the
museum campaign. The letterhead also listed about thirty "sponsoring organizations," including some large and highly respected ones like the ASPCA
and the Humane Society of the United States, some local shelter societies, and
a few more radical animal liberation groups. The coalition brought in some
additional money for the campaign, but that was far less significant than the
impressive letterhead it provided and the access it gave Henry to a network
of supporters. It did not alter the way in which the campaign was run. Henry
consulted widely with those whose views he respected, as he had always done,
but there was no formal structure to the coalition, and the steering committee
never met as a decision-making group.

Around this time, Henry incorporated his own organization, giving it
the name Animal Rights International (ARI). It, too, did not amount to
much more than a letterhead that Henry could use when he was acting on
his own behalf, rather than as part of a coalition. Henry began then to manage his animal work in a way that continues to the present. While he does
not work entirely alone, his operation has always been very lean, with one or
two supporters who spend a few hours a week working for him. Linda Petrie
volunteered her Sundays for thirteen years, but other helpers have come and
gone at shorter intervals. Usually, some external factor has interfered with his
assistants' continued support, like admission to Columbia University for Vicki
Alippe, or the success of his rock band for teenager Mike Galinsky.

When Galinsky left, he found Maureen Cunnie to take his place; and she,
as we will see, played a key role in Henry's later campaign against the face
branding of cattle. When Cunnie in turn left to get married, she linked Henry
up with a French-speaking colleague, Fabienne Ziade, until Ziade returned
to Lebanon. Henry's helper at the time of this writing, Jessica Craig, usually
works in the early morning hours before she heads off to her publishing job.

The status of Animal Rights International as a tax-exempt, nonprofit organization is useful when Henry has a donor who wants to put some money
into his work. For a time, Pegeen Fitzgerald was Henry's main source of
funds. Later, other donors offered financial support. After 1985, when ARI
was granted tax-exempt status, it became possible to get funding from such
organizations as the ASPCA, the Humane Society of the United States, and
the Massachusetts SPCA. Henry also then began to work more closely with
the heads of these organizations, including John Hoyt, Paul Irwin, Fred
Davis, Gus Thornton, John Kuhlberg, and Roger Caras. They were the
heavyweights of the more traditional animal welfare movement, controlling
organizations with assets in the millions, or even tens of millions of dollars, and
able to reach far more supporters than Henry could possibly have reached on

his own. The collaboration between Henry and these leaders helped to draw this long-established side of the movement closer to the newer animal rights movement, with its more far-reaching goals.

Coalition building became Henry's organizational trademark. The groups making up the coalition would have disagreed among themselves on many issues, but they were united on wanting the Metcalf-Hatch Act repealed. By joining together, they made Henry look like much more than a one-man outfit, and they benefited by being able to tell their members that they were participating in the campaign to repeal pound seizure.

The Coalition to Abolish Metcalf-Hatch contacted all its member organizations and urged them to tell their members and supporters to make their views about the Metcalf-Hatch Act known to Senator Lombardi's office. Henry provided them with standard letters to send to the editors of their local community papers. The coalition sent information on the Metcalf-Hatch Act to eve:ry newspaper in the state, and Henry wrote articles for any publications that would place them.[4]

A flood of mail began to pour into the offices of state legislators. Senators reported that they received more mail urging repeal of the Metcalf-Hatch Act than on issues like abortion or the death penalty. But Henry didn't leave it to mail carriers to deliver his message. He went to Albany so often that he became a familiar figure around the corridors of the state legislature. Against a background of power-dressing lobbyists in Albany, he wasn't hard to pick out. "'Did you see that guy Spira, the animal guy?' one legislator asked another in a Capitol hallway last week. 'He wears sneakers, carries a Pan Am bag and wears ratty pants.'"[5] Nor was it only his clothes that made an impression: "His delivery is dramatic, filled with references to abolitionists, philosophers and libertarians; he pulls pamphlets or hideous photographs of experimental animals from the bag to illustrate his claims." Henry wasn't just telling the legislators what he thought. He was also asking them how they would vote and keeping a record of their answers to see how the campaign was doing.

By spring 1979, the issue had become a cause célèbre in Albany. Lombardi was as good as his word, listing it on the agenda of the Senate Health Committee. Lombardi did something else that showed both his influence and the fact that he was playing the game straight. To have the bill pass from the committee to the floor of the state senate, it needed the votes of a majority of all members of the committee. If a member was not present, that individual's vote in effect counted as a negative. So Henry went to all the members of the committee and urged them to attend the hearing:

> Now this one guy had been getting letters from the animal protection community who were hailing him as the greatest thing there is, because he was

saying that when the bill gets to the floor, he'll fight for it. So we went to him and said, "You're going to show up and fight for it, right?" and he says, "No." I said, "But you said you were going to do all this." He said, "Yeah, when it gets to the floor, but it hasn't got to the floor." So I told that to Lombardi, and he said, "Let me call him up and tell him it's OK for him to show up."

The committee discussed the bill, and on April 24, it voted 8 to 3 to move it to the floor of the senate. Lobbying hard against repeal was the New York state biomedical research establishment: the Medical Society of the State of New York, the New York State Veterinary Medical Society, the Council of Agricultural Organizations, and, of course, the National Society for Medical Research, which feared that if New York repealed its pound seizure law, other states would follow suit. Lombardi echoed the arguments of these organizations, saying that repeal would increase costs for medical institutions, since specially bred dogs and cats are far more expensive than those taken from pounds. He also said that repeal would increase the number of animals killed, because as well as the unclaimed strays killed by the pounds, the laboratories would have to kill animals specially bred for the purpose. (Henry's hope was that the effect of the first point would at least partially negate the second: If dogs and cats became more expensive, researchers would not use so many of them.)

When the vote was taken on May 7, 1979, it was overwhelmingly in favor of repeal: 44 to 13. Four weeks later, the assembly approved the repeal by 121 to 17. After the crucial senate victory, Henry took care to avoid making anyone lose face. He made a statement to the press thanking not only the senators who had sponsored the repeal bill, but also "our chief adversary, Senator Lombardi, who gave our position a fair chance to be heard."[6] His relationship with Lombardi and with other New York state legislators remained good after the Metcalf-Hatch Act had been buried.

Now all the repeal bill needed was the signature of Governor Hugh Carey. The state health commissioner, along with his science advisers, opposed repeal; but before his election, in response to a question from an animal group, Carey had written that he would "lead the fight for repeal." Henry asked his supporters to write to Carey, reminding him of that statement. On a television show, Carey was asked if he would sign the repeal bill, but he would not give a clear answer. Henry began to plan a demonstration at the state capitol. It wasn't necessary. Governor Carey signed the bill into law on June 17, 1979.[7]

"For the first time in 27 years," Henry wrote to those who had supported the campaign, "New York animal shelters are no longer storage warehouses for laboratories." The victory showed, he added, that the animal movement had the capacity to organize as effectively as movements that seek to win justice for humans. Nor would the impact of the victory be limited to pound animals:

> Effective actions are the result of people gaining confidence in their ability to effect change. . . .
>
> And so, Repeal of Metcalf-Hatch is one more step in the fight for justice. It will be followed, shortly, by coalitions on other issues, such as abolishing the routine blinding and poisoning of millions of animals for "safety" testing though modern, elegant alternatives are feasible.[8]

THE NEW ANIMAL MOVEMENT

By the time that Metcalf-Hatch had been repealed, it was clear that something new was happening in the animal movement. The campaigns that Henry led were part of a broader phenomenon. In Michigan, in February 1978, a protest stopped car crash experiments on baboons.[9] In England, groups of hunt saboteurs had sprung up across the country, disrupting foxhunts by spraying diversionary scents across the foxes' routes. The oldest of all anticruelty societies, the Royal Society for the Prevention of Cruelty to Animals (RSPCA), elected a new council of young reformers led by Richard Ryder, who became chairman of the RSPCA council in 1977. Ryder was the author of *Victims of Science,* a formidable attack on animal experimentation, and the person who coined the word "speciesism." Under his leadership the RSPCA for the first time opposed foxhunting and began taking stronger positions on every aspect of institutionalized animal suffering. "Animal rights" was moving into the mainstream.

Ryder organized the world's first conference on animal rights, held at Trinity College, Cambridge, in August 1977. Attended by philosophers, politicians, scientists, ministers of religion, writers, and animal activists, it produced a "Declaration Against Speciesism" that was signed by 130 people.[10] Other conferences soon followed. On May 24-27, 1979, the emerging generation of philosophers working on animals and ethics gathered at the Virginia Polytechnic Institute and State University in Blacksburg, Virginia, for a conference on "The Moral Foundations of Public Policy: Ethics and Animals." Among the speakers were Stephen Clark, who had recently published *The Moral Status of Animals;* Tom Regan, later to be the author of *The Case for Animal Rights;* Bernard Rollin, soon to publish *Animal Rights and Human Morality;* and myself. On the other side of the debate was Ray Frey, who was about to publish *Interests and Rights: The Case Against Animals.*

On the list of speakers in the published volume of essays from the Blacksburg conference, all but one of the names has alongside it a department and the name of a university. The exception reads simply: "Henry Spira. New York, New York." Among so many academics, Henry might have been expected to be a misfit. Certainly, he neither spoke nor dressed like an academic. But he showed no sign of feeling intimidated by his audience. With the museum and Amnesty International successes behind him, as well as the Metcalf-Hatch repeal campaign on the brink of achieving its goal, he spoke from his own experience, plainly but with passion, on the topic he knew best:

> We identify with the powerless and the vulnerable—the victims, all those dominated, oppressed, and exploited. And it is the nonhuman animals whose suffering is the most intense, widespread, expanding, systematic, and socially sanctioned of all. What can be done? What are the patterns underlying effective social struggles?

He described his own campaigns and why they had succeeded, then he closed with a rousing call to carry the fight forward:

At the "Ethics and Animals" conference, Blacksburg, Va., May 1979. From left to right, Peter Singer, Tom Regan, James Rachels, Stephen Clark (all philosophers who have written about animals and ethics), and Henry Spira.

We need to remember the words of the Abolitionist leader Frederick Douglass—"If there is no struggle, there is no progress. Those who profess to favor freedom, and yet deprecate agitation, are people who want rain without thunder and lightning. They want the ocean without the roar of its many waters. Power concedes nothing without a demand. It never did and it never will."[11]

New publications began to link the diverse elements of the growing movement. A British magazine called *The Beast* published its first issue in July 1979. Six months later came the first issue of its American equivalent, *Agenda: A Journal of Animal Liberation*. The second issue contained an article by Henry that showed, in its opening paragraphs, the sense that something new was happening:

> Animal rights is in the air. It's a force whose time has come. There is increasing awareness that rights are not dependent on intelligence, sex, age, class, popularity, color or species; that pleasure and pain are as vivid to our fellow humans and our fellow animals as they are to you.

He asked: "What can be done?" and answered the question in terms that summed up his own approach:

> There's a rich tradition to help answer this question. It's the fight for human freedom. And the fundamental lesson is that the meek don't make it. But audacity must be fused with attention to detail, with an awareness of social attitudes, power relations and scientific possibilities.[12]

BLINDING RABBITS ISN'T BEAUTIFUL

The museum campaign saved about seventy cats a year from experimentation; pound seizure in New York State involved thousands of dogs and cats annually; but millions of animals suffered and died every year in safety testing. Henry knew that to make a significant impact on the use of animals for that purpose would do a thousandfold more to reduce the amount of pain and suffering animals undergo than had the campaigns against the Museum or the Metcalf-Hatch Act.

In the 1974 course that Henry attended at New York University, I described a widely practiced safety test that I found particularly outrageous because the pain it inflicted on animals was so grossly out of proportion to the value of the products being tested:

> Cosmetics and other substances are tested for eye damage. Here the standard method is the Draize test, named after J. H. Draize. Rabbits are the

animals most often used. Concentrated solutions of the product to be tested are dripped into the rabbits' eyes, sometimes repeatedly over a period of several days. The damage is then measured according to the size of the area injured, the degree of swelling and redness, and other types of injury. One researcher employed by a large chemical company has described the highest level of reaction as follows: "Total loss of vision due to serious internal injury to cornea or internal structure. Animal holds eye shut urgently. May squeal, claw at eye, jump and try to escape."

By shutting or clawing at the eye, however, the rabbit may succeed in dislodging the substance. To prevent this the animals are now usually immobilized in holding devices from which only their heads protrude. In addition their eyes may be held permanently open by the use of metal clips which keep the eyelids apart. Thus the animals can obtain no relief at all from the burning irritation of substances placed in their eyes.[13]

For thirty years, the Draize test had been widely used to test virtually anything that might get into a human eye. Could anything be done about it?

Opponents of research on animals often argue that experimentation on animals can and should be replaced by alternative methods such as the study of cells or tissues, grown in cultures in laboratories. But defenders of research say that this is wishful thinking, fueled more by the desire to do away with animal experiments than by an objective assessment of the value of the alternative methods. One person who could not be accused of such wishful thinking was Professor David Smyth, chairman of the British Research Defence Society, an organization largely concerned to defend research from attack by opponents of animal experimentation. In 1978, in a book called *Alternatives to Animal Experiments,* Smyth published the results of a study instigated by that society.[14] In most areas of research, Smyth's study deflated claims for alternatives. Nevertheless, Smyth was open-minded enough to see the value of developing alternatives where there was a real prospect of them providing information that was as good as, or better than, that provided by tests on living animals. He singled out one area for special mention: "There does seem to be a good case for a major attempt to find an alternative to the Draize test. . . . Between the cosmetic and the agrochemical industry it should not be difficult to organize something."[15]

Smyth's comment on the Draize test was drawn to Henry's attention by Dr. Andrew Rowan, a biochemist with a doctorate from Oxford University. Rowan had worked on alternatives to animal tests at a British charitable organization called the Fund for the Replacement of Animals in Medical Experiments. He was then hired by the Humane Society of the United States for its newly founded Institute for the Study of Animal Problems in Washington, D.C., and he became one of Henry's circle of advisers. Leonard Rack, Henry's other chief source of scientific advice at the time, had also come to think that the Draize test would be a good target. Two toxicologists, one at Esso's research laboratory and the other at Union Carbide, had some years earlier published a paper in a leading toxicology journal showing that routine Draize testing produced unreliable data—different people, conducting the test on the same chemicals, would get different results.[16] So even putting aside the pain that the Draize test caused, there was a strong case on public safety grounds for replacing it.

The Draize test was a good target for other reasons, too. As Henry said, "people know what it feels like to get a little bit of soap in their eyes," and so they could identify with the rabbits undergoing the Draize test.[17] And if anyone did have trouble identifying with the rabbits, it was easy to show, *very* vividly, just what it was like. The U.S. government's Consumer Product Safety Commission (CPSC) had produced a full-color film showing how to carry out the test. The film was intended to be used to train technicians, but anyone could buy a copy, and Henry did. From the same commission he also got a set of color slides illustrating various grades of damage to the eyes of rabbits who had undergone the Draize test. The slides were issued so that technicians could compare the eyeballs of the living rabbits in front of them with those of the rabbits in the slides. The film and slides were perfect campaigning tools: Their source meant that no one could claim that they gave a false or distorted impression of what the Draize test did to the eyes of rabbits.

Focusing on this test went beyond Henry's previous public campaigns, not only in the number of animals affected, but also in their species. Campaigning for cats and dogs made it easier to get a favorable response from the public, but at the same time, it reinforced the idea that if animals aren't lovable, they don't matter. Henry wanted to break out of that restriction and convey the idea that it is the capacity of an animal to suffer that really matters. But to try to go too far—by campaigning against tests done on rats, for example—would be to risk losing public support altogether. The Draize test was standardly performed on albino rabbits, because their lack of pigmentation meant that any damage caused to the eye was easier to see. White rabbits are a symbol of innocence, though, and probably lie somewhere between rats and dogs in terms of the sympathy they could be expected to arouse.

The Draize test was being performed across the United States by thousands of different corporations, but the success of the museum campaign had reinforced Henry's conviction that a winnable campaign needed a specific target. Cosmetics companies looked particularly vulnerable:

> We could pose the issue this way: is another shampoo worth blinding a rabbit? It was so incongruous for the cosmetics industry to be carrying out these tests. The cosmetics industry is trying to sell dreams, but the reality is that they are creating a nightmare for the rabbits. Exposing the reality of

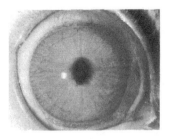

Normal Eye

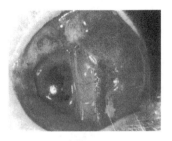

1 Hour

2-3 Redness   > 2 Opacity
1 Iritis   4 Chemosis

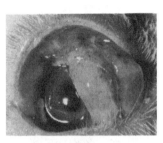

24 Hours

3 Redness   1 Opacity
2 Iritis   > 3 Chemosis

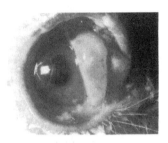

48 Hours

3 Redness   > 1 Opacity
2 Iritis   3 Chemosis

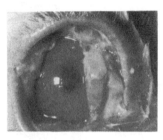

72 Hours

3 Redness   > 1 Opacity
2 Iritis   > 2 Chemosis

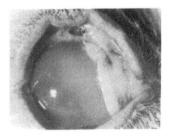

7 Days

3 Redness   4 Opacity
2 Iritis   2 Chemosis

On request, the U.S. government's Consumer Product Safety Commission sent out this set of pictures, in color, to assist technicians carrying out the Draize test in grading the degree of damage that the test substance did to the eyes of rabbits after specified periods. Henry found the pictures a useful campaign tool.

what they are doing threatens the whole image of the industry. Blinding rabbits isn't beautiful.[18]

The frivolous nature of the products the industry was selling was also important: "I think that there are very few people on the street who'll say, 'Yeah, go around and blind rabbits to produce another mascara.'"[19]

Once again, the Freedom of Information Act was essential to the campaign. Organizations carrying out experiments on animals in the United States are required to make annual returns to the Department of Agriculture showing the numbers of animals they are using and—when the experiment causes pain or distress without anesthesia—giving an explanation as to why no anesthetic was used. Henry requested the returns of the two leaders of the cosmetics industry, Revlon and Avon. They confirmed that both corporations were conducting the Draize test. Revlon's 1977 report showed that it had used 2,000 rabbits that year. The report also stated tersely that "no anesthesia is used in any of the above procedures. This is due to the nature of the studies involved."

ONE-HUNDREDTH OF 1 PERCENT

In a cover story on the cosmetics industry, *Time* called Revlon the "General Motors of beauty." The corporation sold $1 billion worth of beauty products in 1978.[20] Though Avon's sales, through door-to-door representatives rather than retail outlets, were slightly larger, Revlon's powerful advertising campaigns had generated an image of beauty that Avon did not even approach. It was this image that made Revlon the obvious target, because an image so carefully constructed could very easily be tarnished by associating it with something as ugly as the Draize test.

What could a campaign against Revlon hope to achieve? The obvious goal was that Revlon should stop testing its products on rabbits. So should that be what the campaign demanded? Barnaby Feder, a business reporter who covered the animal testing issue for the *New York Times,* later described the way in which Henry thought about what would be a suitable outcome for the campaign:

> The thing that was interesting to me, as a business reporter, about Henry's handling of the Revlon campaign was that he was willing to take on a really big-name public target there. For most of the movement, that would have been a real unknown quantity, something that would have been very dangerous. Henry realized that it was a big institution that had interests, and if you could identify what those interests were, and find some little area of

overlap between their interests and your interests, you could actually accomplish something.[21]

To demand that Revlon cease testing its products on rabbits would lead
to head-on conflict. Government regulations required corporations to provide
evidence of the safety of their products, and there was no recognized alternative to the Draize test that would be accepted as evidence of safety for products
that might get in someone's eye. To find an area of overlap between Revlon's
interests and those of the animals, Henry decided not to ask for an immediate
halt to Revlon's use of the Draize test but, instead, to seek Revlon's support
for a research project to develop an alternative test that did not use animals.
After scanning some financial information on the cosmetics industry, he
calculated that if each corporation in the industry gave one-hundredth of 1
percent of their gross revenues, then $1.1 million would be available to fund
a crash research program to develop an alternative to the Draize test. One-
hundredth of 1 percent seemed a modest amount to put toward ending the
suffering that cosmetics companies were inflicting on animals. For Revlon, it
would amount to about $170,000 a year. The company spent $162 million
on advertising alone.[22]

Quite apart from the fact that asking Revlon for one-hundredth of 1
percent of its revenue would make the campaign winnable, whereas asking
it to stop carrying out the Draize test would not, there was another strong
reason for taking the first approach. If the whole cosmetics industry stopped
doing the Draize test, that might save 10,000 rabbits a year; but the number
of rabbits used in Draize tests for household goods, pharmaceuticals, pesticides,
and raw chemicals would be at least ten times that. These industries were not
vulnerable in the way that the cosmetics industry was. They had no elaborately
created image of beauty that could be threatened by exposing what they were
doing to rabbits. In many cases, there was no brand-name company doing the
testing, and in others, the products were not purchased by the general public.
If the ultimate goal was getting rid of the Draize test, then developing an alternative test was more likely to achieve that goal than simply getting Revlon,
Avon, and other cosmetics brands to stop using it.

The campaign began in September 1978 with a letter from Leonard
Rack and Henry to Frank Johnson, Revlon's vice president for public affairs,
outlining some scientific ideas for methods that could replace animal testing in
the cosmetics industry. These methods would, the letter asserted, "be faster,
more economic, and more efficiently protective of the cosmetics user than
current methods." The letter quoted Smyth's comments on the desirability
of finding an alternative to the Draize test and gave detailed references to

scientific papers that offered promising avenues for further exploration. The "humane aspect of substituting alternatives for animal testing" was referred to only in two sentences near the end of the five-page letter.

Months went by without any real response. To try to get the company to move things along, Henry bought one share of Revlon stock and went to the company's annual general meeting. At question time—after Revlon chairman and chief executive Michel Bergerac had announced the largest increase in dividends in the company's history—Henry rose to demand an end to the "cruel and grotesque" rabbit blinding tests Revlon was performing. Bergerac responded that "regrettably" the choice was between "having to harm animals or harming humans."[23]

Until June 1979, Henry was too busy with the Metcalf-Hatch campaign to take the issue further, but once Governor Carey had signed the repeal bill, Henry turned back to Revlon with renewed urgency. Frank Johnson agreed to a meeting, and on the morning of June 28, Henry was ushered into Johnson's impressive office, overlooking Central Park. Johnson was friendly and seemed to listen to what Henry said, but he was vague about what Revlon was doing by way of research into methods of testing its products without the use of animals. Worse still, it became clear during the meeting that he had not passed on Rack's memo on alternatives to those involved in scientific research at Revlon. After the meeting, Henry held a postmortem with Rack, and they concluded that they were not being taken seriously. Henry wrote a letter in which he said that the failure to forward the memo to the company's own researchers "constitutes a breach of communicative faith as well as an inefficient use of our meeting time." He asked for "a timely response" to the specific proposals that he had made.

A month later, Henry wrote to Michel Bergerac:

Dear Mr. Bergerac,

Nine months ago we gave Mr. Frank Johnson a memo on alternatives to the use of live animals in cosmetic safety testing, a revised copy of which is attached. Our last letter, copy enclosed, was hand delivered on 6/28/79. It was followed by three phone calls to his secretary—and no response from Mr. Johnson.

Though pleasant enough on a personal level, Mr. Johnson's actions signify unconcealed contempt and deliberate insult which may, to a considerable extent, represent a failure to recognize the potential value, to Revlon, of our attempted dialogue. It would also be a gross error for Mr. Johnson to mistake our patience and civility as meekness.

We do hope you'll take an intelligent interest in the possibilities suggested.[24]

BUILDING A COALITION

As Revlon continued to make polite but meaningless responses, Henry began to turn his Coalition to Abolish Metcalf-Hatch into an even more impressive Coalition to Stop Draize Rabbit Blinding Tests. The basis for the new coalition was a five-page blueprint dated August 23, 1979, in which Henry outlined the goals of the coalition. From the start, it was clear that they went beyond abolishing the Draize test itself:

- To challenge the archaic ritual whereby regulatory agencies force the testing of every chemical on tens of millions of animals every year.
- To focus on a single, grotesque, massively used—and particularly vulnerable—animal test, the Draize eye mutilations, as a specific, concrete target.
- To set the precedent of replacing crude, painful, and outdated methods with elegant, modern, nonviolent science through a realistic, effective, and winnable campaign.

The remainder of the blueprint described the Draize test; briefly traversed the recent successes of the animal rights movement; discussed the failure, so far, of alternatives to displace a single animal test; and considered a variety of approaches, including pressure on Revlon and/or Avon and the promotion of a bill mandating regulatory agencies to accept nonanimal methods as they are developed.[25] In keeping with his policy of having an up-front, open agenda, Henry sent the plan to anyone who wanted to know about the coalition or the campaign, including members of the cosmetics industry.[26]

The coalition grew to include more than 400 organizations, with a membership in the millions. The basic running costs were met by the larger societies, especially the Humane Society of the United States, the ASPCA, and the Chicago Anti-Cruelty Society. On one occasion the Humane Society sent out a mailing to 250,000 people on behalf of the coalition, and for a time it employed a part-time staff member to assist the coalition. Apart from that, the coalition had no paid employees. Henry himself was still working as a high school teacher and campaigning in his spare time.

Since American animal organizations are notorious for wasting more energy in fighting one another than in fighting for animals, holding this coalition of disparate groups together was an extraordinary achievement. Henry did it essentially by being so successful that everyone wanted to be a part of the coalition, even if they disagreed with what it was doing. Andrew Rowan, the coalition's science adviser and at the time on the staff of the Humane Society of the United States, described the coalition as "Henry's show and Henry's shop." This does not mean that Henry took no notice of the views of others. On the contrary, the method of operation he uses, which has not changed over the years, is to develop some ideas and then bounce them off a group of people, to whom he will speak one at a time, sometimes in person if they are close by, but usually by phone. The people involved vary according to the issue, but Rowan is usually among them, as are Elinor Molbegott and I. So, too, until his death in 1990, was Leonard Rack. In the end, though, Henry makes the decisions.

At the outset of the Draize campaign, there was a disagreement within the coalition about whether to target a single company or the entire cosmetics industry. The Humane Society of the United States—the largest single organization in the coalition—was opposed to singling out Revlon because it feared legal action. The fear was not entirely groundless. A supermarket had successfully sued a group picketing it for racial discrimination in employment and had won because racial discrimination at that supermarket was apparently no worse than at others. Henry went ahead and targeted Revlon anyway. Rowan recalls: "That caused a certain amount of angst and upset within the Humane Society, but the campaign rolled, and the Humane Society wasn't going to step away from it at that point in time."[27]

Newspaper articles about the Draize test and the coalition began to appear,[28] but they were not having sufficient impact to persuade Revlon to take the issue seriously. In December 1979, Henry wrote to Michel Bergerac again, this time on the letterhead of the Coalition to Stop Draize Rabbit Blinding Tests, seeking a meeting with him. Instead, he got another meeting with Johnson, on January 16, 1980. To represent the coalition, Henry brought Andrew Rowan, Pegeen Fitzgerald, and Elinor Molbegott; and in an attempt to pin Johnson down to something concrete, Henry had sent him some specific proposals for a crash program to find an alternative to the Draize test. Nevertheless, the meeting was more show than substance. The guests were shown the view, and a butler came in to ask them what they would like to drink, but they left without any commitments on Henry's proposals. The next month Johnson wrote that he had passed the proposals on to a subcommittee of the industry organization, the Cosmetic, Toiletry, and Fragrances Association (CTFA). This was hardly the decisive action for which the coalition was looking.

The chief obstacle to getting Revlon to do anything about the Draize test was that American business leaders were simply not used to thinking that the use of animals in product testing merited their concern. As Barnaby Feder put it, "it wouldn't have been on the radar screen for most businesses."[29] Henry began to think about a way to make sure that the issue reached the top of Revlon's priority list.

THE ADVERTISEMENT

In 1977, Mark Graham, an advertising executive at Ogilvy & Mather, was walking down Fifth Avenue when one of Henry's volunteers on the museum campaign gave him a flyer with a picture of a cat's head held in a rigid piece of experimental equipment. Graham was outraged at the experiments described, but in his professional judgment, the design of the flyer left a lot to be desired. He gave his business card to the woman and asked her to pass it on to whomever was organizing the campaign. Henry got the card and filed it away. Two years later, he pulled it out and called Graham to ask if he would be interested in helping to design an advertisement against Revlon and the Draize test. That began a series of lunchtime meetings in which Henry and Graham tossed around ideas for an ad. Eventually, they came up with the advertisement described on the first page of this book. Unlike most previous advertising done by the animal movement, it had the style and professional look of the advertising of major corporations like Revlon itself.

With the mock-up advertisement in hand, Henry and Graham visited Pegeen Fitzgerald in her spacious apartment on Central Park South, and she agreed that the Millennium Guild, an organization she ran, would pay for the ad to run as a full page in the *New York Times*. When it appeared on April 15, 1980, the response was enormous. Letters of protest began to flood into Revlon, and donations and letters of support came to the Millennium Guild. The donations were used to pay for more advertising.[30]

Revlon responded with a press statement denying that it "blinds rabbits for beauty." The company did not, it said, test "raw chemicals" or "known irritants" on rabbits. Moreover, the Draize test was "the commonly accepted standard scientific procedure used to test potential eye irritancy of cosmetic products," was "used by agencies of the federal government concerned with the safety of consumer and chemical products," and there was no substitute for it. The statement also claimed that Revlon was "actively looking for alternative test procedures," but to date had found none.[31]

There was some truth in this response. Substances put in rabbits' eyes by the cosmetics industry were less likely to be highly irritating than household cleaners or raw chemicals tested by other companies. It was also true that the Draize test was a standard test for which there was, as yet, no alternative. So Revlon could well feel ill treated in being chosen as the first target of a campaign against the Draize test. Still, thousands of rabbits suffered in cosmetics testing, and Henry did not feel that the cosmetics industry needed his sympathy just because other industries that caused more suffering had not been targeted. As for Revlon's claim that it was actively looking for alternatives,

How many rabbits does Revlon blind for beauty's sake?

WHAT IS THE DRAIZE RABBIT EYE TEST?

Imagine someone placing your head in a stock. As you stare helplessly ahead, unable to defend yourself, your head is pulled back. Your lower eyelid is pulled away from your eyeball. Then chemicals are poured into the eye. There is pain. You scream and writhe hopelessly. There is no escape. This is the Draize Test. The test which measures the harmfulness of chemicals by the damage inflicted on the unprotected eyes of conscious rabbits. The test that Revlon and other cosmetic firms force on thousands of rabbits to test their products.

FOR RABBITS THE ONLY RELIEF IS...DEATH!

There are no if's, but's and maybe's. These bunny rabbits are bred to be blinded. It's happening today. In 1978, 2,692 rabbits were forced into Revlon's Research Center in the Bronx. And now was given any pain relief even though the Draize manual suggests that eye mutilations be observed for 21 days. Their only salvation from eyes slowly eaten away by chemicals, is death.

THE TERRIBLE IRONY: THE RELIABILITY OF THE DRAIZE TEST IS QUESTIONABLE!

And the intense suffering of innocent rabbits victimized by 36 years of Draize rabbit blindings may not even protect our health. Some researchers consider this test crude and unreliable. For instance, a comprehensive study of 25 laboratories by the noted toxicologists, Weil and Scala found "extreme variation" in evaluating the same chemical in the eyes of rabbits (Toxicology & Applied Pharmacology 19,276-360). And we have the potential for developing better, elegant tests. Thus, ending the Draize horror will benefit both the tormented rabbits and ourselves.

IN THE NAME OF SANITY: STOP THE AGONY!

It appears that one public response which Revlon recognizes, would be a decline in sales. We appeal to you as intelligent, sensitive consumers, to speak to Revlon. When you stand at the cosmetics counter, before reaching for a Revlon product, think of the cries, of the unnecessary pain suffered by thousands of rabbits.

THE ALTERNATIVE: NON-ANIMAL TESTING!

Medical labs no longer kill rabbits in pregnancy tests. In fact, the equivalent of the old 2-4 day rabbit test is performed in a test tube in just minutes and with far greater certainty in the results. We want similar innovation for eye irritancy testing. Even Dr. D. H. Smyth, the late chairman of the Research Defence Society, which actively promotes the use of animals in research, suggested that developing non-animal alternatives to the Draize test may be a relatively simple project which should be launched as soon as possible. We urge Revlon to lead the way in developing cell culture systems.

AND HERE'S WHAT YOU CAN DO!

Write Michel Bergerac, President, Revlon Inc., 767 Fifth Avenue, New York City, NY 10022, that you and your friends will not use Revlon products until Revlon funds a crash program to develop non-animal eye irritancy tests.

Focus on the media. Write letters to the editor. Ask your newspaper, radio and TV stations to tell the Draize rabbit test story. A healthy society does not inflict violence on the powerless; does not pursue "glamour" at the expense of innocent animals.

The Millennium Guild
Pegeen Fitzgerald, President
40 Central Park South, New York, N.Y. 10019

☐ Please send me more information on what I can do to stop the Draize blindings.

☐ Here's my tax-deductible contribution to place more ads to stop the Draize eye tests

Name _____

Address _____

City _____ State _____ Zip Code _____

"I knew the stock was going down that day . . ." said Roger Shelley, Revlon's vice president for investor relations, about the moment he saw this advertisement, which appeared in the New York Times on April 15, 1980. The ad triggered developments that led to the end of the Draize test in the U.S. cosmetics industry.

Henry could only wonder why, in all the time he had been meeting and corresponding with the company, Revlon had been unable to show him a single piece of laboratory research into alternatives that it had initiated.

SHIFTING THE BUREAUCRACY

An essential plank of Revlon's defense of its use of the Draize test was that it was "used by agencies of the federal government concerned with the safety of consumer and chemical products." This careful phrasing was necessary, because the test was not strictly required by any federal government agency. Instead, the agencies demanded that companies supply adequate evidence of the safety of a product—or else they required that the product be sold with a label warning that its safety level was unknown. No major cosmetics or household products manufacturer was prepared to put such a label on its products. Since the agencies always accepted Draize test data as adequate evidence, and since no one knew of any other kind of evidence that they would accept as adequate, the manufacturers continued to use the Draize test.

In these circumstances, it was just as urgent to persuade the regulatory agencies to change their stance as it was to persuade the manufacturers to put money into developing alternatives. There would be no point in having alternative tests unless the agencies were prepared to accept results from them. So while the campaign against Revlon was going on, Henry was also lobbying government at various levels. This produced some success. In a move that revealed how utterly mindless the approach to the use of animals in safety testing had been before Henry started campaigning against it, the government's Interagency Regulatory Liaison Group issued a statement that "substances known to be corrosive may be assumed to be eye irritants" and should not be tested on the eyes of rabbits. Even *Chemical Week* applauded the move:

> It is true that the test has been overworked. No sensible person would require a Draize test to prove that caustic soda is an eye irritant—as has been done in the past. But governmental agencies are relaxing their requirements for Draize testing. This appears to be a result of the group's efforts, and for this, the coalition deserves unqualified praise.[32]

In September, Senator David Durenberger, a Republican from Minnesota, addressed the U.S. Senate on the issue:

> The other evening I was watching the television show *20/20*. One of the issues raised was the continued justification for the Draize test. I was embarrassed at the way Federal officials responded to questions posed by the

reporter. For example, the reporter asked why the Federal Government utilizes such a painful test, and why the animal was not given pain medication. The official responded that "No one thought of it."

Durenberger submitted a resolution that referred to doubts about the reliability of the Draize test and then stated:

> Now therefore be it resolved, it is the sense of the Senate that the Consumer Product Safety Commission, the Environmental Protection Agency, and the Food and Drug Administration set aside research time and funding to develop and validate an alternative nonanimal testing procedure.[33]

Such resolutions are not binding, but if they come to a vote—which is uncommon—they carry some weight with government agencies. The resolution was sent to a committee, where it languished for nearly two years. The Senate finally voted on it—and passed it—on August 11, 1982. By then, much else had already happened.

MAKING PROGRESS

Although Revlon did not respond positively to the advertisement, its rival Avon did. On April 25, 1980, Avon announced that it did not use stocks to hold rabbits and that it had recently adopted new guidelines requiring greater use of local anesthetics and the dilution of test substances. Avon also said that it was studying ways of reducing the overall number of Draize tests it was carrying out.[34]

Another positive response came from the industry's peak body, the Cosmetic, Toiletry, and Fragrance Association, which at Avon's urging set up a Test Systems Task Force and began compiling a computerized list of already-tested materials to help eliminate the unnecessary duplication of tests. On October 6–7, the CTFA held a conference in Washington, at which scientists, officials from government agencies regulating product safety, and members of the animal rights movement met to discuss the Draize test. The conference agreed that the test should be modified and that research projects should be developed to find alternatives to it. But no one was actually encouraged to submit proposals, and there was no indication how any proposals that might be submitted would be funded.[35]

It was at this conference that Henry met Professor William Douglas of Tufts University Medical School, an expert in growing cells in culture. Though Douglas made it clear that he was attending the meeting only out of scientific curiosity, Henry found him impressive and was keen to enroll him in the cause.

After the conference, Henry went to Boston to suggest to Douglas that he develop a proposal for research into the use of cell cultures as an alternative to the Draize test. As a result, Douglas wrote a plan to grow cells from human corneas, obtained from an eye bank. The resulting tissues would be human, rather than rabbit, and testing products on them would be cheaper than using rabbits. Henry had in mind that this might be the kind of proposal that either Revlon or a wealthy antivivisection society might finance. Eventually, he persuaded the New England Anti-Vivisection Society (NEAVS) to fund Douglas's research.

A different consequence of the *New York Times* advertisement came through the initiative of Susan Fowler, editor of *Lab Animal,* a trade magazine for the breeders and suppliers of laboratory animals and the technicians who look after the animals in laboratories. Fowler had worked with laboratory animals herself, had been disturbed by things she had seen, and had been thinking that the topic would make her rather dull trade magazine a little more lively. The advertisement provided her with a hook to accomplish this. She called Henry and asked him if he would do an interview for *Lab Animal*—expecting that he would be reluctant to do so for a readership that the animal movement generally regarded as the enemy. But Henry grabbed at the chance to reach people who were in a position to make a real difference to the welfare of the animals under their care. As a result the January–February 1981 issue of *Lab Animal* was easily the most controversial it had ever published. The cover featured the picture of a rabbit that had been used in the *New York Times* advertisement, and the issue began with an editorial in which Fowler defended her decision to give so much space to "the opinions of an anti-vivisectionist." The interview ran over seven pages, sandwiched between advertisements for squirrel monkeys, chinese hamsters, galvanized metal cages, and rodent guillotines. In the photographs, Henry had a friendly smile; and in the text of the interview, he was forthright but cool. He did not disguise the radical nature of the animal liberation position, but he took pains to stress its roots in the human rights movement and to say that it was in no way antiscience.

The publication of the interview, according to Fowler,

> opened up a whole conversation throughout the lab animal industry. It seems that what had been happening was that the people who worked with the animals felt very strongly about the animals—even though they were only rats, they felt strongly about them—but no one had allowed them to say, "I want these animals to do well, I want them to be happy, I don't want them to be injured." You weren't allowed to talk about that. But by publishing this interview with Henry, it opened it up. Because he doesn't demonize the adversary, he made it possible for all the people in the industry to respond to him, and to his ideas. . . . And that conversation has continued to go on in that magazine for at least sixteen years.[36]

To keep up the momentum against Revlon, on May 13, several hundred people gathered outside its head offices. Some were in rabbit costumes. The demonstration impressed Roger Shelley, then Revlon's vice president for investor relations:

> I remember one day at lunch an enormous demonstration on the Fifth Avenue side of the General Motors building, which was probably the most popular four corners in all of New York City, with the Plaza Hotel in the background, the General Motors building in the foreground, Central Park in one direction and Fifth Avenue heading downtown in the other, and there were hundreds and hundreds and hundreds of people . . . and in the middle there was every major science writer, science reporter, newspaper man, or TV science person in New York—all of whom were interviewing people. And that evening on the news and in the next morning's newspapers, we took a beating the likes of which no opponent of Muhammad Ali ever took.[37]

Roger Shelley had good cause to remember that demonstration, because shortly after it, Frank Johnson, who had been handling the issue for Revlon, was removed from his position, and the task was given to Shelley. After working with investors, the change of job must have been a shock:

> I personally had to sign 20,000 letters. I got letters on Saturdays and Sundays prepared by my secretary, in shoe boxes waiting for me to sign, to people who wrote in. [We answered them] whether they were stockholders, whether they were customers, whether they were employees, whether they were animal rights people from all over the country. This produced writer's cramp . . . but more importantly, it gave a real focal point to the board of directors of Revlon . . . that we had to deal with this.

NEGOTIATING

Revlon's decision to replace Johnson with Shelley was a hopeful sign that the corporation might be moving beyond dealing with the issue at the level of public relations. Shelley decided to meet Henry as soon as he could. In contrast to the meetings in Johnson's office, they met privately at a cocktail lounge, where they both ordered soft drinks and began to talk. Shelley was expecting to have difficulty in finding common ground:

> I felt when I met Henry Spira [that] it was going to be a very contentious set of meetings, because Henry espoused—and quite well—the animal rights groups' feelings about animal testing in the cosmetics industry, and I,

on the other hand, represented consumers, stockholders, employees, and a company, and on this issue there was plenty of opportunity for us to have opposite points of view.

The first feeling I had of Henry, though, was that my preconception was wrong. One major and overriding factor about Henry which I and . . . Michel Bergerac felt in those days was that Henry understood the pressures on business. My first impression was: "Here's a man who has a very strong point of view, have no doubt about it, who is going to make peace with us by making us do the right thing in his eye, but who would listen to us and who would be prepared to work something out that we could live with too."[38]

While Shelley and Henry got to know each other and explore what the "right thing" that Revlon could live with might be, Henry took care that the pressure did not abate. Several smaller demonstrations were held, including one at Bloomingdale's. Supporters asked their local stores not to stock Revlon products; a twelve-year-old boy was reported to have persuaded three small department stores to stop selling Revlon cosmetics.[39] The top-rating television network programs, *20/20* and *Speak Up America,* did stories on the Draize test campaign. The trade journal *Chemical Week* ran an article headed "Cosmetics Firms Feel Heat over the Draize Test."[40] On October 7, a second full-page advertisement appeared in the *New York Times,* with a large picture of a hand putting something into the eye of a rabbit and the caption: "There must be a less ugly way for Revlon to test beauty products."

On November 29, the campaign went international, with simultaneous demonstrations in Britain, Germany, France, Australia, New Zealand, and South Africa. "Remember the Revlon Rabbits' Day" was especially big in Britain, where Jean Pink, founder of a rapidly growing organization called Animal Aid, involved at least 3,500 activists in every major British city, picketing High Street stores with Revlon counters and distributing 400,000 leaflets explaining the nature of the Draize test. Stickers saying REVLON TORTURES RABBITS began appearing in public places.[41]

At Revlon, Shelley started talking to his superiors about the futility of hoping that the issue would just go away without any positive move on Revlon's part. Initially, he encountered some resistance from people who didn't want Revlon to be perceived as having backed down under pressure from the animal rights movement, but when he was able to reach past the level of management immediately above him, he found that

those points of view were not held at the top of the company, nor the level just beneath it. . . . [The Board of Directors and the highest level of management] had a different agenda. Their agenda was that Revlon had been around for fifty years . . . , it was going to live a lot of years afterwards, and

there comes a time when this hackneyed phrase of "corporate responsibility" does come into play.[42]

By November, it was clear that Revlon was getting serious in thinking about
putting money into alternatives. In a letter to Roger Shelley that addressed him
as "Dear Roger" (in eighteen months of discussions and correspondence with
Frank Johnson, it had always been "Dear Mr. Johnson"), Henry wrote that
he was "deeply encouraged and grateful for your active interest in developing
alternatives to the Draize eye test." The letter portrayed Revlon's situation in
positive terms, as an opportunity for the industry leader to be "the pioneer in
linking imaginative, elegant science with effective and efficient safety testing."[43]

In getting to this stage, the development of a relationship of trust between
Henry and Shelley had been crucial. As Barnaby Feder commented:

> In any business when you are dealing with people that have values or an
> agenda that's different from yours, it starts to feel like blackmail. They want
> to know: "If we reach some kind of agreement, is this the end of it? Or is
> this just the first step, and is there going to be more and more and more?"[44]

Henry had been able to convince Shelley that all he wanted Revlon to do was
take the first step. When that was done, the campaign against Revlon would
cease. To convince the top levels of management at Revlon of this, Shelley
took Henry to meet them:

> [It took] very little presentation on my part, especially after some of the
> key people at Revlon met Henry. . . . On the top management floor of
> the General Motors building where Revlon was administered, there wasn't
> one person who didn't get to personally know Henry, and like him, dur-
> ing that period.

Crucially, Shelley accepted Henry's view that this could be a win-win outcome for both of them:

> We determined that one of the ways that maybe Revlon could take an
> industry-leading position at that point was to do something that no one
> else had ever undertaken before, and that was to commission a university to
> begin to undertake an alternative to the Draize eye irritancy test.[45]

Henry used his network of science advisers, particularly Andrew Rowan,
to ensure that Revlon received letters from researchers indicating that they
were interested in pursuing promising lines of research into alternatives to the
Draize test if funds could be provided. After considering several proposals,
Henry and Shelley agreed that Rockefeller University, on New York's Upper
East Side, would be an ideal base for the search for an alternative. Previously

known as the Rockefeller Institute for Medical Research, Rockefeller University was devoted exclusively to research and graduate education in the biomedical sciences. The sixteen Nobel Prizes awarded to its scientists were sufficient proof of its international leadership in research. For so eminent an institution to take the lead in research into alternatives to the use of animals would fulfill Henry's highest hopes. The status of the recipient of the funds was important, not only because the better the institution, the better the chance that it would come up with a viable alternative to the Draize test, but also because simply by conducting research in what had hitherto been an extremely low-status area of research, Rockefeller University would give an unprecedented boost to the whole field of in vitro toxicology. As Henry was later to put it: "It transformed the search for alternatives from some kind of flaky anti-vivisectionist issue to something that received large-scale support from a multi-billion-dollar corporation and was linked with one of the most respected medical research institutions in the country."[46]

Henry and Shelley met Dr. Dennis Stark, director of Rockefeller's Laboratory Animal Research Center, to tell him what they were interested in doing. When Stark was receptive to the idea of receiving a grant from Revlon for the purpose of developing an alternative to the Draize test, Shelley arranged a meeting between Bergerac and Dr. Joshua Lederberg, president of Rockefeller University and a Nobel laureate. The upshot was that Revlon agreed to give the univers ity $750,000 over three years—more than the one-hundredth of 1 percent of their gross revenues that Henry had originally sought—to support research into nonanimal safety tests. Bergerac thought the proposal sufficiently important to take it to Revlon's Board of Directors. The board approved it unanimously.[47]

MAKING HISTORY

Shelley organized a major press conference at the Plaza Hotel, at which Bergerac would hand over the initial check to a representativeof the university. The day of the press conference, December 23, 1980, was cold and snowy, and Shelley feared that no members of the press would show up. He needn't have worried: About 200 journalists and television crews arrived to hear Bergerac say that finding an alternative to animal testing was a priority for Revlon and that the grant was "proof of Revlon's social conscience."[48] The words would have brought a smile to Henry's face, but he was not present. Revlon had not invited him, and he tactfully accepted his exclusion from the culmination of his campaign. The next part of Bergerac's speech was the result of a suggestion Henry had made. It served as a starting point for Henry's next task and offered an elegant way for Revlon to get even with the other cosmetic companies that had remained aloof when Revlon was under attack:

> Draize is not a Revlon problem, it is a problem shared by all personal care product companies. I am, therefore, calling on such companies to join us as full partners in this research program. I know that the Chief Executives of Avon, Bristol-Myers, Elizabeth Arden, Gillette, Johnson & Johnson, Estée Lauder, L'Oréal, Max Factor, Maybelline, Noxell and Procter & Gamble share our concern for consumer safety and I trust they will participate with us.[49]

For Shelley it was a memorable day:

> The attitude of the company was . . . a great pride in what we were doing. Everybody in our company felt good when they went home that night because their kids would no longer look at them cockeyed as being someone who does untoward things to rabbits.[50]

The Coalition to Stop Draize Rabbit Blinding Tests issued its own news release. Journalists who picked it up expecting a triumphant proclamation of a famous animal rights victory over a major corporation were surprised to find themselves reading a statement that, from first to last, congratulated Revlon for its "initiative," its "pioneering step," and its "historic breakthrough." The word "victory" was absent, as was any suggestion that Revlon's decision was a response to threats or pressure of any kind:

> We congratulate Revlon and Rockefeller University for making history. This is the first major linkup of a giant corporation with a leading research center to replace crude animal tests with imaginative, humane science. . . . This can be the beginning of ending the suffering of tens of millions of live animals for safety testing.[51]

The statement closed by expressing the hope that "by all of us pulling together . . . the promise of this historic opening will be realized" and by thanking Michel Bergerac, Roger Shelley, and the key figures at Rockefeller University "for constructing a viable program with speed and sensitivity."

BEYOND REVLON

Henry had made a commitment to Revlon that the campaign against it would cease as soon as it made the commitment he was seeking. The campaign had

worked so well, however, that there were some in the animal rights movement who wanted to keep it going as long as Revlon was still doing the Draize
test. In Britain, Jean Pink vowed that "the demonstrations will continue."[52]
For Henry, this was a threat to his credibility, which he would need for the
broader goals he had in mind. He therefore suggested to Pink, as well as
to American groups that were keen to continue to harass Revlon, that—as
Bergerac had indicated in his speech—the ball was now in the court of other
cosmetics companies. Instead of continuing with the Revlon campaign, the
coalition should get ready for a campaign against Avon.

Henry then wrote to David Mitchell, chairman of Avon Products, Inc.:

> Undoubtedly, Revlon has set a standard with its $750,000 grant to Rock-
> efeller University. . . . Revlon has shown that a corporate giant can have
> the vision to be responsive in a constructive, innovative and substantive
> fashion. We expect no less from Avon.[53]

The letter mixed encouragement with a delicately veiled threat of demonstrations. Having watched what happened to Revlon, Avon needed little persuading. On March 18, 1981, the company issued a news release pledging a
matching $750,000 donation to a fund created by the CTFA for research into
alternatives to the Draize test.

Henry turned next to Bristol-Myers, a company that was vulnerable to a
campaign because it too was involved in cosmetics through its Clairol line of
products, but had a much larger business in pharmaceuticals. Henry wanted to
use the company as a means to involve the pharmaceutical industry in the area
of alternatives. Bristol-Myers was more reluctant to put money into alternatives
than Avon had been. Feeling that it was the victim of an extortion attempt, at
first all it was willing to do was contribute $200,000 to the CTFA fund. That
was not enough for Henry, who considered that this was not pro rata given the
size of the corporation and the contributions made by Revlon and Avon. Nor
was it enough for Jean Pink, who was also involved in the negotiations and was
seeking a donation toward the Fund for the Replacement of Animals in Medical
Experiments (FRAME). At one point, Henry had an advertisement featuring
Bristol-Myers drawn up and ready to go to press. On August 21, 1981, Henry
wrote one of his bluntest letters to Richard Gelb, chairman of Bristol-Myers:

> Last year, Bristol-Myers' laboratories confined thousands of innocent
> animals, including 77 primates, 236 dogs, 219 cats, 1,507 guinea pigs, 106
> hamsters, 2,845 rabbits and uncounted rodents—all doomed to a life or
> death filled with pain.
>   And while the animals suffer in agony, Bristol-Myers spent over half a
> billion dollars to promote its products. It is our feeling that most people

believe in fair play, in decent values, in not harming humans nor other animals. And that means that when you deliberately blind, poison and gas animals to death, you have an obligation to plow some of your profits back to phase out the animal suffering you are responsible for as well as to up-grade the archaic tests used to "protect" your consumers.

And we believe that most people, all around our planet, would be will-ing to trade off two minutes of your TV commercials—$1,000,000—in order to phase out the intense suffering of animals.

We attempted, through three months of dialogue with your staff, to establish a collaborative, cooperative approach. But, for Bristol-Myers, ani-mal suffering seems to be a game—a game to be played with clever tricks. . . . And Bristol-Myers has a rotten track record. You were the most persis-tent and the last remaining company to raid New York's animal shelter for some kid's lost and scared to death pet. But from your point of view, this slave trade was eminently profitable. In 1977 you ripped off 558 dogs and 163 cats from the Central New York Society for the Prevention of Cruelty to Animals. . . . You paid $7.14 per dog and $3.44 per cat; commercially, you had to pay $130 per dog and $22 per cat. Curiously, your trafficking in lost pets for profit has not, to date, been publicized.

Please rest assured that the matter of your obligation to the lab animals is not closed. We intend to pursue every avenue to make Bristol-Myers responsive to its moral obligations.[54]

Following this letter there were further meetings and discussions with the company. In November, the final negotiations, with a phone hook-up to Jean Pink in Britain, went on late into the night until Bristol-Myers agreed to contribute a total of $500,000, including $100,000 to FRAME. On that basis, Henry and Jean agreed to drop their plans for a public campaign against the company.[55]

Although Bristol-Myers had initially contributed to the search for alterna-tives only under extreme pressure, it subsequently became a genuine advocate of alternatives. In 1983, it set up its own Biochemical and Cellular Toxicology Department to develop test-tube methods of screening drugs. It sponsored symposia and helped to establish the Industrial In-Vitro Toxicology Group, an industry-wide association of those developing and validating the application in industry of in vitro testing methods. Avon also later became enthusiastic about promoting alternatives. To Henry, that proved that the move into alternatives really was a win–win situation.

Meanwhile, on May 11, 1981, Henry went with ASPCA lawyer Elinor Molbegott and representatives of the Humane Society of the United States and the Anti-Cruelty Society to a meeting with Richard Gross, the executive di-rector of the Consumer Product Safety Commission, and asked him to clarify the commission's Draize test regulations so that industry could no longer claim that it had to perform the Draize test because the CPSC required it. According to the CPSC's record of the meeting, it ended "with an understanding that Commission staff would begin to draft a letter regarding the acceptability of equivalent testing in lieu of the Draize test." It took until January 1982 for the letter to be written, stating that the CPSC would accept "appropriate" data in lieu of the Draize test. This was vague, but the door was now open and the coalition could refute any corporation that tried to use the CPSC regulations to argue that the government insisted on Draize test data.[56] Later, the CPSC issued revised guidelines for the Draize test that had the effect of halving the number of rabbits that corporations needed to use to submit acceptable data. The CPSC also recommended the use of specific anesthetics and ceased its own practice of routinely conducting Draize tests.[57] Shifting the positions taken by the federal government was frustratingly slow, but it was having effects beyond the cosmetics industry, and thus saving much larger numbers of animals from having to go through the pain of the Draize test.

The Cosmetic, Toiletry, and Fragrance Association fund was still growing. Before long Estée Lauder, Max Factor, Chanel, and Mary Kay Cosmetics had joined the other companies in contributing to it. The CTFA announced that it planned to use the fund to establish a new Center for Alternatives to Animal Testing. The recipient would get an initial grant of $1 million, to be followed by a similar amount at a later time. Proposals were sought, and the successful applicant was Dr. Alan Goldberg, a researcher at one of the country's most prestigious medical schools, that of Johns Hopkins University in Baltimore. The first $1 million was given to Johns Hopkins on September 21, 1981.

Henry kept a close watch on the newly established Center for Alternatives to Animal Testing. He knew that such a center could easily develop its own empire-building goals and that these would not necessarily be the same as the goals of those who had worked to establish the center. At first, that appeared to be exactly what was happening. Goldberg, the center's director, was spending more time raising further funds and building an endowment than in getting the research program off and running. Henry felt he had to challenge this way of doing things. Instead of writing directly to Goldberg, however, he wrote a draft of a letter to Goldberg and sent it to a wide range of Goldberg's colleagues and others who had been involved with establishing the center. Along with the draft was a cover note explaining that this was a proposed letter Henry was planning to send to Goldberg and seeking comments on it. The draft was strongly written. Concerning Goldberg's fund-raising efforts, Henry wrote: "We ask ourselves, are you acting in the best long term interest of the lab animals and the concerned members of industry and the scientific community, or are you making a quick killing by selling P.R. kits at bargain basement rates?" The draft was equally critical of the use to which the money already raised was being put:

> The presumed purpose of this funding, we can agree, was to set up innovative research programs which would produce usable results in the shortest time. Yet when we examine the record, to the extent that it has been made available by yourself, we see no signs—or even plans—for innovative programs.
>
> To the contrary, what appears to have taken place is that a considerable sum of money has been used to "pad" existing programs which already enjoy NIH megafunding and which would have been pursued in any event.
>
> The net effect of this approach, it seems, is to render the CTFA funding effort impotent because nothing new is added to existing efforts.

The draft concluded by suggesting that the review and advisory panels Goldberg had set up consisted largely of his friends and cronies and should be replaced by an independent panel of scientists.[58]

The draft never became a finished letter and was never sent to Goldberg. Instead, as Henry had planned, over a period of several weeks, Goldberg kept hearing disturbing things about it from colleagues to whom the draft had been sent for comment. There was no direct confrontation, but Goldberg got the message and heeded it. Relations between Henry and Goldberg were strained for a while, but the center did become a leader in the development of nonanimal methods of testing, and Henry gave it his full support. Ten years later, at a ceremony to mark the center's tenth anniversary, Goldberg was able to laugh about the strategy Henry had used to make him do the right thing.

William Douglas, the cell culture expert from Tufts University whom Henry had met in Washington the previous fall, had also put in an application to the CTFA, hoping that his Cell Culture Unit at Tufts University would receive the million-dollar grant. His application made it to a short list of three but lost out to the greater prestige of Johns Hopkins University Medical School. Douglas had not missed out altogether, however, because NEAVS awarded him $200,000 to develop an eye irritancy test using cells obtained from human corneas. At a ceremony at Tufts Medical School on April 8, 1981, Judge Robert Ford, president of NEAVS, handed over a check for the first installment, in the amount of $100,000. The society's newsletter, *Reverence for Life,* described this as "an historical moment": "Never before has an animal rights organization joined forces with a medical research institution to develop an alternative to the use of animals in experimentation and product testing."[59]

NEAVS also sponsored the first issue, in May 1982, of a newsletter called *In Touch,* containing news about alternative methods in toxicology. William Douglas was a member of the editorial board, and he also contributed the lead story for the first issue, an article on the search for alternatives to the Draize test. The article was illustrated by a photo showing a smiling Douglas overseeing the work of three of his colleagues. One of them, a woman, was peering down a microscope. The caption read "Stan Spillman, Jane Aghajanian and Bill Douglas conducting research at Tufts University."[60] In fact, the woman in the photo was Diane Romeo, a much more junior technician than Aghajanian. The erroneous caption was no accident. Although Aghajanian had nothing to do with the work on the grant from NEAVS, Douglas had put her name on the proposal, rather than Romeo's, in order to be able to justify receiving payment for a higher salary.

That fiddle turned out to be one of Douglas's more minor sins. One morning when Aghajanian was checking expense claims made on the NEAVS grant, she came across receipts from a pharmacy for a large quantity of "biological fluid collection units." As she was wondering what this could be, she noticed that someone had written on one receipt the word "Ramses"—a popular brand of condom. That was odd, but Aghajanian assumed that Douglas must be putting the condoms to some scientific use and passed the receipt on for payment. Soon, even stranger things began happening. Douglas told her that the laboratory would put a graduate student named Robin Benedict on its payroll. She was, Douglas said, working for a colleague at the nearby Massachusetts Institute of Technology. Then Douglas started charging an extraordinary number of travel expenses to the NEAVS grant. Among them were trips to Washington, D.C., and Chicago for Benedict to attend training courses. To send a graduate student interstate, with expenses paid, in order to take training courses was unheard of. When Douglas's staff found other suspicious expense claims amounting to over $10,000, one of them went to Judge Ford with the evidence. Ford, who had lauded Douglas as recently as the previous NEAVS annual general meeting, did not go to the police. Instead, he passed the documents on to Tufts University so that the matter could be handled without publicity. An internal investigation uncovered still more fraudulent expense claims. Douglas was abruptly suspended and locked out of his office. Henry found out that something was amiss when Douglas called and asked him to contact the dean so that he could get on with his work. But there was no question of that. With the threat of a criminal prosecution hanging over him, Douglas agreed to resign.

For a short time, Douglas explored proposals to take his research to another university. These plans stalled when Robin Benedict was reported missing. Newspapers referred to her as the "missing beauty" and mentioned her link with an eminent university professor. Bit by bit, the story emerged. Benedict was a very attractive twenty-one-year-old prostitute. She had no qualifications in biology and did not study at MIT. On the night she vanished, she had told a friend she was going to see Douglas, who was one of her regular clients. Douglas told the police that he was indeed one of her clients, but he added that their relationship was more than this might suggest. They were close friends, he said, and often spent the day together, of which only a small part would involve sexual activity. Despite this "close friendship," Benedict charged Douglas for the time she spent with him, at her usual rate of $100 per hour—much of it drawn from the NEAVS grant. Douglas did not deny that Benedict had visited him at his home on the night she disappeared—his wife was out, he said—but he claimed that Benedict had then left. This story began to look dubious when a man who scavenged in roadside trash cans found a bloodstained shirt wrapped around a sledgehammer. The shirt belonged to Douglas, and the sledgehammer turned out to have been borrowed from his wife's father. As the evidence against Douglas strengthened—despite the absence of a body—he accepted a plea bargain and pleaded guilty to a charge of manslaughter. His story was that he killed her after she had first attacked him with the hammer. Then he threw her body into a dumpster that was later trucked to a landfill site.

Douglas was sentenced to eighteen years in jail. He contacted Henry while he was in prison and asked Henry to be a character reference at his parole hearings. Henry declined. Douglas served his time and is now free. Tufts repaid the misappropriated funds to NEAVS. Robin Benedict's body was never recovered.[61]

· 4 ·

Conflict and Progress

If people are going to develop alternatives, it's the people in the research community who will be developing alternatives. If you're going to get the regulatory agencies to change their requirements, it's going to be animal researchers who are the ones who are going to do it, it's not going to be us who are going to do it. I mean, these are the folks that you need if you're going to be serious about change. . . . You're not going to reprogram them by saying we're saints and you're sinners, and we're going to clobber you with a two-by-four in order to educate you.

Henry Spira

BEYOND THE DRAIZE TEST

By 1982, the Draize campaign was having an impact. In July, Revlon reported that it had established a panel to ensure that unnecessary Draize tests were not performed, and as a result, it had cut back the number of rabbits it used annually in the test from 2,210 in 1979 to 1,431 in 1981. Avon adopted a policy of always using local anesthetics if there was any anticipated discomfort for the animals. Bristol-Myers said that it was using fewer animals than had been used in the classical Draize test. All three of the companies were continuing to contribute to research programs designed to find alternatives to the Draize test.

Both Henry and Jean Pink were anxious to build on the momentum of the undoubted success that the campaign had achieved. But how? The Draize test would not disappear entirely until an alternative had been developed and shown to be at least as reliable as the Draize test itself. That was still some years away. It would be impossible to keep people enthused about a campaign against the Draize test for all the time that it could take for scientists to find alternatives to it. In any case, now that the big cosmetics companies were paying for research into alternatives, they were no longer available as targets. Henry had known for some time what the next campaign would be about. Back in 1978, in a first draft of their initial memo to Revlon, Leonard Rack and Henry had mentioned the need for replacing not only the Draize test, but an even more widely used test known as the LD50—a test that takes its name from its goal, which is to measure the lethal dose of a substance for 50 percent of a group of animals. Perhaps 40 rats would be used, or 200 mice, or 20 dogs- whatever the test animals were, and whatever the substance to be tested was, they would be made to ingest more and more of it until half of them died.

By 1980, the LD50 was being performed on about 4 to 5 million animals each year in the United States alone, making it perhaps twenty times as common as the Draize. To grasp the idea of how much suffering this was causing, consider that in the process of finding the level that killed half of the sample, all of the animals would likely become very ill before some died and some recovered. The tests commonly last fourteen days, but some take up to six months. Symptoms often observed include convulsions, breathlessness, vomiting, internal bleeding, tremors, and paralysis. If the animals will not eat the substance when it is mixed in their food, it will be force-fed to them through a tube down their throat. The same technique will be used if the substance is a relatively harmless one, and enormous quantities have to be given to the animals to make half of them die.

For all the suffering it caused, the growth in use of the LD50 had no sound scientific basis. It was, rather, a case of a bureaucratic liking for mathematical precision, even when it is completely meaningless. The LD50 was first developed in 1927 to measure the potency of drugs like insulin or digitalis with which there is a narrow range between the amount that will cure and the amount that will kill. Since the drugs were not then available in a chemically pure form, it was necessary to find a way of determining their exact strength. But the fact that the test gave a mathematically precise result made it appealing for other purposes, and it soon became the standard way of assessing the toxicity of every new chemical or product. From lipsticks to oven cleaners, from paint thinners to distilled water, from food colorings to fake snow for decorating Christmas trees—all received an LD50 value derived from testing them on animals, usually on at least two separate species.[1] When used in this manner, the LD50's appearance of mathematical precision is illusory. LD50 values vary unpredictably among different species and even among different strains of rats. A precise LD50 value for rats or dogs eating large quantities of a food coloring in fourteen days does not enable us to say anything precise about how toxic the substance will be for humans consuming small quantities of the substance over a period of years. For that reason, as with the Draize test, even those who were not opposed to animal experimentation in general thought that the LD50 was outdated. Dr. Gerhard Zbinden, a World Health Organization toxicology consultant, had written that "most experts considered the modern toxicological routine procedure a wasteful endeavour in which scientific inve ntiveness and common sense have bee n replaced by a thoughtless completion of standard protocols."[2] Henry needed only to put this more pithily to suit it to his campaign materials: "The test defies common sense. Does one really need to know how many bars of pure Ivory soap it takes to kill a dog?"[3]

One aspect of this new initiative made Henry uncomfortable. In the museum campaign, he had stressed that the protests would not end until the experiments were stopped completely, and he had kept his word. The Amnesty International and Metcalf-Hatch campaigns had also been brought to a successful conclusion. Yet the Draize test was still being carried out. Was Henry quitting without winning? In January 1982, he wrote to members of the Coalition to Stop Draize Rabbit Blinding Tests that "our track record will be maintained. We stay with a campaign until it is won." The Draize coalition would remain intact until the Draize test had been abolished, he promised, but the momentum developed would be used to challenge other animal tests.

As part of his commitment to keeping up the momentum of the Draize campaign while taking on a new target, Henry took early retirement. While he still enjoyed high school teaching, it was not what he most wanted to be doing. From this point on, he was a full-time campaigner for animals. In addition to the $500 a month he receives from his retirement fund and—after he turned sixty-five—his social security payments, he pays himself $15,000 a year from Animal Rights International and reimburses himself for up to $4,800 worth of expenses annually. Luckily, he doesn't need to spend time raising money for his efforts because he has attracted the support of a small number of people who are prepared to make substantial donations to Animal Rights International. In 1980, for example, Helaine Lerner came across a brochure publicizing a demonstration against Revlon at Bloomingdale's. She knew nothing of the Draize test at the time and was shocked by the photograph of rabbits in stocks. She went to the demonstration and afterward asked Henry how she could help. She and her husband, Sid, both got involved, becoming advisers to Henry's campaigns as well as paying for advertisements and other expenses. She finds it much more effective than giving funding to large organizations, where the money "can go down a deep hole and you never know what the results of it are." Later, Barbara Clapp also found her way to Henry, initially planning to leave money to him in her will. He told her that she would do better to give some money now, so that she could judge for herself what use he made of it. She agreed and has been so pleased by the results Henry has achieved that she now works with Henry on projects that particularly interest her and supports them financially. Sometimes she might herself suggest a project or put Henry in touch with people who she thinks might have something to contribute. Henry, in turn, keeps his donors involved in what he is doing, frequently calling or sending them reports and clippings, and getting feedback and ideas from them.[4]

During the campaign against the Draize test, Henry had come to appreciate the value of an international approach. The toxicology community is an international one, and products are traded across national boundaries. If one significant market for an American-made product requires the use of a particular test before allowing that product to be sold within its borders, then the test will be done, even if it is not required in the United States. So the campaign against the LD50 had to be an international campaign. In May 1981, at the invitation of Animal Aid, he traveled to England, and at a rally in Birmingham, he and Jean Pink told a cheering group of supporters that they were jointly establishing an international campaign for the abolition of the LD50 test.[5] Like the Draize test campaign, it was to be run by a coalition. To create the American wing of the Coalition to Abolish the LD50, all that was needed was a change of title at the top of the letterhead. The steering committee and sponsoring organizations remained the same.

For his work on the LD50, Henry added another adviser to the loose group of people he would call from time to time to check out his ideas. Myron Mehlman was the director of toxicology and environmental health at Mobil Oil, in New York, when Henry heard that he had set up a review of the usage of animals at his laboratory. Mehlman was trying to determine the long-term effects of chemicals without spending the usual three to five years feeding them to animals. Under his direction, Mobil became an early leader in moving to computer models, tissue culture, and bacterial testing to generate information about the toxicity of materials.[6] Mehlman agreed to talk to Henry, and they soon began to meet frequently over coffee at the end of the working day. Mehlman thought that the use of animals in toxicology could easily by reduced by 90 percent, and in some areas by as much as 98 percent, without the loss of any significant information. This confirmed Henry's hunch that the LD50 continued to be the standard toxicity test only because of "cultural lag." As in the case of the Draize test, less painful tests were not used because, as the federal official quoted by Senator Durenberger had said, "No one thought of it."

How, then, to make them think of it? While Henry was still looking around for the best lever to pull in order to get things moving in the right direction, the Pennsylvania Animal Rights Coalition announced that on October 14, 1982, it would demonstrate against animal testing in front of the international head offices of SmithKline Beckman, in Philadelphia. The

Pennsylvania Animal Rights Coalition had been formed in January 1982 for the purpose of working with Henry's LD50 coalition, but it had planned this event on its own, after obtaining documents showing that SmithKline, the pharmaceutical arm of SmithKline Beckman, had used 31,839 animals in 1980. The corporation was a sensitive target, because, as a SmithKline executive recalled, "We'd just built a new hotel next to our headquarters, so we weren't delighted with the idea of pickets marching back and forth."

Henry contacted SmithKline, sending it a copy of the Pennsylvania Animal Rights Coalition's newsletter, in which the planned demonstration was announced, together with a letter suggesting that SmithKline might like to take some positive steps that could head off the demonstration. Jim Russo, a SmithKline executive, sought the advice of Frankie Trull, executive director of the Association for Biomedical Research, who said that they should talk with Henry, because "rather than standing outside and pointing a finger and saying everyone's terrible," Henry would try to understand their point of view. SmithKline took Trull's advice and agreed to talk to him. Henry got together with the Pennsylvania Animal Rights Coalition and worked out a package of proposals that Henry would ask SmithKline to accept; if it did, Henry would agree to intercede to have the demonstration called off. On October 5, Henry met Stanley Crooke, vice president of research and development at SmithKline & French Laboratories, the corporation's research subsidiary. After more than two hours of discussion, Crooke accepted all of the proposals and, on October 8, put their agreement in writing:

> Within my organization, I will elevate the status of the effort to reduce animal use by discussing it at my next executive committee meeting later this month and ask that a formal plan be developed.
>
> We have agreed to recommend the development of a symposium jointly sponsored by your organization and the Pharmaceutical Manufacturers Association or a group of pharmaceutical companies. The symposium will address progress in the task of reducing the use of animals and attempt to develop scientific and regulatory recommendations for future action in this regard.
>
> We shall continue efforts in the appropriate forum to encourage collaboration between the industry and the FDA [Food and Drug Administration] on the use of animals. We shall also continue to work through the appropriate professional organizations to publicize our work when it may help reduce reliance on animals while meeting the scientific and regulatory requirements.[7]

The demonstration was canceled.[8]

The Pharmaceutical Manufacturers Association (PMA), mentioned in Crooke's letter, represented 149 research-based American pharmaceutical companies, together accounting for most of the new prescription drugs developed in the United States. Crooke was a member of the PMA's research and development section. He told Henry that the PMA had already been discussing the issue of the classic LD50 and was ready to come out with a statement recommending that it should not be required by federal government agencies. On October 11, Henry sent the association a memo seeking a review of all testing procedures. The association, with Crooke urging it on, moved swiftly. On October 21, 1982, it issued a news release saying that "the classical LD-50 test which utilizes many animals to determine an LD-50 value with mathematical precision lacks justification. . . . Regulatory requirements should accommodate this position."[9]

In rapid succession, other organizations issued similar statements. Among them were the CTFA, the Soap and Detergent Association, and the National Society for Medical Research.[10] In February 1983, Henry wrote to Dr. David Rall, director of the Department of Health and Human Services' National Toxicology Program, asking him to "perform a leadership role in reviewing the massive use of the classical LD50 and promoting change in regulatory procedures." On March 3, Rall replied, describing the test as "an anachronism" that "does not provide much useful information about the health hazards to humans from chemicals." He added that the National Toxicology Program does not use the LD50.[11]

Now Henry was ready for an assault on the bureaucracy. At a community benefit in Trenton, New Jersey, he had won a raffle, for which the prize was free advertising space in the local paper. On May 3, 1983, a full-page advertisement appeared in the *Trentonian* featuring a photograph of a dog looking sadly through bars. Above the photograph was the question, "Would you pay someone to kill this animal?"; alongside the photo were the words: "The LD50 causes agonizing death for millions of lab animals . . . And you pay for it!" The text below described the LD50 and asked readers to write to their congressional representatives and ask them to contact the appropriate regulatory agency and demand an end to the LD50.

The ad wasn't intended only for the people of Trenton. NBC's *Today Show* had been interested in doing a segment on the LD50 and the ad gave them a hook. On the day after it appeared, Henry was on the *Today Show,* telling Jane Pauley and 7 million viewers about the LD50 and putting the blame for it squarely on the bureaucrats:

> *Henry:* It's not that anybody gets their jollies out of seeing animals suffer.
> . . . You have this enormous bureaucratic inertia. This is the way it's been
> done for the last fifty-five years, and how do you move a bureaucracy at
> a time when industry says you don't need [the LD50], the Pharmaceutical
> Manufacturers Association says you don't need it, the Cosmetic, Toiletry,

and Fragrance Association says you don't need it, the National Society for Medical Research says you don't need it . . .

Jane Pauley: Who says you need it?

Henry: I don't know what you did to arrange this program, but I would tend to imagine that you would have had a very hard time getting anybody from the regulatory section to come up here . . .

Jane Pauley: EPA, FDA?

Henry: . . . and defend the LD50.

Jane Pauley: That's true. We tried.

Henry: They refuse to defend it in public debate, yet they require it. Even though it might not be written in their rules.

Jane Pauley: They did point that out, that it's not written regulation.

Henry: The point is, nobody's ever gotten a chemical accepted without having the LD50, it's the most routine thing.

Not all things during the interview, however, went Henry's way. Pauley threw at him one of the real difficulties that a campaign against the LD50 had to face:

> *Jane Pauley:* Is anybody really interested, to be cold and blunt about it, about rats? If we could see your ad again . . . [the advertisement appears on screen] . . . You use a beagle. But in point of fact, it's almost exclusively a test performed on rats, because rats are cheaper. Beagles are expensive. So isn't it a little misleading to play on our emotions with beagle faces?
>
> *Henry:* I think you've got something of a point there. Most of the animals are rodents, there's no question about that. There are also some dogs used, some primates, some guinea pigs, et cetera. What we are trying to connect up with is that the vast majority of people would much prefer that animals not be harmed, and a dog is part of the household, it's a popular animal, et cetera. But I think that people can also relate . . .
>
> *Jane Pauley:* So you're intentionally being manipulative—that's the strategy?
>
> *Henry:* You're going to have a hard time, people looking at an ad with a rodent on it, basically. . . . The criteria really should be, I think, not how popular is an animal, but can it tell the difference between pain and pleasure?

The advertisement was also run in the *Washington Post,* and Henry had several other media appearances. Many people responded to the suggestion that they write to the federal agencies that required the LD50 to be performed.

Would you pay someone to kill this animal?

This ad, which appeared in the Trentonian *on May 3, 1983, gave Henry the opportunity to talk about the LD50 to 7 million viewers of the* Today Show.

An article in *Science* reported that a "hapless official from the Department of Transportation's Office of Hazardous Substances said his office has been besieged with more than 1,000 letters in the past year protesting the agency's alleged requirement for LD50 testing."[12]

Meanwhile, the European side of the campaign was keeping pace with progress in America. In August 1983, the expert committee on drug testing of the European Commission reported that the number of animals killed in Europe could be cut by a quarter by amending a 1975 European Economic Community directive that required all new drugs to be put through the LD50 test. The experts said that the test was clumsy and should be replaced by a more detailed study of the mechanism of toxicity.[13]

New York Congressman Bill Green wrote a letter that was signed by seventy-three other members of Congress, asking federal agencies to eliminate the LD50. Since Green was on the House committee that allocated funds to the regulatory agencies, he had some leverage with them. The pressure from Congress and the public, together with the growing consensus against the LD50 within the science community, led the FDA to hold a day-long workshop on November 9, 1983, that featured officials of the FDA and five other federal agencies, as well as scientists and representatives from the cosmetics and drug industry. Henry attended, and at his urging, two long-standing and prominent members of the animal welfare movement, Cleveland Amory and Christine Stevens, were also there.

The meeting saw a succession of regulatory agency officials standing up and saying what Henry had been saying for the past year. The FDA, said Gary Flamm, an official from that organization, "does not have any regulation specifying the need for LD50 testing. . . . The LD50 test is of limited value and we would prefer other testing." According to a report in the CTFA's newsletter, "a consensus emerged that the classical LD50 test has 'limited' value in safety evaluation, and that limit tests or range-finding studies requiring fewer animals can provide sufficient oral toxicity data."[14] A representative of the PMA said later that "the meeting was the first time FDA stated its position clearly."

New Scientist described the meeting as "an important victory" for the movement to end unnecessary research on animals. Nevertheless, the meeting did not resolve the contradictions within the federal bureaucracy as a whole, because the Environmental Protection Agency continued to require some form of the LD50 for pesticides and toxic substances, while the Department of Transportation required a modified form of the LD50 to be performed in order to determine how a substance such as a chemical should be shipped.[15] The agencies promised to issue more formal statements on their positions, and these appeared during 1984.[16] The EPA then fell into line, saying that it "discourages the use of animals solely for the calculation of an LD50," and instead suggested a "limit" test using fewer animals.[17]

GOING FOR THE LESSER EVIL

The growing consensus, both outside and then within the regulatory agencies, that the classical LD50 should not be used was welcome news, but as people in the animal movement began to understand its implications, Henry came under fire from some elements of the movement. Jane Pauley put the problem to Henry during the same *Today Show* segment:

> *Henry:* The science community is saying . . . you can get the same amount of data with six animals as you can out of two hundred.
>
> *Jane Pauley:* So you're not unilaterally banning lethal dose testing on live animals? You're just saying, don't kill millions when hundreds of thousands would do?
>
> *Henry:* Well I think it's almost like a triage system. . . You have a certain universe of pain and death. What's the most rapid way to bring this universe of pain and death down? And the most rapid way is, right now, . . . let's do away with the classical Lethal Dose 50, which uses sixty to two hundred animals, and the other thing that they could be using instead, for instance, is an approximate lethal dose where you use six animals, because all you do is get a range finding anyway, and nobody is really interested in killing half of the population.

For many activists in the animal rights movement, this was heresy. All animal testing was a violation of the rights of animals and should be stopped. Henry's ultimate goal was as radical as anyone's, but he also thought that it was simply unrealistic to expect that goal to be achieved in the near future. So what should he do? Say that the approximate lethal dose test—a test carried out by administering increasing doses of the substance to perhaps six animals—is no better than the LD50, and thereby abandon the very real prospect of making a 90 percent reduction in the number of animals suffering painful deaths in safety testing? For what? Would this bring the total abolition of testing on animals any closer? It was hard to see why it would. All his experience in the human rights movement told Henry that change came about step-by-step, not in a single, revolutionary stroke. If refusing to countenance any animal testing at all did not bring the total abolition of animal testing any closer, why take that stance? Was it just a matter of keeping ourselves morally pure? Henry didn't care for that style of morality. His thought was: The animals are suffering now, and if we can change things so that some of them don't suffer, we should do so.

As long as Henry's campaigns were tackling the corporate giants of America and winning, his critics were few and easily ignored. They remained on the sidelines, though, ready to emerge as soon as things were not going so well.

PROCTER & GAMBLE

In addition to getting the regulatory agencies to move away from the LD50, Henry was keen to get the big corporations involved. After his successes in persuading so many cosmetics companies to put money into the search for alternatives to the Draize, it would have been relatively easy to proceed along the same lines with regard to the LD50. Instead, he considered a different approach:

> At this point we realized that we had the formula for liberating money from just about every company that experiments on animals and wants to keep its image clean with consumers. But then we decided to reevaluate what we were doing . . . we thought that perhaps our strategy was not going to be the best way rapidly to bring down the total amount of pain and death. Our reasoning was that the real expertise for reduction and replacement might reside in the corporations themselves rather than in the universities. The universities, after all, are interested in obtaining more money and doing more research. Perhaps that will prompt them to achieve quick success so that they can boast of their achievements, but then again perhaps it won't. Anyway, we didn't want to be simply unpaid fundraisers for every medical school in the USA. So from this point we switched our strategy. We went to Procter & Gamble, and we told them we weren't interested in bucks; we wanted an internal plan and programme to reduce and replace the use of animals, and we wanted the plan publicized so that it could be used as a model for other companies to follow.[18]

If Revlon had seemed a corporate giant when Henry tackled the Draize test, it was puny compared to Procter & Gamble, which made laundry detergents such as Tide, soaps like Ivory, toothpastes, and over-the-counter drugs. Procter & Gamble was a true multinational, producing 260 different brands in 140 companies. Its attitude to reducing the use of animals would make a crucial difference to a huge industry that so far had not been touched by the animal rights movement.

Henry wrote some initial letters that got a polite brush-off. He bought a share of Procter & Gamble stock and went to the 1982 annual meeting at the company's head office in Cincinnati, Ohio:

> You've got to imagine, P&G is this enormous institution, physically it's enormous, like a whole city by itself. When you go to the bathroom, every piece of soap around is identical, so they're very much into predictability. So there I go into the shareholders' meeting, everybody is in suits and ties and stuff, and I've got on a pair of open sneakers, khakis, and an open shirt, and I raise my hand. The guy tells me I'm out of order. I've had a lot of experience with a microphone in the maritime union and I know my rights with a mike and I know how to hold on to a mike, and there's this one lady who goes to every shareholders' meeting, and she starts talking about how she met with the chairman, and she had a cocktail, and she said this and he said that, and they figure she's part of the *scenery,* and she had spoken before I did, so there's hardly any way he could call me out of order because what I had to say wasn't relevant to the thing he had brought up after this lady had spoken, so I made that point. . . . I had a piece of paper with all the data on the animals they were using, and I questioned them on all of this. They spend an enormous amount of time preparing for all the questions they were going to be asked and basically they hadn't prepared for this question, so the guy didn't know whether he was coming or going. I just kept pulling out papers and documents and stuff. And the windup was that he said he would set up a meeting for me with the people at P&G; so before he left the stage, I blocked his way and said, "Who is the person I'm going to be dealing with?"

On the day after the meeting, Henry wrote the chairman, Owen Butler, a friendly letter that began:

> Enjoyed meeting you and thanks for the opportunity to air some of our concerns at yesterday's annual meeting. As you implied, we have common interests in reducing and replacing the use of lab animals, while improving the efficiency of testing systems.[19]

Henry ended the letter by saying that, "as per our conversation after the meeting," he would contact Geoffrey Place, vice president for research and development. He met Place and P&G scientists in January 1983. The scientists described work they had already done on testing without using animals, because that was the cutting edge of toxicology, offering the prospect of quicker, cheaper, and more reliable ways of screening new products. They also agreed to take a more active role within the industry in promoting nonanimal tests and in reducing the number of animals, or the severity of their suffering, in tests in which they did not consider that animals could be replaced.

Procter & Gamble made its efforts public at a symposium at the Center for Alternatives to Animal Testing in May 1983, when it presented its proposal for replacing the classical LD50 test with what it called an "up/down" test, using high and low doses alternately on a much smaller number of animals, to find the approximate range within which a substance poisoned an animal. In September the corporation made its own employees more aware of the issue when it published the article "Taking Animals Out of the Laboratory" in its in-house journal. In that article, Henry publicly expressed his support for what the corporate giant was doing:

> News of the Company's efforts has reached not only the science community but also leaders of the animal rights movement. "Procter & Gamble's serious initiatives and commitment to replace and reduce the use and suffering of lab animals is both visionary and practical—believing that it can be done, followed by planning and then action," says Henry Spira, coordinator of a national coalition of animal rights groups. "We hope and expect that others will follow your lead."[20]

As with Revlon, if a company was moving in the right direction, Henry was willing to be quoted in support of what it was doing. He saw that P&G was getting behind the quest for alternatives, not in a minimal way, but wholeheartedly, and he wanted to encourage it to go further. The way to do that was not, as Henry put it in a passage quoted at the head of this chapter, to say, "we're saints and you're sinners, and we're going to clobber you with a two-by-four in order to educate you." But for much of the animal movement, the "we're saints and you're sinners" mind-set was hard to escape.

DRAMATIC EVENTS AND STEADY PROGRESS

In 1981, Alex Pacheco, co-founder with Ingrid Newkirk of a Washington, D.C.-based group called People for the Ethical Treatment of Animals, or PETA, volunteered his services as an assistant at the Institute for Behavioral Research, in Silver Spring, Maryland. There he compiled evidence of shocking neglect and maltreatment of monkeys used in experiments. This led to the first police raid on an American laboratory, followed by the trial of the institute's director, Dr. Edward Taub, and the beginning of a long-running saga over the custody of the "Silver Spring monkeys." The case sharpened public awareness of the nature of animal experimentation and catapulted PETA into the major league of American animal rights organizations.[21]

The U.S. animal movement reached new heights in 1984 when members of the underground Animal Liberation Front (ALF) broke into the laboratory of Dr. Thomas Gennarelli at the University of Pennsylvania Medical School. The raiders stole thirty-four videotapes, made by the experimenters themselves, which showed conscious baboons being strapped to an operating table where their heads were moved very rapidly in order to inflict severe brain damage. The experimenters were taped mocking the frightened animals, and one even said, "You better hope the anti-vivisection people don't get hold of this film." When an edited compilation of the tapes was shown on national television, millions of viewers were outraged. PETA waged a year-long campaign to close Gennarelli's head injury laboratory. The campaign came to a climax on July 15, 1985, when 100 people took part in a sit-in at the offices of the source of Gennarelli's funds, the National Institutes of Health. On the fourth day of the sit-in, the secretary of health and human services announced that the experiments would be stopped.[22]

A flood of media publicity followed. "Animal Rights: A Growing Movement in the U.S.," headlined the *New York Times*.[23] "Animal-rights groups are gaining clout and respect," wrote *Newsweek*.[24] There were feature stories on the animal movement in magazines from *New Woman* to *Hustler* and from *Omni* to the chemical industry's *Chemical Week*. There was also plenty of television coverage.[25]

The new scientific culture in safety testing that Henry had set in motion did not make for dramatic headlines, but it did lead to significantly less animal suffering. The change was noted by Bernard Dixon, the editor of the popular English science journal *New Scientist,* in an essay in *The Sciences,* a publication of the New York Academy of Science:

> Animal rights has become a fashionable issue, and this has greatly stimulated the search for alternative techniques. Scientists who until relatively recently argued that such special steps [to find alternatives not using animals] were unrealistic and unnecessary are now beginning to join a virtually new crusade.[26]

During the years that followed, the previously neglected field of alternatives and in vitro toxicology blossomed. Conferences and symposia were frequent, publications skyrocketed, and new scientific journals specifically dealing with alternatives were established. In 1984, the initially reluctant Bristol-Myers, by now an enthusiastic supporter of nonanimal testing, gave a further $200,000 to the Center for Alternatives to Animal Testing at Johns Hopkins, for research into alternatives suitable for the pharmaceutical industry, and Revlon contributed an additional $250,000 to Rockefeller University for trials with some promising alternatives to the Draize test.[27]

Several major corporations cut their animal testing. Bristol-Myers replaced the classical LD50 with the limit test, in which the trial substance was

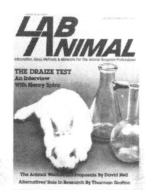

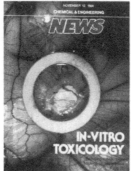

Nine cover stories from magazines aimed at scientists, physicians, and the chemical industry indicate the increasing awareness, in the early 1980s, of alternatives to the use of animals.

fed up to a certain quantity—perhaps 10 grams per kilo of body weight—and if that did not cause any harmful effects in a group of six to ten animals, there was judged to be no need to proceed to a level that killed half the animals. In this way, it was possible to dispense with the absurdity of force-feeding animals vast quantities of harmless substances—equivalent, perhaps, to a human being consuming kilos of toothpaste or hundreds of cans of soda per day. In April 1984, Avon said that it had reduced the overall number of animals used in safety testing during 1983 by 31 percent over the previous year. This followed a 33 percent reduction between 1981 and 1982. Revlon reported a 20 percent reduction. Colgate-Palmolive said it had reduced animal usage by more than 50 percent between 1982 and 1983, and by 1986, it was able to report an 80 percent reduction as compared with 1981.[28] In several areas of pharmaceutical testing, animals had been replaced with alternatives.[29] By October 1984, there were no more rabbits in Bristol-Myers' Mead Johnson division, which previously had used 300 a year to test the quality of intravenous drugs. Now the rabbit tests had been replaced with a cheaper, faster, and more sensitive test that used an enzyme taken from the horseshoe crab. (The crabs were, the company said, returned unharmed to the ocean floor after some blood had been taken from them.) The FDA had accepted the use of the test and agreed with Bristol-Myers' findings concerning its advantages.[30] In June 1985, the CTFA issued a news release stating that the cosmetic industry as a whole had ceased to use the classic LD50 test and was now using the limit test instead. As a result, the number of animals used by the industry in acute oral toxicity tests had been reduced by an estimated 75–90 percent.[31] By October 1985, Procter & Gamble had "virtually eliminated" the classical LD50 from its laboratories, using only six to ten animals for its up/down test, instead of the forty or fifty required for the LD50.

Henry called a public meeting in New York, in January 1984, "to organize the final push to bury the LD50." I had a visiting appointment in Boulder, Colorado, at the time and, at Henry's urging, flew to New York to speak at the meeting. Henry spoke, too, along with representatives of many grassroots animal groups from around the country and long-standing supporters of the coalition, such as scientists Andrew Rowan and Leonard Rack, broadcaster Pegeen Fitzgerald, writer Cleveland Amory, and Congressman Bill Green. Behind the platform there was a huge banner with a picture of a tombstone on which was written:

LD50

1927–1984

The epitaph was premature. In a society in which corporations are always fearful of multi-million-dollar lawsuits lest they not comply with usual testing procedures, it proved extremely difficult to persuade corporations to do away with these traditional animal tests altogether. By 1989, Henry and Leonard Rack were writing of "phasing down" the classic LD50 and Draize tests, rather than abolishing them.[32]

DISSENSION IN THE MOVEMENT

The big cosmetics companies were, Henry believed, making reasonable progress in reducing their use of animals; but others in the animal movement took a different view. The campaigns that Henry had run against the cosmetics companies had been so successful, not only in changing the practices of the targeted companies, but also in winning popular support, that many leaders of new and radical animal rights groups wanted to continue along the same path. For them, as long as a company continued to test on animals, it was a potential target. In October 1985, PETA launched a "Compassion Campaign" featuring a logo of a rabbit undergoing the Draize test and targeting the major cosmetics companies, including Avon and Bristol-Myers. After the campaign was featured in *Animals' Agenda*, Henry wrote a letter to the editor taking issue with it:

> I believe that *Agenda*'s call for further ultimatums to the cosmetics industry may well be counterproductive. It seems to me that when an industry or corporation is responsive, we want them to continue to be responsive and use their responsiveness as an example for others. Why spend your energies hitting people who are working with you on common goals?
>
> The cosmetics industry uses less than 1 percent of animals used in product testing. But it was the cosmetics industry that opened up the whole field of nonanimal toxicology through the Johns Hopkins Center for Alternatives to Animal Testing and Revlon's project for developing alternatives at Rockefeller University. These efforts have spread to major research facilities around the world. In fact, the cosmetics industry and such household product leaders as Procter & Gamble have surely been responsible, through their impact on other industries, for rescuing more animals from pain and suffering than the cosmetics industry itself uses.
>
> Why not go after other industries which use many more animals and that have not been responsive to animal concerns? These include the pharmaceutical and chemical industries, public education systems and agriculture, which is still responsible for the suffering of four billion animals per year. While ultimatums to the responsive cosmetics industry could prove counterproductive to expanding negotiations, adequate and fresh energies in these so-far neglected areas could be pivotal to the creation of new victories. Let's apply our energies where they can really make a difference.[33]

Relations between Henry and a number of other organizations, especially PETA, deteriorated in 1987, when PETA bought stock in Procter & Gamble and moved a shareholder's proposal at its annual meeting, asking the company to stop the use of live animals in product testing. Outside the meeting, seventy-five animal rights activists picketed and a PETA-chartered helicopter

flew overhead trailing a banner reading "Stop Product Testing on Animals."
Inside nearly half of the two-hour meeting was taken up by a discussion of the
proposal. When Henry heard that PETA was going to make a major event
of the meeting, he decided to stand by the corporation, which had reduced
animal usage in testing consumer products by 60 percent between 1984 and
1986 and had cut overall usage by 22 percent despite taking over a pharmaceutical company. Henry flew to Cincinnati, attended the meeting, and heard
PETA spokesperson Susan Rich say that while P&G should be commended
for using fewer animals in testing than previously, the number should be reduced still further. Rich estimated that the company continued to use 70,000
to 100,000 animals a year. Henry then stood up. He began by saying that he
supported the objective of phasing out painful animal testing, as suggested in
the proposal, but he added:

> I do not support PETA's campaign which attempts to portray P&G as
> villain when, in fact, P&G has the best record to date in developing,
> implementing, and promoting alternatives to the use of animals in product
> testing. It seems to me that when a corporation is responsive to our con-
> cerns, it makes no sense to clobber them over the head. Rather, we want to
> encourage them to continue to be responsive and use their responsiveness
> as an example to others.
>
> It would be unfortunate to give industry the impression that it is use-
> less to deal with and respond to animal rights concerns—that if they do
> respond, they'll just make themselves a more visible target.

Henry then spoke about the positive initiatives that P&G had taken and
congratulated the corporation on its commitment to develop and implement
alternatives. His comments were made available to the media in a news release,
and the "tactical splits within the animal rights movement" were noted in the
New York Times and other media.[34] PETA's proposal was supported by only
2.2 percent of the shares voted.

Ingrid Newkirk, national director of PETA, responded by sending a letter to all the advisers listed on Henry's letterhead. Attached was a copy of the
news release Henry had issued at P&G's meeting, as well as a document called
"Seeking Change Together: An Activist Manifesto," by the philosopher and
activist Brian Klug. Klug's document was a call for groups in the movement
to avoid conflict with one another, and Newkirk's letter stated that Henry's
points "could have been made without attacking another group. . . . I hope
you find this behavior less than satisfactory."[35] Another attack came from
Helen Jones, president of the International Society for Animal Rights. Jones
had originally supported Henry's campaign against the American Museum of
Natural History, but she withdrew her support after a disagreement over tac-

tics[36] and had kept her society apart from his coalitions ever since. Now she drew attention to the events at P&G's meeting in her society's newsletter and suggested that organizations that were members of Spira's Coalition to Abolish the LD50 may want to withdraw in view of those remarks.[37]

Neither Newkirk's nor Jones's attempts to influence Henry's supporters met with any success. None of his advisers suggested that he change course or stop his criticism of PETA, and no groups resigned from the coalition. Nevertheless, many activists in the animal movement wondered why the very person who had built unity in the movement—through the coalitions he had drawn together to fight pound seizure, the Draize test, and the LD50—was now siding with a corporation that tested on animals, and against other animal rights groups. Henry's view, though, was that some organizations were merely using the cosmetics companies and P&G, not because they were the worst animal abusers, but because they were convenient and popular targets to campaign against-and to seek donations from their supporters for doing so. Even more worrying, from Henry's point of view, was the concern he had made plain at the P&G meeting: If companies that he had once campaigned against were, after they had delivered what the campaign had sought, still the focus of attacks, no company would have any incentive to give him anything.

A decade later, the verdict on Procter & Gamble remained in dispute. The corporation's opponents considered themselves vindicated in May 1997 when Michele Rokke, a PETA undercover investigator, reported on what she had seen during her eight months' employment in the laboratory of Huntingdon Life Sciences in Millstone, New Jersey. The laboratory undertook tests for many major corporations, including P&G. According to an Associated Press report, Rokke "videotaped the alleged abuse that showed technicians cutting monkeys while they were still alive, slamming them into cages and suspending them in air while pumping fluids through their noses." PETA filed a thirty-seven-page complaint against Huntingdon with the United States Department of Agriculture (USDA), alleging failure to comply with the Animal Welfare Act.[38] P&G, clearly embarrassed by the disclosures, took its work away from the laboratory.

On the other side of the ledger, P&G claims that since 1984 it has reduced its use of animals for nondrug consumer product safety testing by 85 percent—even though the company has tripled in size during this period. The corporation has adopted a policy of commitment to the ultimate elimination of animal testing, and has shown that this is more than rhetoric by leading the search for alternatives. Since 1984, P&G calculates that it has spent $64 million on the development, validation, and acceptance of nonanimal testing—roughly three times as much as any other corporation or institution—and its scientists have published more than 450 papers on alternative methods. In

1990 P&G instituted an International Program for Animal Alternatives, which provides a total of $450,000 a year in grants for scientists in projects that will result in the development of new alternative test methods. Recognizing that one of the major obstacles to greater use of alternatives is the refusal of regulatory agencies to accept them, P&G has funded conferences to develop agreed standards for validating alternatives. P&G was the only company to testify before the U.S. Congress in favor of legislation directing the U.S. government to actively support the development, validation, and regulatory acceptance of alternative methods. This led to the formation of the U.S. Interagency Coordinating Committee for Validation of Alternative Methods, which will review alternative methods and recommend them for acceptance by regulatory agencies. To ensure that information about alternatives to animal testing is available to researchers around the world, P&G has provided financial support for the development of Altweb, the Alternatives to Animal Testing Website, in association with the Center for Alternatives to Animal Testing at Johns Hopkins University. At its October 1997 annual shareholders' meeting, P&G took the search for alternatives into new territory by announcing that it was giving $1 million to the Supercomputer Center at the University of California at San Diego for the development of a computer model known as Biology Network of Modeling Efforts, or BioNOME. The model seeks to predict biological responses to new drug compounds. P&G's associate direction of human and environmental safety, Katherine Stitzel, acknowledged that the supercomputer project was in its infancy, but said "we can't see any other way you can get to complete elimination of animal use. It can't ever happen if we don't start."[39]

More friction between PETA and Henry—and this time, not only Henry—occurred in 1987 when PETA engineered takeovers of the New England Anti-Vivisection Society and the Toronto Humane Society. Between them, the two long-established and generally conservative organizations had assets worth about $22 million—money that the leaders of PETA thought was not doing as much for animals as it could. That may well have been true, but Henry, along with the leaders of several other animal rights groups, was concerned that PETA—which did not itself have the kind of democratic structure that made some other groups vulnerable to takeovers—was achieving an unhealthy degree of dominance in the animal movement. PETA's need to raise large sums of money to pay for its soaring number of paid staff continued to be a sore point with Henry, who was running his coalitions on about $75,000 a year at a time when PETA's operating budget was over $6 million.[40] Henry may also have been influenced by the fact that NEAVS had given financial support to projects he had suggested to them. With a PETA-controlled board, this support was likely to disappear. So he didn't mind telling Ian Harvey, a writer for the *Toronto Sun,* that the takeover of traditional and conservative humane societies by more radical groups was helping to create "bureaucracy for bureaucracy's sake, and to massage the egos of those in charge."[41]

Newkirk saw the situation differently. In 1989, she told a *New York Times* reporter who was doing a profile on Henry:

> He is hobnobbing in the halls with our enemy. Six or seven years ago, we had a lot in common. Everything he did then was putting down gravel for other people to pave roads, which was crucial. But I think Henry was deceived by the industry response. Henry was unable to cut himself loose from the mire of having become an industry mediator. The search for alternatives is a quite transparent ploy to maintain the status quo.[42]

Was the search for alternatives, on which Henry had invested so much energy in the past decade, really "a transparent ploy to maintain the status quo"? The way in which the major American cosmetics companies ended their animal testing throws light on that question.

THE END OF COSMETICS TESTING?

On January 10, 1989, Noxell, the maker of Noxzema skin creams and Cover-Girl cosmetics, became the first major American cosmetics corporation to announce that it would replace the Draize test by a tissue culture test. The decision followed two years of study on the ability of a cell test known as "agarose diffusion" to predict eye irritation. Henry hailed the decision as an important breakthrough in the drive to eradicate the Draize test.[43]

Less than two months later, PETA made Avon the prime target of a new campaign against cosmetic testing on animals. PETA called for a worldwide boycott of Avon products and distributed 3 million door-hangers, like those left by Avon's salespeople, except that instead of saying "Avon calling," they said "Avon killing." Within a month, Avon announced that it would no longer use the Draize test and was ceasing all animal testing. In June, Revlon followed suit. By the end of the year, eleven of the biggest American cosmetics firms had completely stopped testing their products on animals. The list included Chesebrough-Ponds, Fabergé, and Christian Dior, while Amway and Mary Kay Cosmetics had declared moratoriums on animal testing.

This should have been a moment for Henry to savor and celebrate. Wasn't it the culmination of the decade of work that had begun with his first letter to Revlon? Instead, there was an edge of acrimony about what had happened. To those with no knowledge of the history of the issue—and since the animal rights movement was young and had grown rapidly, that meant most of its supporters—it looked as if it was PETA's boycott that brought about Avon's announcement. In the end, what really seemed to count was a serious threat from a powerful organization with hundreds of thousands of supporters in the United States and branches overseas as well. To those who knew the history of the issue, however, the story was very different. Cosmetics companies were in a position to stop animal testing only because of the development of alternatives. That is why Noxell had been able to switch to a cell culture test. Avon could avoid using the Draize test by substituting Eytex, an in vitro method developed by National Testing, a company founded by Christopher Kelly.[44] Kelly told *Chemical Week* that Eytex "takes less time, is more reproducible and less subjective than the Draize." It also cost only $50 as opposed to $500 for the Draize.[45] Those advantages were just what Henry had hoped the new methods would bring when he first decided to ask Revlon to fund research into alternatives.

PETA's role in the cessation of cosmetics animal testing, then, was no more than that of icing the cake. Far from being a "transparent ploy to maintain the status quo," the development of alternatives was an essential prerequisite for the success of PETA's boycott. But even that assessment of PETA's role in Avon's decision to end cosmetic testing may give too much weight to its actions. A more Machiavellian analysis was suggested by the *Animal Rights Reporter,* a journal that boasts the subtitle *An Objective Analysis of the Animal Rights Movement.* That description is highly dubious: The *Reporter* was published by a security consulting firm that worked for companies targeted by the animal rights movement.[46] Nevertheless, it is significant that, even before Avon had announced that it was stopping animal testing, the *Reporter* wrote of PETA's boycott:

> PETA's action appears to be both a media ploy and an attempt to minimize the work of ARI's Henry Spira. . . . Spira has developed a working relationship with Avon's management and his efforts have clearly been a factor in Avon's decreasing dependence on animal testing.
>
> Now that Avon is on the verge of dropping animal testing entirely, PETA steps forward and announces a boycott. The boycott will allow PETA to claim a . . . "victory" when Avon announces that it has stopped animal testing entirely. Regardless, Avon officials say that PETA's boycott will not impact their decision making. One Avon representative stated: "The company can only assume that PETA called this boycott in a self-serving attempt to take credit for Avon's plans to eliminate testing."
>
> PETA is also likely to claim that its confrontational style had greater impact on Avon abandoning product testing than the steady, low-key pressure by Spira. Avon's actions indicate otherwise.[47]

Was it, then, just a coincidence that Avon announced an end to animal testing just a month after PETA called its boycott? That seems barely credible; even if Avon had planned to end animal testing at some indefinite time in the future, surely PETA's boycott advanced the date on which it did so. Were the Avon officials quoted simply trying to deny that they had been influenced by their strongest adversary? That is one way of explaining the speed with which Avon's announcement followed PETA's boycott. But in June 1989, in an interview with *Life* journalist Alston Chase, Avon's chairman, Jim Preston, offered another explanation:

> Last February, Susan Rich [director of PETA's campaign against cosmetic testing] called me to ask if she could be allowed to speak to the board of the CTFA. I'm chairman of the CTFA. I thought we should hear her out, and we did. . . . When I spoke to Miss Rich before the CTFA meeting, I told her that Avon was close to making an announcement that would be good news for PETA and all animal rights activists. That could only have been interpreted to mean that we were about to be able to announce an end to animal testing.
>
> The boycott against Avon began the next week. This couldn't have been a coincidence. They were trying to take credit for Avon eliminating animal testing of our products, a program that had begun eight years ago.[48]

Henry had become sufficiently cynical about the way in which some animal rights groups operated to find this account entirely believable. Others would no doubt take his willingness to believe the head of a cosmetics corporation as further confirmation that he had spent too much time "hobnobbing in the halls with our enemy."

AN UNFINISHED STORY

In April 1992, the Center for Alternatives to Animal Testing celebrated its tenth anniversary. The center was doing well. It had broadened its range of sponsors to include such corporations as Exxon and IBM and such federal agencies as the EPA and the NIH, as well as the cosmetics and drug companies that continued to support it. At a ceremony at the Baltimore Museum of Art, the center presented Henry with a Founder's Award in recognition of his central role in getting it started. But Henry let his audience know that he was not satisfied. While noting the enormous change that had taken place in the previous decade and praising those responsible for it, he called for a new sense of urgency, saying, "I founded the coalition to abolish the Draize test, not to refine it."[49]

But how is abolition to be achieved? Corporations that make only cosmetics and toiletries can end their own animal testing programs because their products are relatively harmless and the regulations that apply to them, both in the United States and elsewhere, do not require data from animal testing. For companies with a wider range of products, however, the regulations are much stricter. In many countries, household cleansers and other products with nasty chemicals in them cannot be transported without an indication, derived from animal testing, of the degree of hazard they involve, and environmental protection agencies may also insist on animal tests to determine the environmental safety of a product. Pharmaceuticals, too, are subjected to much stricter standards than cosmetics. Since corporations like Procter & Gamble and Unilever sell their products all over the world, they are bound by the regulations of each nation in which they sell their products. This means that unless they are willing to give up markets, they must comply with the regulations of the nations that have the most extravagant or archaic requirements for animal testing.

A few months before the tenth anniversary celebrations at the Center for Alternatives to Animal Testing, Henry had rejected invitations from both PETA and the Doris Duke Foundation to join them in new campaigns targeting cosmetics testing. The goal of the campaigns was the final abolition of the Draize test. Henry's response to both groups was that the days of making progress for animals by "bashing cosmetics companies" were over. It had never been the case—and it still wasn't—that cosmetic testing made up a large proportion of the Draize tests carried out on animals. Henry cited figures from the United Kingdom showing that for each animal suffering in cosmetics tests there, an estimated 80,000 animals were being used in testing in other industries. (He added that there were no comparable U.S. figures but that there was no reason to believe that the proportion would be significantly different.) Nevertheless, a decade earlier, it had made sense to pressure cosmetics companies to develop alternatives because there were no alternatives, and the cosmetics companies were the most vulnerable to pressure to get them to put up some money for getting the whole field of alternatives started. Now that alternatives existed, and more were being developed, the real issue was no longer in the hands of the cosmetics companies:

> In order for the Draize to be replaced, the regulatory agencies must approve batteries of alternative tests, and the acceptance must include all major trading nations. But the regulatory agencies won't approve these tests until there's a clear consensus within the toxicology community. And there will be no consensus within the science community until there is a coordinated

effort to assess newly developed alternative tests, one by one, and to assign batteries of tests to various objectives for various groups of chemicals.[50]

Henry failed to persuade other animal groups that it was no longer fruitful to keep going down the trail that he had pioneered. Some of them joined PETA in a campaign against the French cosmetics giant L'Oréal, which unlike the major American cosmetics companies, was still doing animal tests. In 1993, PETA claimed victory when L'Oréal agreed to a permanent ban on animal tests. But the victory was later denounced as deceptive by the British Union for the Abolition of Vivisection, because L'Oréal had not agreed to stop using ingredients that had been tested on animals.[51]

The complete abolition of the Draize and the LD50 test remains an elusive goal. In 1992, the European Community took a step ahead of the United States when it passed a law requiring that alternatives must be used whenever possible. It also established the European Centre for the Validation of Alternative Methods at Ispra, in Italy, to determine which alternatives were available to replace tests using animals. The first study of alternatives to the Draize test was published in 1995, but it found, disappointingly, that none of the nine alternative methods tested met the performance targets for replacing the Draize. The study reported that further research was required before it could conclude that there was an adequate alternative to the Draize.[52]

Though the coalitions to stop the Draize and the LD50 have yet to fully achieve their stated objectives, they have made an enormous difference to the culture of product testing and have contributed to a huge reduction in animal use. In 1985, the *United States Pharmacopeia* and the *National Formulary,* the compendia of standards and methods of analysis for drugs and related items, required use of animals in 11 percent of their tests. By 1993, this figure had dropped to 2 percent. The National Cancer Institute replaced several million mice used to screen potential drugs with human cell culture assays that were not only less expensive, but were also not affected by differences in species. Andrew Rowan surveyed the numbers of animals being used in experiments generally and found a decline of up to 50 percent in some countries since the 1970s. While many factors are involved in the drop, the replacement of animals in product testing is certainly one of them.[53]

By the 1990s, Henry had come to see that product safety testing on animals would not cease completely until our attitudes toward animals changed in other areas as well. In an interview published in the newsletter of a pro-research lobby group, he was asked if he thought that eventually all animal use in product safety testing would be eliminated:

> As long as six billion animals are being consumed as food, I don't think you're going to have a point where there's not even one animal being

used [for product testing]. But if the whole science community and the regulators and those involved with product liability move in harmony, then instead of having 20 to 60 million lab animals, we can keep chopping off some of the zeros from the end and wind up with a very minimal number of animals that are being used as a last resort in matters of life and death, and put all the resources into alleviating the pain and suffering of those animals that are being used.[54]

As this statement shows, while Henry had not given up his commitment to reducing the number of animals used in product testing, his focus had shifted to animals being consumed as food.

• 5 •

The Forgotten Animal Issue

You're right if you think the animal rights movement made a big splash in the 1970s and 1980s. Unfortunately, you're also right if you think that the big splash was only a drop in the bucket.

Henry Spira[1]

REVELATIONS ABOUT "CHICKEN HEAVEN"

While the American animal movement reached new levels of public awareness in the first half of the 1980s, it was narrowly focused on animals used in research, with some concern for stray dogs and cats and for wildlife. Farm animals were almost entirely neglected. Yet for each one of the 20 to 60 million animals then used in research in the United States each year, at least 200 farm animals were killed during the same period. Moreover, whereas the number of animals used in research seems to be falling, the number of farm animals used is rising rapidly. Farm animals may not suffer the acute pain or distress that some experiments cause, but the hens who produce our eggs are so closely confined in wire cages that they cannot stretch their wings or move away from more aggressive birds in the same cage. Chickens raised for meat are crowded into large sheds, and each year millions of them are slaughtered without being stunned first. Veal calves destined for the white veal trade are taken from their mothers just a few days after birth, then locked into stalls so narrow that they cannot turn around or walk a single step. There they will spend the rest of their lives, deliberately kept anemic, to keep their flesh pale and soft. They are given no straw for fear that, craving roughage, they might eat it and turn their flesh a more natural red. Breeding sows, too, are confined in stalls that prevent them from turning around or walking and are forced to give birth to their piglets on concrete, with no bedding materials.

By 1985, Henry was keen to tackle farm animal issues. In January of that year, he organized a "planning and strategy" meeting of the heads of all the major animal groups in the country (including the ASPCA and the Humane Society of the United States, as well as representatives of the newer activist organizations like PETA and Student Action Corps for Animals), and they agreed that it was time to take action for farm animals.[2] The ultimate solution to the abuse of farm animals is, as Henry told a journalist, that "animal rights and eating animals don't mix." The realist in him then added: "However, while it's going on, you want to at least reduce pain and suffering."[3]

Could animals be raised in ways that provided for their basic needs and yet were commercially viable? European research on more humane methods of farming looked promising, but in America, the whole trend was in the opposite direction. Agribusiness enterprises kept getting bigger. Some egg producers now numbered their caged hens in the millions, and pig operations had tens of thousands of pigs, all kept indoors. The animal was being reduced to a cog in the machine. Profitability was the only thing that mattered. The welfare of the individual animal was irrelevant to the profitability of the enterprise as a whole.

Henry thought that the kind of campaign he had waged against Revlon could be effective for farm animals too, if he could find a corporation that had to be as sensitive about its image as Revlon was. Then he could pressure that

"Chicken heaven"? This photo, taken in a shed used to raise chickens for Perdue, shows the crowded reality of confinement for a bird who will never go outdoors or be part of a normal-sized flock.

corporation into donating funds to find ways of raising animals that allowed them freedom to move around and live a reasonably normal life for their species. The problem was to find a corporation that would be responsive. When shopping at the supermarket for meat, poultry, and eggs, people just bought the cheapest they could get. Unlike the cosmetics industry, there was relatively little brand-name advertising for these products. But Frank Perdue is an exception. Perdue Farms is not the biggest chicken producer in the country—it ranks about third—but it is the best known, thanks to its $20–$30 million annual advertising budget. Frank Perdue is, as Mark Graham put it, "a poultry mogul who looked and talked like his product." His advertising agency made him the up-front salesperson for his chickens, so when you switched on your television, there was Frank Perdue telling you in his folksy style that "My chickens eat better than people do." "Chicken heaven" was the term Perdue used to describe the conditions under which his birds lived. In a full-page newspaper advertisement, he told consumers:

THE WAY TO MAKE GREAT CHICKENS IS TO SPOIL THEM

> Perdue chickens lead such a soft life they can't help but turn out tender. They live in $60,000 houses, get eight hours' sleep and eat princely meals that include cookies for dessert!

The advertisement goes on to describe in detail the "spacious, specially constructed houses" with "expensive tinted windows" where there is "no overcrowding" and "every bird has plenty of room to roam. To make friends, or find a quiet place of its own."[4]

This was blatant nonsense. As in the case of Revlon, the gap between the image that the corporation was trying to foster and the reality of what it was doing was huge. That had made Revlon vulnerable. Could the same be true of Perdue?

In April 1987, Henry wrote Frank Perdue a polite letter seeking "initiatives which will reduce farm animal stress."

> Your involvement in these efforts to improve the lives of factory farm animals would be highly consistent with the tone and thrust of your advertising:
>
> > Every Perdue chicken travels first-class. Which is nothing more (and nothing less) than what a first-class chicken deserves. (Besides, why deny a bird a tasty treat? Frank Perdue may be tough, but he's not mean.)
>
> Our coalitions, in the last decade, have been engaged in a variety of activities, functioning as catalysts to promote reduction of the suffering of animals in a variety of contexts.

> We have included enclosures to illustrate some of our activities and that also may serve to illustrate further the nature of the opportunity that we are suggesting to you.
>
> We would very much appreciate the opportunity to meet and exchange ideas with you and look forward to your early response.[5]

The sting to the letter was in the enclosures: the full-page ads Henry had done on Revlon. Avoiding similar treatment was "the nature of the opportunity" that Perdue was being offered. But Perdue's slogan was "It takes a tough man to make a tender chicken," and he proved that at least one part of his advertising was true: He ignored the letter.

Henry gathered material about Perdue. With Mark Graham, he planned a full-page advertisement that featured a picture of Perdue with a very long nose and a headline that read: "Frank, Are You Telling the Truth about Your Chickens?" The advertisement first ran in the *New York Times* and described the reality behind Perdue's advertising:

> Resort life for a "pampered" Perdue chicken begins painfully with dismemberment as the young bird's beak is burned off with a hot knife. . . . Growers typically crowd 25,000 birds into one long windowless shed (and sometimes as many as 75,000 or more). In these conditions each bird can expect about one square foot or less of living space for its entire life. Obviously as the bird reaches its full size of about four pounds, living conditions and the attendant problems become even more stressful. Attacks on each other, cannibalism, disease and sudden death are all by-products of this severe overcrowding and the "farmer" resorts to drugs and debeaking to discourage these man-induced "vices." . . . The farms of yesterday with contented animals in natural surroundings are almost extinct. They have been replaced by corporate factories—cramped indoor facilities—where nature, biological necessity and any reasonable consideration towards animals are spurned in favor of the massive profits that can be realized by treating animals as a commodity. . . . Is there anyone who has exploited this inhumane system more profitably than Mr. Perdue with his misleading depiction of "Chicken Heaven"?[6]

The advertisement asked readers to tell Perdue that they would not buy his chickens until he stopped misrepresenting the realities of poultry farming, gave each bird a two-by-two foot living space, and started a research program to investigate more humane methods of raising poultry.

In the weeks after the advertisement appeared, several TV and radio shows contacted Henry and ran stories about Perdue. Henry again wrote to Perdue, suggesting that "constructive negotiations are more productive than ongoing confrontation." He referred to his experience with Revlon and

FRANK, ARE YOU TELLING THE TRUTH ABOUT YOUR CHICKENS?

Is Frank Perdue's advertising just a pile of poultry puffery hiding the brutal realities of an inhumane industry?

For nearly 20 years, Frank Perdue has crowed about the creature comforts of his chickens, painting a picture of pampered pets living in "resorts" which he likes to describe as "chicken heaven." He says in one ad that they "eat better than you do" and in another that "your kids never had it so good!" This farmyard fantasy has clearly helped Mr. Perdue to parlay the misery of millions of chickens into a jumbo nest egg. And many of us have been happy to sit back and pay up to 20 cents more per pound to gobble up this feathery fiction.

In reality, life in Mr. Perdue's chicken "resorts" begins with painful dismemberment and ends with electrocution—with a lifetime of stress crowded in between.
Resort life for a "pampered" Perdue chicken begins painfully with dismemberment as the young bird's beak is burned off with a hot knife. Mr. Perdue is not, strictly speaking, a farmer at all. He breeds chicks that are "designed"—genetically speaking—to grow as rapidly as possible on the least amount of food. This technique often produces chickens that are so oversized for their age that they are unable to support their own weight and live out their lives on painfully crippled legs. Mr. Perdue's main business is slaughter and packaging. The actual raising of chickens is left to contract growers to whom the debeaked chicks are trucked when they are a few days old.

After having their beaks burned off with a hot knife, chickens struggle through life —often with less than *one* square foot of living space per bird.
Contract growers typically crowd 25,000 birds into one long windowless shed (and sometimes as many as 75,000 or more). In these conditions each bird can expect about one square foot or less of living space for its entire life. Obviously as the bird reaches its full size of about four pounds, living conditions and the attendant problems become even more stressful. Attacks on each other, cannibalism, disease and sudden death are all by-products of this severe overcrowding and the "farmer" resorts to drugs and debeaking to discourage these man-induced "vices".

Mr. Perdue proudly markets his birds as oven stuffers, but the bird in your oven may have four times the space it had when it was alive!
The unnatural density of today's poultry sheds (and filthy litter which can not be cleaned while so many birds occupy the shed) often results in overheating, suffocating air which, when combined with abnormally warm weather, can lead to death and disease. Technology frequently allows just one person to "take care of" tens of

thousands of chickens and provides little opportunity for real interaction between farmer and bird. On a daily basis he may move through the shed to remove dead chickens, but the sudden intrusion of strangers or even a loud noise can set off mass hysteria which moves in waves from end to end of the barn as the jittery chickens pile up against the walls ten deep with hundreds dead or injured.

Yellow skins or purple prose? Mr. Perdue says his birds are healthier because of their yellow skins—consumer studies say foul!
Mr. Perdue copied the yellow skin gimmick from a company in Maine which found it could charge a few more cents per pound after putting skin coloring additive in their chicken feed. He has since been restrained from making any health claims based on yellow skin. A lot of strange things go into Mr. Perdue's chicken feed, including ground up dead chickens. Not surprisingly, Mr. Perdue has chosen to focus on marigold petals.

Back at Mr. Perdue's plant, chickens approach the gates of "chicken heaven" pinned upside down as their heads are dragged through an electrified water trough prior to having their throats cut.
The farms of yesterday with contented animals in natural surroundings are almost extinct. They have been replaced by corporate factories—cramped indoor facilities—where nature, biological necessity and any reasonable consideration towards animals are spurned in favor of the massive profits that can be realized by treating animals as a commodity. And the high mortality rates associated with intensive confinement are merely considered an "incidental cost" in an insensitive business. Is there anyone who has exploited this inhumane system more profitably than Mr. Perdue with his misleading depiction of "Chicken Heaven"?

Mr. Perdue appears to be equally callous to his workers. And when they tried to organize, he quickly winged his way to the mob for help.
Recent reports on National Public Radio and in the Washington Post depict a work environment at Perdue's Lewiston, NC plant where employees unable to function due to work-related injuries were routinely fired. According to a National Health Service doctor, up to 30 percent of the workers in that factory are afflicted with repetitive motion syndrome, a potentially crippling disorder of the hands or wrists, caused by having to cut up to 75 chickens per minute. A Perdue personnel memo stated that it was normal procedure for

about 60 percent of workers to go to the nurse for pain killers and to have their hands bandaged. Donna Bazemore, a former employee, told NPR that she'd seen women urinating and vomiting on the work line because they were not allowed to leave it to go to the bathroom. None of the Perdue factories is unionized. And in 1986, Frank Perdue told the president's commission on organized crime that he sought help from organized crime figures to keep it that way.

Here's how you can help

Mr. Perdue's chicken literature says that when you're unhappy you should "squawk to Frank". You can write to Mr. Perdue at: PERDUE FARMS INC., P.O. BOX 1537, SALISBURY, MD 21801. **Tell Mr. Perdue that you will not buy his chickens until he does the following:**

1. Tells the truth
Provides a complete list of his slaughterhouses and contract farms, and allows the media unannounced access to film and report what life is really like for the Perdue chicken.
Stops misrepresenting the realities of factory intensive poultry "farming" in his advertising.

2. Gives the birds some quality of life
Guarantees each bird two feet by two feet of living space. Doesn't sound like much to ask, does it?

3. Starts a research program
Investigates more humane methods of raising poultry. Almost all animals including calves, pigs and cattle raised for food suffer on factory farms. Your involvement and opinion can change this inhumane system.

You can run this ad. This ad was produced by the Coalition for Non-Violent Food, a project of Animal Rights International, and is not copyrighted. We invite you or your organization to run it with your name. Contact us if you would like a camera-ready copy of this ad.

This full-page New York Times *advertisement was the opening salvo in Henry's campaign against Frank Perdue.*

proposed that they meet to discuss "opportunities for developing realistic solutions to pressing problems" so that Perdue could "play a pioneering role similar to that of Revlon in 1979." This time, Perdue did reply: "While we respect your right to seek a meatless society, Perdue Farms sees no value in meeting with people with that goal who also are engaged in the dissemination of half-truths and distortions that border on extortion."[7]

Henry put the Perdue campaign on hold, but he continued to gather information on Perdue's way of running business. He passed his material on to the Council on Economic Priorities, which each year rates American corporations on the extent to which they show "corporate conscience." Perdue Farms received a "dishonorable mention" in 1990 for its treatment of its workers and of its chickens. After this, the council expanded its questionnaires, sent to all major corporations, to include farm animal issues.

An opportunity to make more explicit use of the material Henry had collected came in 1991, when the University of Maryland appointed Frank Perdue to its Board of Regents. Henry and Mark Graham wrote a new advertisement that began:

THE P. WORD

There's a word for someone who does bad stuff for money.

Perdue.

In commenting on Frank Perdue's appointment to the Board of Regents, President William Kirwan of the College Park campus of the University of Maryland asserted that *Frank Perdue's business background will benefit the school.*

Which business background is he talking about?

His business with the Mafia?

In 1986 Perdue admitted to the President's Commission on Organized Crime that when his workers tried to organize, he went to New York's Gambino crime family to get their help.

The business of endangering the lives of his workers?

Perdue's business has been described as even more dangerous than mining. Workers, mostly poor black women, who cut up to 90 chickens per minute for low pay, face a variety of hazards including skin diseases, toxic air and crippling arm and hand injuries. National Public Radio reported that women were urinating on the workline because they were afraid to leave it.

The business of lying to the government?

Not content with endangering the welfare of his employees, Perdue systematically covered up injuries to his workers. Perdue has received record fines for *wilfully* concealing worker injuries from the federal government.

The advertisement continued in that vein, highlighting Perdue's false advertising, his conviction for polluting Virginia's waterways, his abuse of animals, and his evasion of a manslaughter charge after he killed someone when speeding the wrong way up a one-way road. The text ended by asking:

Is this the kind of business background that the University of Maryland plans to hold up as a model for their students?
Or is it Perdue's large cash donation to the school that has allowed him to buy a seat on the Board of Regents?

Because if the student body is for sale, there's a P. word for that too!

Like its predecessor, this advertisement was widely reported and discussed in the media. Through a public relations firm, Perdue issued a statement asking, "Do we want to allow a small group who claim animals have the same rights as people to impose their will on the majority and banish meat from the tables of America?" His spokesperson claimed that the ad was "filled with misinformation, misstatements and untruths" but was unable to show that any of the specific claims made in the advertisement were false. The *Washington Times,* which ran the ad, said that its legal department had checked the advertisement against documentation that Henry had provided.[8]

Henry wanted to run another advertisement focusing on the health hazards of eating Perdue chicken. At a 1991 Senate hearing, expert witnesses testified that eight out of ten chickens in America tested positive for salmonella and other bacteria. Contaminated chickens were estimated to be responsible for making 4 million Americans ill each year and killing 2,000 of them. A microbiologist who had worked with the U.S. Department of Agriculture told the Senate committee that "the final product is no different than if you took a bird . . . stuck it in the toilet and then ate it." This was not too far from what did happen to some chickens: A former Perdue worker described how workers had to relieve themselves on the floor because they could not leave the line, and supervisors instructed workers that chickens that fell into the muck on the floor were to be put back on the line. At the time the major health issue in the United States was AIDS. Health advertising focused on "safe sex," but some right-wing moralists stirred controversy by claiming that outside of a monogamous relationship, "there's no such thing as safe sex." When Henry and Mark Graham were brainstorming in a coffee shop about an ad on the health dangers of chicken, Graham suddenly sketched the outline of a condom around a Perdue chicken, and above it wrote: "There's No Such Thing as Safe Chicken." It was, Henry thought, a stroke of genius. They still had the problem—in a time when there were no computer graphics—of how to get a picture of a chicken inside a condom. Graham recalled their next move:

> We went down to Greenwich Village to see if we could find a condom that we could get a four-pound bird into. . . . In one place we stopped long enough to explain that we needed to get a chicken into a condom, and they just looked at us like we were mad. So we gave up explaining why we wanted them; we just went in and asked, "Do you have extra-large condoms?" People seem to look at you with a new respect when you ask that. We finally wound up in a place where this young guy said yes, we've got some brand—I can't recall now what it was, but apparently it was some humungous-size product—and he put his arm around my shoulder and said in a conspiratorial whisper, "Only kind I use."[9]

Even with the biggest condoms in New York, they broke dozens before they succeeded in squeezing a chicken into one. Then the teat wasn't standing up in a way that made the condom recognizable, so Graham used a compressed air gun to blow some air into it. Finally, they got the picture they wanted. On September 9, 1992, readers of the *Washington Times* opened their paper to find themselves looking at a picture of a chicken inside a condom, its Perdue label clearly visible. Once their attention had been caught, the text below told them why "There's No Such Thing as Safe Chicken." Henry ran the ad in many other newspapers and magazines, and it became such a conversation piece that he had T-shirts made up with the ad printed across the front.[10]

After the chicken-in-a-condom ad appeared in the Baltimore *City Paper,* Henry was contacted by the advertising manager from the *Catholic Review,* the newspaper of the Catholic Archdiocese of Baltimore, who offered to run the ad at a reasonable price. Henry thought that to have a Roman Catholic newspaper running an ad with a condom in it might attract some media attention, so he accepted the offer and paid for the ad. He was astonished to find, when the paper appeared, that the teat of the condom had been painted out, so that the chicken appeared merely to be wrapped in cellophane.[11]

Henry continues to give Perdue as much bad publicity as he can. For *Her New York,* he and Graham designed an ad focusing on the sexual harassment that female workers at Perdue had to endure (if they resisted supervisors who groped, they were given the most demeaning jobs in the plant).[12] In March 1993, one of Henry's friends received an invitation to a lecture Frank Perdue was giving at New York City's University Club. She passed the invitation on to Henry, who stood up at question time and began to ask Perdue a few questions about the way he did business. Bedlam ensued. The organizer of the event screamed, "How dare you!" at Henry and looked ready to assault him physically. Meanwhile, Henry kept challenging Perdue with questions that Perdue refused to answer. Eventually, Henry was surrounded by staff from the club, who ushered him out.

Though Perdue did not yield, Henry doesn't consider the campaign a wasted effort:

We got absolutely nothing from him. But . . . after the Revlon campaign everybody we talked with was ready to be responsive to us, so for about ten years we never had a negative campaign on anybody, and I think a negative campaign makes it easier to get phone calls returned. . . . So I think the Perdue campaign worked well in that sense.

VIOLENCE IN THE MOVEMENT

The issue is not the occasional sadist who gets his jollies out of torturing animals. The problems we need to solve involve structural social change—they involve literally billions of animals. We are seeking a revolution in people's thinking—that animals are not edibles, and that animals are not lab tools. The animal rights movement's focus must be on achieving real cultural change. Terrorism and threats of violence can only hinder the process.

Henry Spira[13]

During the 1980s, the animal movement began to have its own image problem. A spate of militant actions by the Animal Liberation Front and other groups threatened to spill over into serious violence against people who exploited animals. The ALF broke into farms and laboratories, releasing animals or taking them to secret hiding places where they could be cared for. Equipment was smashed, and in some cases, the homes of experimenters were painted with slogans or vandalized.

Henry did not keep entirely aloof from illegal action—in fact, he had had some involvement in what was probably the first raid on an animal research unit in the United States. After the cat experiments at the American Museum of Natural History had been stopped, someone who had worked for that campaign told Henry that she and a few others were planning to break into a laboratory at the New York University Medical Center, on the corner of Thirtieth Street and First Avenue, in Manhattan. The aim was to free some animals and let the public see what was going on there. She asked Henry's advice, not on whether to do it—that decision had already been made—but on how to do it most effectively. He suggested that they set up a media contact in advance, and have homes ready for the animals they would take out. Before the raid, the group went into the lab to check everything out. The lab was unlocked because in the early days of the animal rights movement, it did not occur to those in charge of animal facilities that anyone might want to break into them. Henry went with the group on one occasion and took some photographs that were later circulated to the media. The raid itself took place on March 14,

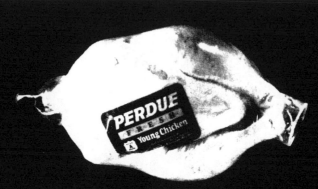

There's No Such Thing As Safe Chicken

Eight out of ten USDA-approved chickens are contaminated with salmonella and campylobacter bacteria . . . Each year, these bacteria sicken at least 4 million Americans and kill 2,000. Raw poultry is now the most common source of these bacteria . . . Poultry producers say cleanliness is the consumer's problem . . . But should we have to treat chicken like hazardous waste?

Senator Howard Metzenbaum, USA Today (6/28/91)

The final product is no different than if you took a bird . . . stuck it in the toilet and then ate it . . . (p. 236*)

Gerald Kuester
Former USDA Microbiologist

The first thing they go through is the scald tank. There it's nothing but boiling fecal soup. . . . It's a mass accumulation of bacteria on top of bacteria.

Today, basically, the consumers eat it. (pp. 341-342*)

USDA Poultry Inspectors

Workers get sick to their stomachs in the drain. The drain is a lot less sanitary than anyone's toilet. The Perdue inspectors told us to take (chickens that fell) out of the drain and send them back down the line . . . (p. 70*)

Former Perdue Worker

The waste is not always even from the chickens . . . (workers) sometimes have to relieve themselves on the floor. Chickens regularly fall off the line and into all the muck . . . supervisors have workers put them back on the line . . . (p. 70*)

Former Perdue Worker

. . . cancerous birds come through with tumors regularly, sometimes all day long . . . right after I'd put them in the condemned barrel foremen have the floor workers hang

the birds back on the (processing) line . . . (p. 61*)

Former Perdue Quality Control Inspector

I've heard that Frank Perdue ads talk about how tough his quality control inspectors are. He wouldn't dare run those ads in North Carolina . . . (p. 71*)

Former Perdue Worker

Can you imagine Frank Perdue's face when you go to him and say, "I want to put a warning on your chicken that says 'This chicken may be contaminated'?" (p. 346*)

Jim Vance, Co-anchor
News 4 WRC-TV (NBC) (4/26/91)

You are risking more than your health every time you eat chicken. You are supporting an industry which cripples workers, destroys the environment and creates an unending horror for birds. Twenty-five thousand birds at a time, are crammed into a dark warehouse, with less than one square foot of living space per bird, choking from accumulated ammonia fumes.

Perdue workers, mostly poor minority women, have to cut up to 90 chickens per minute, for minimal pay. When this unnatural speedup cripples the workers' arms and hands, they are fired and left to fend for

themselves. The government has fined Perdue for deliberately concealing worker injuries and for polluting the Virginia waterways. Perdue is a pioneer of intensive chicken confinement, which means misery for the birds and an epidemic of dirt and disease for consumers.

One More Thing To Worry About . . .

Rather than clean up the industry, current proposals call for covering up the dirt and disease by irradiating the birds. But using nuclear waste to irradiate chickens effectively turns consumers into individual toxic waste dumps. While this may help to dispose of nuclear waste, it introduces additional unknown health risks and encourages the poultry industry to further lower already abominable standards.

You can run this ad. This ad was produced by the Coalition for Non-Violent Food, a project of Animal Rights International. Henry Spira, coordinator, and is not copyrighted. For additional information about Frank Perdue and the poultry industry send a SASE to: ARI, Box 214, Planetarium Stn., New York, NY 10024. Your tax deductible contribution to ARI will make it possible to rerun this and related ads.

*Testimony from the June 28, 1991 Hearing of the Committee on Labor and Human Resources, U.S. Senate on Poultry Safety: Consumers at Risk.

The famous "chicken in a condom" advertisement was used in newspapers, magazines, and on T-shirts, but when Baltimore's Catholic Review ran it, the condom was painted out.

1979. Two dogs, a cat, and two guinea pigs were rescued.[14] Henry kept his distance, but he raised some money to pay for a vet to remove electrodes that had been implanted into the skull of the cat.

By 1984, illegal actions against labs, farms, and fur shops had become an almost daily occurrence in Britain and were increasingly common in the United States as well. In one of the most dramatic incidents, British activists told the media that poisoned Mars candy bars had been placed in supermarkets to protest against dental experiments on animals paid for by the confectionery's manufacturer. The poisoning scare was later revealed to be a hoax, but this did not stop millions of people from getting the impression that animal liberationists cared more about animals than they did about children. By 1985, many within the animal movement were worried that a few fanatics would destroy the public goodwill on which the movement's prospects of continued gains for animals depended. Henry phoned me to suggest that we co-sign a letter opposing the use of violence, to be published in *Animals' Agenda,* the leading publication of the animal movement. Together we drafted a letter that expressed our joint views on violence:

> In light of the sensationalist media coverage given to acts such as bomb threats, poisoning of food and contamination of consumer products—acts said to have been committed by animal movement activists—we believe the time has come to explore the possible repercussions of such tactics.
>
> While our society's present legal structure reflects a relatively narrow speciesist viewpoint which needs to be challenged in forceful ways, there are fundamental moral principles that should not be violated. Respecting the interests and rights of others is foremost among these. We do not place animals before people; all should be given equal and fair consideration. Threatening the lives and health of any human or non-human is an act of unjustified violence and contrary to our basic beliefs.
>
> We are asking people to extend their moral horizons, to accept the notion of fair play; if we violate our own principles of non-violence we may relinquish our most powerful means of persuasion and thus risk alienating those very people on whom the success of this movement depends. We should follow the lead set by Gandhi and Martin Luther King and not that of international terrorists.[15]

While illegal break-ins continued, virtually all those who practiced undercover activities drew a line between damage to property and violence to people. But no one in the American movement was prepared for the sensational news that broke on November 11, 1988, when Fran Trutt, a thirty-three-year-old animal rights activist from New York, was arrested and charged with attempted murder, possession of explosives, and manufacturing a bomb. Police alleged that she had hidden a sophisticated radio-controlled pipe bomb near a pathway leading to the offices of the United States Surgical Corporation, in Norwalk, Connecticut. Had they not arrested her, they claimed, she would have detonated it as Leon Hirsch, the corporation's chief executive, entered the building. The police added that the bomb, along with three other bombs found in her apartment, was supplied by "a terrorist group."[16]

Hirsch and his corporation had been the target of protests from the animal rights movement because U.S. Surgical's sales representatives used live dogs—about 1,000 a year—to demonstrate a surgical stapling device sold by the company. The major organizer of the protests was Friends of Animals, a group that was headquartered in Connecticut. Trutt had taken part in these protests. She was known to be devoted to dogs, taking in and feeding strays, and sometimes even going hungry so that her dogs could eat.

Three days later, Trutt appeared in court at a bail hearing. Though Henry had never met her or even heard of her before the story broke, he went to the bail hearing and was surprised to find himself the only animal rights person there. Everyone else had stayed away, apparently fearful of being linked to a terrorist. Henry's presence was widely reported:

> Prominent activist Henry Spira of Animal Rights International attended Trutt's arraignment and said he was surprised that more animal rights activists "didn't show up as observers to make sure she got a fair shake." Said Spira, "The animal movement is against violence and harm, but one can understand the frustration of individuals when they run into the Leon Hirsches of the world. The Hirsches are responsible for the violence." Spira speculates that Trutt may have been set up by animal rights opponents. "The question is, who benefits from things like this? The answer is, the Hirsches of the world."[17]

Bail was set at $500,000, which Trutt could not raise. She remained in jail, where Henry visited her occasionally. Priscilla Feral, head of Friends of Animals, said that Trutt had nothing to do with her organization, which worked within a legal framework. Trutt had occasionally attended meetings of other animal groups. They described her as "disruptive" and prone to make irrational demands. Pauline Kehlenbach of the Bronx Animal Rights Coalition said that Trutt was "unstable, but not capable of murder. She was an irrational person, but she was unable to do anything like this by herself." Trutt's parents said that the bomb was supposed to be "a scare," nothing more, and that their daughter "would never under any circumstance hurt anyone."[18]

Enterprising sleuthing by a journalist for the local newspaper *Westport News* soon showed that Henry was right to ask "who benefits?" The paper discovered that Trutt was driven to the headquarters of U.S. Surgical by a man named Marc Mead, who had been hired by Perceptions International, a security firm, to get to know Trutt and report on her activities. Mead was paid $500 a week plus expenses and had been told that the bill was being covered by U.S. Surgical. He had approached Trutt after being called by his contact at Perceptions International and told that she was using a phone in a pizza parlor, and that he could get to know her by saying that he needed to use the phone because of a problem with his dog. The ruse worked. Trutt took an interest in Mead's dog problem, and afterward, they continued to meet two or three times a week. Trutt had picketed U.S. Surgical several times and, Mead claimed, had told him that she wanted to "get even" with Leon Hirsch for what his company was doing to dogs. Mead claimed that he had no idea what that meant until one day she showed him the bomb. (Trutt, on the other hand, claimed that Mead had given her the money she needed to buy the bomb.) Mead then reported back to Perceptions International and was told to arrange to have Trutt bring the bomb to U.S. Surgical on a particular time and day. Mead suggested the time to Trutt and offered to drive her there in his van. She agreed, the police were tipped off, and Trutt was arrested as she placed the bomb at a spot Mead had suggested. Mead was neither arrested nor questioned by police.[19]

U.S. Surgical called a media conference to deny that it had "set up" Trutt and to warn Americans that "terrorists are on the loose." But Hirsch abruptly ended the meeting when reporters pressed him for details about U.S. Surgical's connection with Perceptions International.[20] A week later, *Westport News* revealed that seven months before her arrest, Trutt had been befriended by another Perceptions International undercover agent, Mary Lou Sapone. Sapone had long been suspected of being an infiltrator in Friends of Animals and other activist animal groups. She had urged them to smash the windows of fur shops and throw paint on the furs, even offering to pay for the paint. Trutt phoned Sapone before leaving for the U.S. Surgical offices to plant the bomb and said that she was having second thoughts about going with Mead. "Trust Mead," Sapone was reported to have said. "He knows what he is doing." Trutt took Sapone's advice. Even after she was arrested, she was so far from suspecting Sapone that she arranged to have her care for her dogs.[21]

Henry was no longer alone in thinking that U.S. Surgical had targeted a lonely, emotionally unstable person and had encouraged her to plant the bomb. Hirsch's goal was to be able to paint all animal rights activists as terrorists. Henry called William Kunstler, a brilliant attorney who had successfully defended unpopular accused people in many trials, and asked him to take Trutt's case. Henry's hope was that Kunstler would be able to show that U.S. Surgical's role in setting up the bombing went even further than had been reported so far. Kunstler agreed to take the case, but to Henry's disappointment, Trutt instead accepted a local lawyer recommended by other animal rights groups.

While Trutt remained in jail, awaiting trial, Henry wrote a column for *Animals' Agenda* opposing violence and warning against agents provocateurs:

> I believe that on the basis of both principles and good strategy we need to oppose violence and threats of violence because: 1) it runs counter to the very foundation of the animal protection movement which maintains that it's wrong to harm others (be they human or nonhuman animals); 2) it shifts attention away from the massive institutionalized violence routinely inflicted on billions of animals; and 3) it offers defenders of tyranny the opportunity to position themselves as victims.[22]

He concluded that the animal movement must maintain "an intransigent position that refuses to be seduced into violence."

Trutt's trial on a charge of attempted murder began in April 1990. In tape-recorded conversations played in court, Mary Lou Sapone repeatedly assured Trutt that she was her friend and offered to help her get money for the bombs, but Trutt's case was damaged by a recording in which she said that Hirsch is "going to have to go." The trial ended dramatically when conversations about Trutt's lesbian sex life were played, in which Trutt talked about killing her lover. Tearfully, Trutt asked her lawyer to accept a plea bargain that she had earlier refused. Trutt changed her plea from "not guilty" to "no contest" and was sentenced to one year in prison, with a ten-year suspended sentence. The opportunity for cross-examining Sapone, Mead, or anyone from Perceptions International or U.S. Surgical was lost.[23] Three years later, Henry found himself on a panel with Leon Hirsch at a Boston meeting of a group called Public Responsibility in Medicine and Research. In the wake of the Trutt affair, Hirsch had founded a lobby for animal experimentation called Americans for Medical Progress, which accused animal activists of using terrorism to stop animal research. Hirsch spoke first and mentioned U.S. Surgical's interest in alternatives. Henry challenged him to redirect some of the advertising budget of Americans for Medical Progress away from attacks on the animal movement and toward promoting alternatives. Hirsch responded that he would be happy to consider advertising copy promoting valid alternatives to animals in research and testing. Henry and Hirsch then spent the remainder of the session exchanging notes about potential advertising copy. In his closing remarks, Hirsch got a laugh when he commented on the unlikeliness of the interaction.[24]

The beginning of the 1990s saw a backlash against the animal movement. Louis Sullivan, secretary of health and human services, referred to 25,000 animal rights activists, assembling in Washington, D.C., for a peaceful "March for the Animals," on June 10, 1990, as "terrorists." The next day, grandmothers marched holding up placards saying, "I am a terrorist." As Sullivan continued to use this absurdly inflated rhetoric, Henry took out a full-page advertisement in the *Washington Times* asking the question "Are You a Terrorist" and answering that you are, according to Sullivan, if you oppose needless cruelty to animals. The ad went on to ask why Sullivan was evading the real issues of his portfolio, including the fact that the United States was not even on the top-twenty list for health care among industrialized countries.[25] After that, Sullivan's language became a little less hysterical.

ENDING SHACKLING AND HOISTING

Jewish and Moslem ritual slaughter laws prohibit stunning before slaughter. Nevertheless, the manner of killing prescribed by the laws of both these religions should lead to a rapid loss of consciousness. In American slaughterhouses, however, by far the greatest part of the suffering associated with ritual slaughter was caused by the fact that sanitary laws require that a slaughtered animal must not fall in the blood of a previously slaughtered animal. Since the floor of a slaughterhouse is usually covered with blood, slaughterhouses killing large animals like cattle deal with this by putting a chain around one of the back legs of the animal and hoisting it off the floor so that it hangs upside down. This is known as "shackling and hoisting." Animals not intended for ritual slaughter are stunned before shackling and hoisting, then have their throats cut before they recover consciousness; but in the case of ritual slaughter, fully conscious cows and steers are shackled with a chain around one of their back legs and then hoisted off the floor before they are killed. Since steers may weigh up to 2,000 pounds, it is easy to imagine the shock and pain they feel when suddenly jerked off their feet and hung upside down by one leg.

In 1987 Henry came across an article in the trade publication *Meat and Poultry* in which a livestock consultant wrote:

> Shackling and hoisting of conscious animals for ritual slaughter is an area of our profession in need of major housecleaning.
>
> I have been in hundreds of slaughter plants, but I had nightmares after visiting one plant in which five big steers were hung up in a row to await slaughter. They were hitting the walls, and their bellowing could be heard out in the parking lot.[26]

The author was Temple Grandin, a remarkable person in many ways. A silent, withdrawn, and sometimes destructively violent child, she was diagnosed as autistic, and it was thought that she might have to spend her life in an institution. She learned to cope with her disability, although she still lacks the

"Their bellowing could be heard out in the parking lot,"
wrote livestock consultant Temple Grandin of steers shack-
led and hoisted before slaughter. The practice ended when
Henry contacted brand-name companies buying meat from
animals slaughtered in this cruel way.

normal range of emotions and has problems empathizing with others and understanding their motives and intentions. (Oliver Sacks has written about her
in *An Anthropologist on Mars*—the book's title is Grandin's way of describing
her inability to understand the nuances of what most of us take as ordinary
social behavior.) As a child growing up on a farm, Grandin always had good
rapport with animals. At college, this interest led her into the animal sciences,
and she ended up with a doctorate and a teaching position at Colorado State
University. She also runs her own consulting business. Many people find her
ability to enter into an animal's point of view uncanny; it is certainly an asset to her in pointing out how poor design of animal-handling facilities may
cause animals to become distressed and difficult to manage. She has written
her autobiography, titled *Emergence: Labeled Autistic,* and has published over a
hundred papers, some on autism and others on animal behavior and animal
management.[27]

After reading Grandin's article, Henry commissioned her to prepare a report on the issue of "Pre-Slaughter Restraint for Religious Slaughter." The report gave an overview of the practice and argued that it violates the humane intent of both Jewish and Moslem teachings on ritual slaughter, which were originally supposed to ensure that slaughter was carried out swiftly and without suffering to the animal. Grandin described viable alternatives to shackling and hoisting, including an "upright restrainer system" that she had designed and installed at a plant in upstate New York in 1986. The upright restrainer enabled religious and sanitary requirements to be met, while eliminating the agony of shackling and hoisting for animals. It also dramatically reduced injuries to workers caused by the flailing, hanging animals. In the following years, some other slaughterhouses switched over to it, but several of the largest slaughter-houses in the country continued to shackle and hoist fully conscious animals.

Grandin's report had pointed out that many rabbis who are not directly involved with slaughter do not know about shackling and hoisting and sug-gested that grassroots support from the Jewish community would put pressure on plants to change the system. So in February 1988, Henry spoke to a rabbi affiliated with the Benjamin N. Cardozo School of Law, who had a reputation for being concerned about some uses of animals in research. But he turned out to be totally unsympathetic to any attempt to tackle the issue of shackling and hoisting, and Henry's plans to work through the Jewish community made no progress. Instead, in January 1991, Henry wrote to Milton Schloss, chair-man of the board of the Cincinnati-based corporation John Morrell & Co., one of America's largest "meatpackers" (as slaughtering operations are known in the industry). Henry chose Morrell & Co. because it had a reputation for progressive thinking and had already sought Grandin's advice on some matters. Nevertheless, Morrell's Alabama slaughtering operation continued to shackle and hoist conscious cattle. Henry also wrote to Mike Fagel, of Aurora Food Services, in Illinois, because Fagel was a member of the American Meat Indus-try's Safety Committee, and Henry thought that someone who was concerned about worker safety might also be concerned about the suffering of animals, or if not, could be persuaded to get rid of shackling and hoisting for safety reasons alone. To give these executives added interest in taking action, Henry's letters always included what he referred to as "some background materials to iden-tify ourselves and our concerns." These materials included his advertisements about Revlon and Perdue.

Two weeks after mailing his letter, Henry was flying to Cincinnati to meet Schloss at Morrell's headquarters, where Schloss told him that he had employed Grandin to improve the situation at the corporation's Alabama plant. By the end of May, the upright restraining systems were in operation

At a July 1989 "Agriculture and Animal Rights" conference in Albany, N.Y., Henry was told that there would be no questions from the audience. He caused a commotion, calling out "Let the public in. Let the public decide about veal farms." This picture appeared in Country Folks West, *August 7, 1989, p. A2.*

there. Fagel was even faster. Barely a month after Henry's letter, Aurora Food Services had gotten rid of shackling and hoisting.

Other meatpackers were not so quick to respond. When a letter to Federal Beef Processors, of West Fargo, North Dakota, brought no response, Henry needed to find some way of putting pressure on them. He recalls:

> There had been a lot of campaigns [on shackling and hoisting], and they went nowhere. The reason they went nowhere is that these slaughterhouses are not really concerned about the image they project. So what we did is, we went to some of their corporate customers and used that as leverage on the slaughterhouses.

Among the corporate customers supplied by Federal Beef was Hebrew National, the country's leading vendor of kosher sausages and other meat products. Henry sent its chief executive, Harvey Potkin, a letter, with the usual enclosures, telling him what its supplier was doing to animals killed for kosher slaughter and inviting him to discuss the matter. Potkin replied that he had contacted Federal Beef Processors, and they had agreed to find a way of eliminating shackling and hoisting. Henry waited two months and then wrote to Potkin asking what progress had been made. Potkin phoned Henry to tell him that he was going to fly to West Fargo himself to find out what was happening. When he got there, Potkin judged that Federal Beef was not seriously pursuing the matter. So on his return, he found an alternative supplier that was not using shackling and hoisting and switched over.

In a similar way, Henry wrote to Sinai Kosher Sausage Corporation in order to find a way of influencing one of its suppliers, Long Prairie Packing Company. This time, both the packer and the sausage maker tried to ignore him, but luckily, Sinai Kosher Sausage had just been taken over by the much larger and more visible Sara Lee Corporation, whose slogan was "Nobody doesn't like Sara Lee." Henry wrote to John Bryan, Sara Lee's chief executive, suggesting that "widespread public awareness of shackling and hoisting could convince many people they don't like Sara Lee quite so much any more." Six weeks later, Long Prairie was installing a suitable upright restraining device.

The last of the major slaughterers to fall in line was Brown Packing Company, of Illinois. In April 1994, it installed restrainers in accordance with Grandin's designs. Some small operations may have escaped Henry's net, but the shackling and hoisting of large conscious animals was virtually over.

FACE BRANDING: CHANGING GOVERNMENT POLICY

Henry's next campaign for farm animals was sparked by an obscure notice in the *Federal Register,* the government publication that carries announcements about proposed regulatory changes. The notice stated that the USDA intended to expand an existing program that required cattle imported from Mexico to be branded on the face with a hot iron in the shape of the letter M. In the existing program, only steers (castrated males) were being branded; but in November 1993, the department proposed branding females as well. Since about 1 million cattle entered the United States from Mexico, this would mean that about 2,700 cattle were being branded on the face every day. The branding was part of a program to eliminate tuberculosis from the U.S. cattle herd. It was supposed to make cattle of Mexican origin easy to identify, so that if one of them came down with TB, the source of the disease would be clear.

Henry thought that even though cattle did not have the public appeal of cats or rabbits, hot iron branding on the face was something that the general public would not accept. He contacted the USDA and suggested that there must be better ways of identifying cattle than facial branding. He commissioned Temple Grandin to write a brief position paper suggesting several less painful alternatives, including branding on the rump and punching a distinctive symbol in the ear, and sent the paper to the Department of Agriculture. Henry describes what happened next:

> We attempted to have a dialogue with the people at the U.S. Department of Agriculture. They set up a meeting. Then they canceled the meeting— at which point we figured that with 3,000 animals getting their faces scorched each day, this lackadaisical attitude isn't appropriate. We needed to photograph face branding in progress, so the public could actually see and feel the terror on the faces of these animals as the hot iron poker gets pushed onto their jaw. At the time, I was working with a young woman, Maureen Cunnie, who arranged a trip to the Texas–Mexico border with a photographer friend, David Kagan. The two basically charmed their way into a face-branding facility and took pictures.

The photographers came back with a sequence of images that Mark Graham turned into an extraordinarily powerful full-page advertisement: four black-and-white photographs running down the side of the page show a terrified steer, its head clamped and metal pincers in its nostrils, as the hot iron nears its cheek; then a cloud of smoke bursts from its face as the brand makes contact with the flesh. The text reads: "This is what USDA policy looks like. Can you imagine what it *feels* like?" Readers were asked to phone or write to the secretary for agriculture, Mike Espy, "before one more calf has his face torched," to tell him to stop such a barbaric method of identifying cattle. The advertisement appeared in the *New York Times* on March 15, 1994. Within two days, more than 1,000 readers had called, and more calls and letters kept coming in as the advertisement appeared in other newspapers. According to a member of Espy's staff, the secretary received more calls on this issue than on any other since he had taken office.

Henry decided it was time to take the matter up with Espy himself. Getting through to him was not easy. He made half a dozen phone calls to the department, but he couldn't even reach Espy's appointments secretary. Then he recalled an article from the *Wall Street Journal* that referred to Espy's "open-door policy" for people in agriculture who had problems with the government. He faxed Espy's office the quote from the article, but he still got no response. Remembering that the *Wall Street Journal* article had also referred to the "gentle treatment" that the USDA was giving to Tyson, the nation's biggest chicken producer, Henry called once more, asking for Espy's appointments secretary. Asked who was calling, he replied, "Don Tyson." In a flash he was put through, and an eager voice was saying, "Mr. Tyson?" "No," Henry replied, "it's Henry Spira. I thought I could get through using that name." There was an explosive reaction, and Henry was chewed out

THIS IS WHAT USDA POLICY LOOKS LIKE.

CAN YOU IMAGINE WHAT IT *FEELS* LIKE?

Or what it sounds like. Or smells like. Imagine a red-hot frying pan pressed against your cheek, — the searing pain, the heat and smoke of sizzling flesh. Even the melt down of your eye.

Face Branding Is Barbaric!

Hidden from the public, this organized atrocity is how the USDA currently identifies Mexican steers. Now the USDA proposes to expand this horror to all Mexican cattle in a pathetic gesture at monitoring tuberculosis.

In branding, the terrorized steer is first trapped between bars. Then his head is immobilized with steel pincers painfully clamped on to his nostrils and pulled to one side. If that's not enough the cowboy steps on the steer's face with his boot. As the red hot iron is pressed into his face, the steer bellows, his eyes bulge as he disappears into a cloud of his own burning flesh.

It's Completely Unnecessary!

There are far less painful ways of satisfying the USDA's desire to trace Mexican cattle. Experts say face-branding is not only barbaric but unnecessary. Far more humane alternatives have been suggested, including punching a distinctive symbol in the ear, notching the ear or branding near the edge of the hide on the rear.

In an age of DNA fingerprinting, why is the USDA using pre-historic brutality to identify cattle? Why is the USDA attempting to expand face branding when we should be outlawing such barbarisms? Is it just bureaucratic inertia, the convenience of doing things the way they've always been done at the USDA? Is it possible that Secretary Espy is not even aware of his organization's face branding program?

Stop The Face Branding Now!

Secretary of Agriculture Mike Espy: You can halt the red hot irons with one decisive word.—STOP! Face-branding is wrong. It's unethical. And there are easy alternatives.

This ad was produced by the Coalition for Non-Violent Food, a project of Animal Rights Int'l, Box 214, Planetarium Stn., New York, NY 10024, Henry Spira, Coordinator.

(left) A terrified young steer disappears in a cloud of smoke from his own burning flesh. Trapped between metal bars, his head is immobilized by metal pincers clamped to his nostrils and pulled to the side. He is now at the mercy of the USDA's red-hot iron. (Photos February, 1994)

This dramatic advertisement led the United States Department of Agriculture to reverse its plans to expand face branding, and to instead get rid of face branding altogether.

for misrepresentation. When he asked why he had not heard back, he was told that it was because they had been "reviewing Secretary Espy's calendar." Later, he received a call from someone in the USDA inspector general's office threatening to file a formal complaint over the misrepresentation. Henry told him to go ahead. No complaint was ever filed.[28]

Although Espy continued to avoid meeting Henry, the angry public reaction to what had previously been considered a routine procedure made an impression on the Department of Agriculture. It canceled its plans to expand the face-branding program. Then it invited public comment on a new proposal to stop the face branding of Mexican cattle altogether. Henry ran the same series of pictures in a new advertisement, this time with text headed: "The USDA wants to know how you feel about this. Tell them. Quickly." Twelve thousand written comments were sent to the USDA office, virtually all calling for an end to face branding. In December 1994, the USDA heeded the public demand and abolished the face branding of Mexican cattle. A million animals a year had been spared an acutely painful procedure. But the national disease control program still required some domestic cattle to be branded on the face. The Department accepted the logic of its own previous decisions, and on September 19, 1995, the *Federal Register* published the department's "Final Rule" completely eliminating the face branding of all cattle.

Henry's response was another full-page advertisement. This time a much more contented steer looked straight at the reader and asked, "Who's listening?" The answer was given below: "The USDA is listening!" The ad went on to thank all of those who had spoken out against face branding and to thank the USDA for listening. It was a gesture that USDA officials appreciated: When Henry visited their offices later, he saw his advertisement hanging on the wall.

Keen to build on the relationship he had achieved with the USDA, Henry talked to officials about making concern for animal well-being a permanent part of the department's work. As a result, Patricia Jensen, then assistant secretary for marketing and regulatory programs, convened a USDA Interagency Animal Well-Being Task Force, which began the work of developing voluntary guidelines to improve conditions for farm animals.

A HELEN KELLER BIRD SHOOT?

On Friday, September 15, 1995, Henry opened his mailbox to find an envelope with no return address. Inside was a photocopy of an invitation to "Shoot for Sight" at a "1,000 bird combination duck and pheasant driven shoot" to aid Helen Keller International. The organization was named after the celebrated blind and deaf woman who had dedicated her life to raising money to assist people who are blind or in need in other ways. It had programs in twenty-three countries to prevent blindness, restore sight, and rehabilitate the blind, "the most vulnerable people in the human family." Also in the envelope was a list of Helen Keller International's Board of Trustees, advisers, and sponsors.

Henry got to work and prepared a letter to John Palmer, Helen Keller International's executive director, with copies to other leading officials:

Dear Mr. Palmer,

HELEN KELLER'S GOOD NAME

Helen Keller is surely one of the most remarkable people this country ever produced. She exemplifies bravery, sensitivity, indomitable will—a triumph of the spirit.

You can therefore understand how taken aback we were to see a copy of your invitation to a day of killing on October 27 in Dutchess County in return for donations to Helen Keller International [HKI]. Would not Helen Keller have paid almost any price for a mere glimpse of the natural wonders you so casually propose blowing away in her name, for the sake of fund-raising? Is this not a mockery of Helen Keller's love of life—a travesty that the public and your financial supporters would condemn?

We think HKI's programs, here and abroad, are admirable. But killing for pleasure is no way to combat the terrible tragedy of blindness. Are there not more creative ways to save the sight and lives of the "most vulnerable" other than sponsoring the pleasure-killing of the absolutely defenseless?

We think that much can be accomplished by meeting with you. We have an established track record for preferring constructive dialogue over public confrontations. Unfortunately, in this instance, the time frame for your scheduled fund-raiser necessitates that we speak immediately if we are to achieve a mutually satisfying resolution. I'll call as soon as you've received this letter.

The letter, with copies of the advertisements on face branding and articles discussing Henry's track record, was brought by courier to Helen Keller International on Monday, September 18. Two hours later, Henry called Palmer and asked for his initial response. He said that he needed to consider it and would get back to Henry on the following Wednesday.

On Wednesday, Palmer thanked Henry for his "consciousness-raising." He offered a written statement that there would be no more such shooting events. Henry insisted that the shoot on October 27 must also be canceled. Palmer said that he had problems with one member of his board—probably, Henry guessed, the one who had initiated this fund-raiser. Henry offered to fax him some preliminary drawings of advertisements they might run if the shoot went ahead. The advertisements had headings like "Helen Keller was a miracle. Not a killer" and "Guns cause blindness. They don't cure it." Henry also made it clear that if the shoot was not canceled by Friday, September 22, he would start contacting the media.

Palmer called him back on September 21 to say that Helen Keller International had decided not to proceed with the Shoot for Sight fund-raising program and had no intention of undertaking similar events in the future. Henry thanked him in a letter and enclosed a personal donation as a token of his support for the work of Helen Keller International.

Henry's track record had been responsible for a remarkably quick victory, first in leading his unknown informer to send him a copy of the invitation (Palmer was curious about how Henry had known of the shoot, since invitations had gone to only a small and select group) and second in making it clear to Helen Keller International that Henry had the capacity to do it much more harm than the fund-raiser was worth. Henry never found out who had sent him the invitation.

THE BIG MAC

By the early 1990s, McDonald's restaurants were serving up more than 1 billion eggs and half a billion pounds of beef a year. That volume, and the icon status of the hamburger chain, made McDonald's an obvious target for bringing about change for farm animals. If McDonald's were to give one hundredth of 1 percent of its gross revenues to fund a research center dedicated to finding alternatives to the stressful confinement of factory farming, that could do even more to reduce suffering than the similar percentage that Revlon had given to the search for alternatives to the Draize test. But McDonald's has a reputation for having a corporate culture that is aggressive and politically well to the right. It was never going to be easy to get it to take animals seriously.

Henry's opening move was a low-key meeting with McDonald's general counsel and executive vice president, Donald Horwitz, held in February 1989 at the offices of the American Society for the Prevention of Cruelty to Animals. The purpose of the meeting was to ask McDonald's to investigate the effect of factory farming on the animals whose meat and eggs it used, and then to use these findings to develop less stressful ways of raising these animals. Horwitz seemed remarkably ready to cooperate. He agreed that McDonald's would survey its suppliers in the United States and Canada and take a look at the situation in Europe, where there was legislation setting minimum standards for farm animals that was in advance of anything in the United States. The research would, he said, be a guide to further action.

Horwitz went away to contact McDonald's suppliers, and he apparently received some negative feedback about the plan. He suggested some dialogue between advocates of farm animal reform and the animal producers. That led to a Farm Animal Well-Being Workshop, sponsored by McDonald's and its suppliers, and organized by the Tufts University Center for Animals and Public Policy, headed by Henry's friend Andrew Rowan. The workshop, held in November 1990, seemed to be a useful exploration of common ground between the animal movement and the producers, but it did not lead to any further action by McDonald's or its suppliers.

Over the next eighteen months, Henry wrote to, and met with, Horwitz's successor, Shelby Yastrow, suggesting various steps that McDonald's could take to reduce the suffering of the animals used in its products. In May 1992, Yastrow wrote to Henry saying, "We have taken all the steps that we said we would take." McDonald's had, he said, surveyed suppliers and received assurances that "they are in compliance with the laws, regulations and industry guidelines concerning the humane treatment of animals." But this was meaningless, for the "laws, regulations and industry guidelines" in virtually all countries continued to allow the most inhumane confinement of factory farmed animals. Yastrow's letter also referred to "an understanding" between McDonald's and its suppliers that if the existing guidelines "do not show sufficient concern for the humane treatment of animals," the suppliers will "take all reasonable additional measures to assure that animals raised, transported and slaughtered for McDonald's products are treated humanely." That sounded good, but who was to decide what additional measures were "reasonable"? Apparently, the suppliers themselves. In any case, Henry wanted McDonald's to make a more public commitment. As with Revlon, his plan was that McDonald's would set a standard that he could take to other corporations using farm animals and ask: "Do you want to be seen as less concerned about animals than McDonald's?"

Henry wrote to Mike Quinlan, McDonald's chief executive officer, asking McDonald's to honor the commitment that Horwitz had made at the 1989 meeting to make the survey the basis of some real action to reduce animal suffering. Quinlan passed the task back to Horwitz, now working independently with a Chicago law firm. Horwitz wrote denying that McDonald's had entered into any agreements with Henry regarding the well-being of farm animals, but offering to work with him for that goal anyway. Henry accepted the offer, and suggested to Horwitz that McDonald's do the following:

- set standards for its suppliers that would, with minimal expenditure of time and money, ensure more humane standards of handling and slaughter;

- investigate alternatives to the worst forms of confinement in factory farms;
- add a meatless burger to its menu; and
- establish a Center for Farm Animal Well-Being to assess alternative systems of raising farm animals, in use elsewhere, for their suitability for adoption in the United States.

By February 1993, these proposals had gone nowhere, and Henry wrote again to Yastrow expressing his frustration "that after three years of on-again, off-again dialog there's nothing to show for it." The letter ended with both a carrot and a stick:

> We believe that we are looking at a problem which is capable of a quick and easy solution if dealt with promptly. From our perspective there are no complex decisions that need to be agonized over, nothing that justifies weeks, months and even years of debate. We also believe that you are looking at a problem which, with benign neglect, will quickly escalate into a global and multi-faceted PR nightmare for McDonald's.[29]

This brought about, in March, a breakfast meeting between Henry and Yastrow, after which Yastrow wrote, "I'm glad I had a chance to meet with you and live to tell about it." At the meeting, Yastrow had said that he would try to organize a coalition of other quick-service restaurants to get behind some of Henry's proposals. The next few letters between Henry and Yastrow were on a "Dear Henry/Dear Shelby" basis, and markedly more friendly in tone, but still nothing happened. By June, Henry was once again bluntly pointing this out to Yastrow. In reply, Yastrow wrote that he was still trying to establish the coalition: "We will either act as part of a coalition or we won't act at all—especially in view of all you are asking."

A year earlier, Henry had bought sixty-five shares of stock in McDonald's. The time had come to make use of them. Together with Franklin Research & Development, a firm that provides advice to socially concerned investors, Henry filed a shareholder's resolution to be voted on by all McDonald's shareholders at their 1994 annual meeting. The resolution had a preamble describing the treatment of animals used by McDonald's and then asked shareholders to vote for a recommendation asking the Board of Directors to endorse the following principles and encourage the company's suppliers to take all reasonable steps to comply with them:

1. Least Restrictive Alternative—animals should be housed, fed, and transported in a practical manner least restrictive of their physical and behavioral needs.

2. Individual Veterinary Care—animals should be afforded individual veterinary care when needed.
3. Humane Slaughter—methods used should be designed to produce a quick and humane death.

The resolution was phrased so as to be difficult to argue against. How could McDonald's deny that animals should have individual veterinary care when needed? Yet intensively reared chickens and laying hens have no individual veterinary care at all. Inspection is so cursory that sick birds are usually not noticed until they die. Giving all animals individual veterinary care would mean a radical change in modem methods of animal production.

McDonald's was unhappy about Henry's resolution being put to shareholders. Armed with a long legal opinion, it gave notice—as required by law—to the Securities and Exchange Commission that it intended to omit the proposal from its proxy materials for the 1994 annual meeting. Henry gave notice of his intention to contest this decision, but at the same time, Yastrow was asking him what would persuade him to withdraw the resolution. In February 1994, a deal was struck. McDonald's agreed to mail a copy of a policy statement on the humane treatment of animals to all its meat and poultry suppliers and to print an excerpt from the statement in its annual report.

The statement that McDonald's agreed to mail to its suppliers read as follows:

MCDONALD'S AND THE HUMANE TREATMENT OF ANIMALS

Just as McDonald's works hard to maintain the trust and confidence of its customers, it takes seriously its obligation to the communities in which we do business. We are already well-known for our efforts with respect to children and young people. Our commitment to the protection of the environment is also well-documented. However, because McDonald's restaurants buy all their food products from independent suppliers, the Company's commitment to the humane treatment of animals may not be as well-known.

McDonald's believes the humane treatment of animals, from the time of their birth and throughout their lives, is a moral responsibility. The Company fully respects the independence of its suppliers and requires them to adhere to pertinent laws, regulations, and industry guidelines concerning the humane treatment of animals such as those recommended by the American Meat Institute. Additionally, where those guidelines do not show sufficient concern for the humane treatment of animals, McDonald's suppliers should take all reasonable steps to assure that animals raised, transported and slaughtered for McDonald's products are treated humanely. Additionally, we require that each supplier submit to us an annual written statement, signed by its Chief Executive Officer, confirming that it is in compliance with this statement (or explaining where and why it is not in compliance, and when compliance can be expected).[30]

Henry accepted the deal and withdrew his shareholder's resolution, not because he thought this statement was going to bring about dramatic changes to the treatment of animals used by McDonald's, but because he didn't think he was going to get any more out of the company by pushing on with the resolution, which the big shareholders were sure to vote down by a comfortable margin. As Henry told *Vegetarian Times,* the statement "doesn't necessarily mean a lot," but it was a first step in setting an industry standard: "If McDonald's moves a millimeter, everyone else moves with them."[31] In other articles, however, Henry took a more optimistic view, describing McDonald's action as "a fundamental breakthrough in corporate thinking."[32]

Whatever he said publicly, Henry had his doubts about whether anything had really changed in the way McDonald's suppliers were handling their animals. Over the next three years, he tried frequently, but without much success, to find out. Temple Grandin told him that she noticed a difference around that time. You could, she said, tell by looking at them whether particular slaughterhouses were McDonald's suppliers. They were better maintained, and they avoided handling the worst of the "downers"—cattle who arrive at the slaughterhouse so weak that they cannot stand and therefore have to be dragged off the truck with a rope. But these were, at best, marginal improvements. In commenting on the campaign in 1996, Henry wrote, "Long term results of this initiative are unclear, since McDonald's is not yet making any substantive information available to the public. Stay tuned."[33]

The public did not need to stay tuned for much longer. When McDonald's sued Helen Steel and Dave Morris, two activists from London Greenpeace, for defamation over a leaflet titled "What's Wrong with McDonald's?" they gave Steel and Morris the chance to prove in court that the allegations in their leaflet—which included cruelty to animals—were true. The outcome was the longest trial in British legal history, pitting a $32 billion corporation against two activists who, unable to afford a lawyer, represented themselves throughout a trial that ran for 313 days and heard 180 witnesses. To meet the charge of cruelty, Dr. Fernando Gomez Gonzalez, McDonald's manager of meat products, was in the witness box for seven days. In handing down his verdict, Mr. Justice Bell said:

> [McDonald's] evidence of an animal welfare policy, or at least a written animal welfare policy, was curious to say the least. . . . On the seventh and last day of his evidence Dr. Gomez Gonzalez said that he had seen "a small statement, half a page, regarding animal welfare, the concept." This turned

out to be a one page statement headed "McDonald's and the Humane Treatment of Animals," which reads as follows:

Mr. Justice Bell then read the statement already quoted above, and further commented:

> This statement is in the most general terms. It reads more like a public relations hand-out than a serious policy statement and that interpretation is consistent with it not being so well known as to be at Dr. Gomez Gonzalez' fingertips during the greater part of his evidence, although it may have dated from 1989. . . . In my judgment [McDonald's] policy . . . was primarily for public consumption in case anyone enquired.[34]

The judge got the date wrong, and the statement may have been more than just a public relations exercise. Nevertheless, the fact that Gonzalez was not at first aware of the statement does show how little concern there was among McDonald's executives for the welfare of the animals whose flesh and eggs it served.

The "McLibel trial" opened a new chapter in Henry's dealings with McDonald's. When the verdict was finally handed down, on June 19, 1997, McDonald's claimed victory because Mr. Justice Bell ruled that Steel and Morris had not demonstrated the truth of all of their wide-ranging criticisms. They had not, for example, shown that McDonald's played a role in the clearing of tropical rain forests. McDonald's received a modest award of damages, which it made no attempt to get from Steel and Morris. It did not even bother to apply for costs, writing off the $15 million it had spent on legal fees. In public relations terms, the trial was a disaster. The corporate giant lost on several points, most notably on the issue of cruelty, for the judge found that:

- Chicken served by McDonald's comes from hens who have so little room to move that to keep them in this way is cruel, and McDonald's "are culpably responsible for that cruel practice."
- "A proportion of the chickens used to produce the . . . food are still fully conscious when they have their throats cut. This is a cruel practice for which the Plaintiffs [i.e., McDonald's] are culpably responsible."
- Bacon served by McDonald's involves keeping sows who "spend virtually the whole of their lives in dry sow stalls . . . without freedom of movement." Again, McDonald's was found to be "culpably responsible for that cruel practice."
- Eggs served by McDonald's come from hens who "spend their whole lives in battery cages" and McDonald's "are culpably responsible for that cruel practice."

Only three months before the McLibel verdict, Yastrow had told Henry bluntly that "farm animal well-being is not high on McDonald's priority list." When Henry called immediately after the verdict, Yastrow's interest in farm animal well-being had risen sufficiently for him to fly to New York to talk about it. They arranged to meet on July 3. Before the meeting, Henry called me for some feedback on how to handle it; he realized that McDonald's was now much more vulnerable than it had ever been before and wanted to make the most of it. We discussed different possible tactics. Around the world, on the Saturday after the verdict, there had been demonstrations outside McDonald's restaurants. Would it be best to try to launch an international campaign against McDonald's immediately, focusing on what the trial had shown about the cruelty involved in the food it served? Or should that be held in reserve, to be used only if the discussions between Yastrow and Henry came to nothing? Yastrow himself had said that once a public campaign began, it would be harder for McDonald's to make changes, because it would not want to appear to be yielding to protesters. This might be a ploy to fend off protests until the issue had cooled, but it could also be true. Henry decided to hold off on the protests.

At Yastrow's suggestion, he and Henry met over breakfast in the Waldorf Astoria's Peacock Alley. Yastrow told Henry that he had been against taking on Steel and Morris in the British courts but that he had been overruled. Now he was only six months away from retirement and wanted to do something about animal welfare issues before he left. The final decision, though, would depend on how others in the top management group at McDonald's responded. Henry showed him an advertisement that he and Mark Graham had designed—but not yet used—for a campaign against one of McDonald's rivals, KFC (formerly Kentucky Fried Chicken). It pictured a toilet with a KFC tub where the bowl should be and the heading "Do KFC's Standards Meet Your Standards?" The text used the quote from a government microbiologist that Henry had already used in a Perdue advertisement: "The final product is no different than if you took a bird . . . stuck it in the toilet and then ate it." Yastrow looked at it and said, "I suppose you've prepared ads on us as well?" Henry confirmed that he had. Yastrow admitted that his earlier efforts to do something about the treatment of animals had lacked any real commitment, and—as if to demonstrate that he was serious this time—he showed Henry an internal company memo in which he bragged that he had been able to fend off Henry's threats without doing much. At the end of the breakfast, the two men had a power play over who would pay the exorbitant bill. Over Yastrow's undoubtedly true protests that he earned a lot more than Henry did, Henry, who had been quicker at catching the waiter's eye, won. The most significant outcome of the meeting was that Yastrow agreed to meet Temple Grandin to discuss some practical and feasible changes.

The meeting left Henry hopeful but wary: Was Yastrow's new frankness just a way of trying to fool him again? While staying in close contact with McDonald's, Henry and I formed an International Coalition for Farm Animals, modeled on the Draize and LD50 coalitions. By September, some major animal organizations had agreed to be part of it, including the World Society for the Protection of Animals, the Humane Society of the United States, the American Society for the Prevention of Cruelty to Animals, Compassion in World Farming, and the American Humane Association. At the same time, McDonald's seemed to be moving forward. It commissioned Grandin to do an animal welfare survey of its suppliers, and Yastrow told Henry that it would appoint someone to a full-time position to take responsibility for animal welfare issues. That person would report to Bob Langert, McDonald's director of environmental affairs, who in turn reported to the chief purchasing officer, who was directly under the chief executive. So, Yastrow was saying, this would be a high-level position. At McDonald's, being only four rungs down the hierarchy was a big deal.

The next meeting with McDonald's was arranged for October 1997, at a time when I would be visiting the East Coast. Langert had told Henry that he would come to New York with the person appointed to the new position of animal welfare director. Henry arranged a breakfast meeting for the four of us.

When I arrived in New York, Henry and I talked about what we wanted the meeting to achieve. We were worried that McDonald's strategy might be simply to delay things until the McLibel decision was so dated that nobody would get excited about it anymore. Hiring someone to deal with animal welfare didn't, in itself, help a single animal, and for a company as big as McDonald's, the cost of another salary was peanuts. We would need to tell McDonald's that we wanted to see, soon, some tangible steps toward reducing the pain and suffering of the animals it used. We talked about what we could ask McDonald's to do. The way it responded to Grandin's criticisms of its suppliers' facilities would be one test of its sincerity. But we wanted more far-reaching changes. What, for example, could McDonald's do about the confinement of sows? Before our meeting, we called Osborne Industries, a corporation based in Kansas that manufactured systems for keeping sows that allowed them to roam freely over a large indoor area. Confining sows individually was a crude—and cruel—response to the problem of ensuring that dominant sows do not take more than their share of food. Osborne's response was much more sophisticated. In its system, each sow activates a feeding device by entering a pen, one at a time. The sows wear collars with a bar code suitable for electronic scanning. If a dominant sow enters twice, a scanner detects this and stops the feeder. Our conversation with Osborne Industries confirmed that this system was already in commercial operation in the Unit

Today's chicken has been compared to hazardous waste. In fact, former USDA microbiologist Gerald Kuester describes the final product as "no different than if you took a bird... stuck it in a toilet and then ate it..."

Another USDA poultry inspector told a Senate committee that birds were processed in "boiling fecal soup...it's a mass accumulation of bacteria on bacteria." And the waste is not only from the chickens. At one KFC supplier, workers have been forced to relieve themselves on the floor because they are not allowed to leave the work line. Chickens regularly fall into the muck. And supervisors have workers put them right back on the line. And it's not only the outside of the bird that's contaminated. Chickens are fed an unwholesome diet which includes the remnants of diseased chickens.

So, it's probably no surprise that, according to the Centers for Disease Control, food-borne disease kills 4,500 Americans each year and sickens another 5 million.

Today's assembly line chicken is also an environmental disaster. The waste produced by factory farmed chickens and other animals pollutes land, air and water. CBS' 60 Minutes compared whole areas of North Carolina to a gigantic toilet. And in Virginia, a KFC supplier received record fines for destroying an entire waterway.

A KFC supplier has also been fined by the government for deliberately concealing worker injuries. Workers, mostly minority women, have to cut up to 90 chickens per minute for low pay. They face hazards like skin disease, toxic air, crippling hand injuries and sexual harassment.

Between the egg and the KFC bucket stretches one of the most brutal existences imaginable. Today's chickens are genetically manipulated to grow unnaturally fast. Young oversized birds can barely walk on their flimsy, crippled legs. They squat much of the time or breast-stroke their way lizard-like across filthy contaminated litter. Tens of

thousands of chickens are crowded into each dark shed—each bird with less than one square foot of "living space." Slaughter is often a horror in which millions of unstunned birds are thrown into the scald tanks alive.

We have suggested to KFC that they have a public obligation to upgrade food safety, protect the environment, improve working conditions and promote humane standards for the birds. KFC says they already require suppliers to adhere to all humane laws and guidelines—conveniently ignoring that there aren't any laws or guidelines.

Nobody has more influence on the poultry industry than KFC. And nobody has more influence on KFC than you. So if you think your food should come without lethal toxins, crippled workers, environmental damage or animal cruelty, you may want to slam the lid on the KFC bucket. Because if KFC won't pull the chicken industry out of the toilet, who will?

Do KFC's Standards Meet Your Standards?

Whereas McDonald's was prepared to enter into discussions on how to minimize the suffering of the animals it serves, KFC was not. The result was this ad, which ran in the Washington Times *on March 31, 1998.*

Animal production today: a typical pig production unit, in which sows are locked for months into stalls in which they cannot walk or turn around.

ed States. We would therefore be able to tell McDonald's that if it was serious about overcoming the cruelty described by Mr. Justice Bell, it could ensure that its suppliers switched over to this system whenever they put in new facilities for sows.

The meeting took place at a cafe on the Upper West Side, and it did not begin well. We were surprised to find that the new animal welfare director was none other than Fernando Gomez Gonzalez, who from the witness stand in the McLibel trial had resolutely denied that there is any cruelty in the raising of the animals used by McDonald's. That Gonzalez began by ordering bacon with his breakfast was scarcely calculated to endear him to us. But we did not waste time on either pleasantries or unpleasantries. We told Langert and Gonzalez that they needed to deal rapidly with the issues of cruelty identified in the McLibel trial because there were some major animal rights organizations that were keen to campaign against McDonald's. (This was entirely true: Since McDonald's restaurants are easily accessible in every major city, they are an ideal target for both national and international campaigns.) We suggested practical ways in which this could be done, ranging from gas stunning for chickens to Osborne Industries' system of keeping sows.

A lively discussion followed, which ended with Langert telling us that he couldn't give us specific commitments now, but by the end of the year McDonald's would have in place an action plan that would include:

- using Temple Grandin to develop an animal welfare auditing system that would be integrated into McDonald's food safety audits;
- a way to implement some of the more simple and practical steps to improve the treatment of animals, which could be done immediately or at least during 1998;
- a list of more complex issues that McDonald's would regard as longer-term goals; and
- procedures for working with suppliers to ensure that these changes took place.

Langert accepted our view that the real test of McDonald's sincerity would be whether it brought about significant improvements in the treatment of animals. But at the same time, he was saying, "We have big plans, but we can't move as quickly as you want. Give us until next year, and then see what we have done."

After the meeting, Henry and I puzzled over the conflicting messages McDonald's seemed to be sending us. The appointment of Gonzalez as animal welfare director was astonishing. Of all the people employed by McDonald's, he had been the most public in defending its treatment of animals. Was his appointment a calculated slap in the face for the animal movement? But then, why would Langert have bothered to come to New York with him to meet us and try so hard to convince us that McDonald's is serious about treating animals better?

If McDonald's had been totally intransigent, we would have begun planning a campaign against it, drawing on the millions of members of the organizations that had joined our International Coalition for Farm Animals. But since it had said that it would draw up a plan to improve the treatment of animals, we had little choice but to wait until 1998 to see what it did. To launch a campaign against McDonald's now would invite the response that McDonald's had been willing to talk to us but that we had not been prepared to give it the time it needed to change practices affecting millions of animals. At the time of writing, the McDonald's discussions are at a "wait and see" stage.

FOR THE SEVENTH GENERATION

I think one way of looking at it is expressed by the saying of Native Americans, that what they're concerned about is the impact of what's happening not on this current generation, or the next generation, but the seventh generation from now.

Henry Spira

When Henry was collecting material to use against Frank Perdue, he had been struck by the many different grounds on which factory farming could be condemned: "Not just bad news for the animals, but bad news for the environment, bad news for feeding the billions, bad news for the water, the air, and it used up non-renewable resources." If he could draw people concerned about each of these issues together, the opposition to factory farming would be much more powerful.

Early in 1993, Henry began a series of advertisements that, in contrast to all his previous advertising, had no target more specific than meat itself. Under the heading "There's a world of misery in every mouthful of meat," the first ad begins by describing "the preferred meal of affluent societies" as a "proven killer" linked to cancer, heart disease, and diabetes. The text then goes on:

> It kills people in other ways too. The grain which fattens animals for our dinner tables is oft times "appropriated" from the peoples of Third World countries; it enriches dictators while vast populations starve.
>
> Meat production destroys the environment, squanders dwindling water reserves, pollutes our rivers and lakes with toxic animal wastes, and is causing the destruction of rain forests.

Two paragraphs on the suffering of confined factory farm animals follow, and the ad ends with a request to "Cut it out or cut it down. You'll be taking a bite out of misery."

The "world of misery" ads were well written, but they were not especially eye-catching. With Mark Graham, Henry then devised something much more striking: Over a picture of an appealing cat going into a meat grinder, with ground-up meat coming out of the grinder, the ad offers "Five Good Reasons to Eat Your Dog or Cat." Among the reasons given are:

> **You'll be taking a stand against cruelty.**
> Right up to the moment your furry friend disappears into a crockpot, he'll have led a pampered and happy life. No such luck for the seven billion farm animals consumed in the U.S. each year! Their lives are a never ending nightmare. The millions who drop dead from stress are considered just a routine business expense.

Three of the other "Good Reasons" take aim at meat on health, environmental, and worker exploitation grounds, while the last says that "You'll help solve the dog and cat overpopulation problem" and points to the need to do something serious about controlling unwanted breeding of cats and dogs. In the last paragraph, Henry appeals to the thinking that drew him into the animal movement more than twenty years earlier:

Finally, let's not allow anything as irrational as personal attachment to stand between us and that tasty poodle casserole. Loving and cuddling some animals while ignoring the suffering of others, who feel exactly the same pain, is what's *really* irrational. We are programmed from our first meals to pet some animals and eat others. But this need not be so. A meatless diet will improve your health, the environment and the lives of farm animals. Best of all, with your new nonviolent diet you can keep cuddling your four legged friend while sending a powerful message to the meat industry's moguls of misery.

This was one ad that the *New York Times* flatly refused to run. It said the image of the cat going into the grinder would offend its readers. Henry submitted another version, without the meat coming out of the bottom of the grinder, but was still asked to "come up with something a little less repulsive." So Henry scrapped the cat and the meat grinder, substituting a puppy as the "hot dog" in a hot dog roll, with a bottle of ketchup standing in the background. Thus sanitized, the ad appeared in the *New York Times* on November 7, 1996.

There was a curious sequel. In February 1997, someone sent Henry a copy of the *Weekly World News,* a supermarket tabloid, which had an article titled "Hottest New Fast Food in Japan—Smoked Puppies on a Bun." Under the heading was the picture Mark Graham had made up for use in Henry's advertisement. The article below described the "outrage" of animal lovers the world over at this horrifying new Japanese food fad, stating that 4,000 had been sold in the past three weeks. The reporter quoted "famed animal rights activist Martha Serensen of Sydney, Australia" saying that she wanted to throw up when she thought about it. No one in Sydney, or anywhere else, had ever heard of Martha Serensen. The entire article appeared to have come out of the imagination of the reporter who wrote it, obviously inspired by Henry's photograph, which was copied without his permission.

Henry's aim is to do to meat what has happened to tobacco: change it from an accepted part of life to the mark of a social pariah. But reaching Americans, or even the entire population of the developed nations, would not be enough. While Americans are cutting down on meat, people in countries that have traditionally eaten very little meat are using their increasing prosperity to eat more. A continuation of present trends toward eating more meat in China, for example, would mean a consequent spread of factory farming and a huge increase in the "world of misery" caused by eating meat. This global situation led Henry to think about how he could have an impact on dietary trends in China, India, or Indonesia: "A lot of people had been talking about looking to the future as doom and gloom, nobody was working on what are

It could save your life! Has anyone ever died from salmonella or E. coli after eating their companion animal? But thousands of Americans die from toxic meat, poultry and eggs each year. And millions become seriously ill, according to the Centers for Disease Control (CDC). Because raising food animals in dark, squalid cages where they can't even turn around, lie down or breathe normally isn't just cruel and abusive. It's a recipe for lethal disease.

You'll be taking a stand against cruelty. Right up to the moment you slip your furry friend into a hot dog roll, he'll have led a pampered and happy life. No such luck for the eight billion farm animals consumed in the U.S each year! Their lives are a never ending nightmare. The millions who drop dead from stress are considered just a routine business expense.

You'll help save the environment. Factory farms destroy the environment. The dumping of millions of tons of animal waste and rotting body parts is poisoning once pristine waterways and underground water supplies. Putrid air is making entire communities uninhabitable.

You'll help exploited workers. Eating Rover or Muffin won't leave you feeling that you contributed to the abuse of the human victims who cut up slaughtered animals. Many workers, particularly in the poultry industry, are crippled by having to cut up to 90 chickens a minute. When they can no longer work, they are discarded like worn out tires.

You'll help solve the dog and cat overpopulation problem. Unwanted dogs and cats are put to death by the millions. Until we can implement a national spay/neuter program and stop the endless cycle of unwanted animals starving in the streets, why not just attack the problem with a hot skillet and a dash of garlic?

Finally, let's not allow anything as irrational as personal attachment to stand between us and a *real* hot dog. Loving and cuddling some animals while ignoring the suffering of others, who feel exactly the same pain, is what's *really* irrational. We are programmed from our first meals to pet some animals and eat others. But, a meatless diet can save your health, the environment and the lives of farm animals. Best of all, with your new non-violent diet you can keep cuddling your four legged friend while sending a powerful message to the meat industry's moguls of misery.

Why Would Anybody Eat Their Best Friend?

One of Henry and Mark Graham's more amusing ads, but with a serious point behind it. A tabloid newspaper later used the photograph, without permission, to illustrate an article allegedly exposing a shocking new Japanese food fad: "smoked puppies on a bun."

some practical things that they can do right now in order to have quality of life in the future."

In January 1996, Henry talked to Alan Goldberg, director of the Center for Alternatives to Animal Testing, about getting Johns Hopkins' world-renowned expertise in public health involved in the biggest public health uestion of them all: the health and environmental aspects of a diet heavy in animal products. Goldberg in turn spoke to Dr. Robert Lawrence, associate dean of the School of Hygiene and Public Health, who set up a meeting with Henry and some other members of the school. In Lawrence, Henry found a sympathetic expert in public health who well understood the link between the Western diet and an epidemic of cardiovascular disease and cancers of the digestive system. They agreed on the need to do something to bring about change in the direction of a more ecologically sustainable lifestyle. Henry suggested that the links between factory farming, public health, human nutrition, and the environment provide an entry point, something that could draw experts from many areas and bring about changes from the governmental level to the consumer. If Johns Hopkins were to organize small, tightly focused conferences, drawing on its global network of public health graduates, it might influence thinking not only in America, but all over the world.

Lawrence and his colleagues liked the idea. Toward the end of February, Lawrence visited Henry in New York to discuss it further. A few weeks later, he wrote Henry a letter, supporting the creation of a Center for a Livable Future and setting out some ideas about the work it might do. Here is Lawrence's account of what happened next:

> I sent Henry the letter by fax, about midday Tuesday. The hard copy was still in the outbox, waiting to be picked up by the university's mail collection service, when the phone rang on Wednesday at 9:30 A.M. It was a donor in New York who said, "Henry shared with me the letter you sent him Tuesday, and I need to speak to whoever it is who can take $50,000 to help you get the Center for a Livable Future started." I hadn't even asked Henry for money![35]

The Center for a Livable Future held its first conference in November 1997. Titled "Equity, Health, and the World's Resources: Food and Social Justice," its speakers included a former Canadian cabinet minister, a North Carolina activist who leads campaigns against pollution caused by factory farming in his own neighborhood, and scientists and academics specializing in public health, nutrition, agriculture, environmental engineering, animal welfare, and ethics. Among the scientists were two Nobel Prize winners: F. Sherwood Rowland, who received the prize for his work in identifying aerosol sprays as the cause of damage to the ozone layer, and Henry W. Kendall, whose work confirmed the existence of particles known as "quarks," and who had now turned his attention to environmental issues. After three days of presentations and discussions, the center issued a "Consensus Statement" calling for a concerted effort to bring about greater equity in the availability of food and condemning the current American diet as unhealthy, not environmentally sustainable, and based on cruel treatment of animals.

Henry hopes that the Center for a Livable Future will become a "do tank" rather than a "think tank." The center cannot tell people in other countries what to do, but it can invite them to assess where their policies are heading. It will take five years to know whether the center is making a difference. In the end, there has to be change, because the world cannot sustain a population of 10 billion eating a diet as heavily based on animal products as the standard Western diet. The earlier the change comes, the less painful it will be.

· 6 ·

Pushing the Peanut Forward

It is not the theoretic question if life has any purpose. It is the practical question which purpose do we put into life.

Margit Spira, in a Letter to Henry Spira, 1954

$\mathcal{I}$n the preface to this book I mentioned two widely accepted assumptions: that the individual is powerless to change the world, and that life is essentially meaningless. We have seen how Henry's determination to do something about the needless suffering inflicted on billions of animals each year has changed the world. Because his persistence was combined with intelligent thinking about how best to make a difference, each year millions of animals do not go through the agonies of the Draize test, the LD50, shackling and hoisting before slaughter, or face branding. He did not do this alone, but he was the inspiration, the strategist, and the coordinator of the campaigns that achieved these results. Now that the story has reached the present time, we can go back over these campaigns and distill some key points for others who want to use Henry's methods. That is the aim of the first part of this final chapter. In the second part of the chapter I will return to the second assumption I mentioned in the preface, and ask what kind of meaning Henry has been able to find in his life.

TEN WAYS TO MAKE A DIFFERENCE

The whole forward thrust of the movement Henry has created rests on his shoulders. If Henry disappears tomorrow, there's an interesting question as to how much of it will survive, how much will be nipped in the bud, how much will be lost by there not being some mechanism in place for someone

173

else to pick up that mantle. In the time that I have talked to Henry, he has never come to grips with the issue of who is going to carry on in his footsteps and continue fighting the fight the way he fought it.[1]

This comment was made by Barnaby Feder, who profiled Henry for the *New York Times Magazine*. But Henry doesn't see the continuation of his work in terms of grooming individuals to take over from him. In many interviews, and in articles he has written himself, Henry has described the methods he has used to bring about change. His methods are what count, not who uses them. The following key points are, therefore, set out here so that others can continue to fight as he has done, whether for animals or for the oppressed and exploited more generally.[2]

1. Try to understand the public's current thinking and where it could be encouraged to go tomorrow. Above all, keep in touch with reality.

Too many activists mix only with other activists and imagine that everyone else thinks as they do. They start to believe in their own propaganda and lose their feel for what the average person in the street might think. They no longer know what is achievable and what is a fantasy that has grown out of their own intense conviction of the need for change. Henry saw this in the Socialist Workers Party, where members were so used to the Marxist–Trotskyist framework that they all accepted that they lost contact with the real world in which they were trying to make a revolution. As Henry put it: "You need to have a crap detector rotating all the time."

Henry grabs every opportunity to talk to people outside the animal movement. He'll start up a conversation with the person sitting next to him on a bus or train, mention an issue he is concerned about, and listen to their responses. How do they react? Can they feel themselves in the place of the victim? Are they outraged? What in particular do they focus on?

2. Select a target on the basis of vulnerabilities to public opinion, the intensity of suffering, and the opportunities for change.

Target selection is crucial. Henry knows that he can run an effective campaign when he feels sure that, as he said about the New York state law allowing laboratories to take dogs and cats from shelters, "it just defies common sense that the average guy in the street would say, 'Hey, that's a real neat thing to do.'"

You know that you have a good target if, by merely stating the issue, you put your adversary on the defensive. During the museum campaign, for example, Henry could ask the public: "Do you want your tax monies spent to mutilate cats in order to observe the sexual performance of crippled felines?"

The museum was immediately in a very awkward position. Cosmetic testing made another good target, because you only had to ask, "Is another shampoo worth blinding rabbits?" to put Revlon officials on the defensive.

Keeping in touch with reality is a prerequisite for selecting the right target: If you don't know what the public currently thinks, you won't know what they will find acceptable and what will revolt them.

The other elements of point 2 suggest a balance between the good that the campaign can do and its likelihood of success. When Henry selected the cat experiments at the American Museum of Natural History as his first target, he knew that he would directly affect, at best, about sixty cats a year—a tiny number compared to many other possible targets. But the opportunity for change was great because of the nature of the experiments themselves and the location and vulnerability of the institution carrying out the experiments. In 1976, it was vital for the animal movement to have a victory, no matter how small, to encourage its own supporters to believe in the possibility of change and to gain some credibility with the wider world. With that victory gained, Henry began to give more weight, in choosing his targets, to the amount of suffering involved. Even so, that was never the dominant consideration. If you multiply x by y, but $y = 0$, then no matter how large x may be, the product will also be 0. So, too, no target should be chosen without considering both the amount of suffering and the opportunities for change.

3. Set goals that are achievable. Bring about meaningful change one step at a time. Raising awareness is not enough.

When Henry first took an interest in opposing animal experimentation, the antivivisection movement had no goal other than the abolition of vivisection and no strategy for achieving this goal other than "raising awareness"—that is, mailing out literature filled with pictures and descriptions of the horrors of vivisection. This was the strategy of a movement that talked mainly to itself. It had no idea how to get a hold on the levers of change, or even where those levers might be located. It seemed unaware of its own image as a bunch of ineffective cranks and did not know how to make vivisection an issue that would be picked up by the media. Henry's background in the civil rights movement told him that this was not the way to succeed:

> One of the first things that I learned in earlier movements was that nothing is ever an all-or-nothing issue. It's not a one-day process, it's a long pro-cess. You need to see the world-including individuals and institutions—as not being static but in constant change, with change occurring one step at a time. It's incremental. It's almost like organic development. You might say, for instance, that a couple of blacks demanding to be seated at a lunch

counter really doesn't make a hell of a lot of difference because most of them don't even have the money to buy anything at a lunch counter. But it did make a difference, it was a first step. Once you take that first step and you have that same first step in a number of places, you integrate a number of lunch counters, you set a whole pattern, and it's one of the steps that would generate the least amount of resistance. It's something that's winnable, but it encourages the black struggle and it clearly leads to the next step and the next step. I think that no movement has ever won on the basis of all or none.[3]

Some activists think that accepting less than, say, the total abolition of vivisection is a form of compromise that reduces their chances of a more complete victory. Henry's view is: "I want to abolish the use of animals as much as anybody else, but I say, let's do what we can do today and then do more tomorrow."[4] That is why he was willing to support moves to replace the LD50 with tests like the approximate lethal dose test, which still uses animals, but far fewer of them.

Look for targets that are not only winnable in themselves, but where winning will have expanding ripple effects. Ask yourself if success in one campaign will be a stepping stone toward still-bigger targets and more significant victories. The campaign against Revlon is an example: Because it made research into alternatives respectable, its most important effects have been felt beyond Revlon and even beyond the cosmetics industry as a whole. While raising awareness is essential if we are to bring about change, Henry does not usually work directly at raising awareness. (His advertisements against meat are an exception.) Awareness follows a successful campaign, and a successful campaign will have achievable goals.

4. Establish credible sources of information and documentation. Never assume anything. Never deceive the media or the public. Maintain credibility, don't exaggerate or hype the issue.

Before starting a new campaign, Henry spends several months gathering information. Freedom of information legislation has helped enormously, but a lot of information is already out there, in the public domain. Experimenters report their experiments in scientific journals that are available in major libraries, and valuable data about corporations may also be a matter of public record. Henry is never content simply to quote from the leaflets of animal rights groups, or other opponents of the institution or corporation that he is targeting. He always goes to the source, which is preferably a publication of the target itself, or else a government document. Newspapers like the *New York Times* have been prepared to run Henry's advertisements making very specific allegations of wrongdoing against people like Frank Perdue because every allegation has been meticulously checked.

Some organizations describing experiments will conveniently omit details that make the experiments less shocking than they would otherwise appear. They may, for example, neglect to tell their readers that the animals were anesthetized at the time. But those who do this eventually lose credibility. Henry's credibility is extraordinarily high, both within the animal movement and with its opponents, because he regards it as his most important asset. It is therefore never to be sacrificed for a short-term gain, no matter how tempting that may be at the time.

5. Don't divide the world into saints and sinners.

When Henry wants to get someone—a scientist, a corporate executive, a legislator, or a government official—to do something differently, he puts himself in the position of that person:

> [The question to ask yourself is:] If I were that person, what would make me want to change my behavior? If you accuse them of being a bunch of sadistic bastards, these people are not going to figure, "Hey, what is it I could do that's going to be different and make those people happy?" That's not the way the real world works.

Being personally hostile to an opponent may be a good way of letting off steam, but it doesn't win people over. When Henry wanted to persuade scientists working for corporations like Procter & Gamble to develop nonanimal alternatives, he saw their situation as similar to that of people who eat animals:

> How do you change these people's behavior best? By saying you've never made a conscious decision to harm those animals. Basically you've been programmed from being a kid: "Be nice to cat and doggy, and eat meat." And I think some of these researchers, that's how they were taught, that's how they were programmed. And you want to reprogram them, and you're not going to reprogram them by saying we're saints and you're sinners, and we're going to clobber you with a two-by-four in order to educate you.

As Susan Fowler, editor of the trade magazine *Lab Animal* at the time of the Revlon campaign, put it:

> There is no sense in Henry's campaign of: "Well, this is Revlon, and no one in Revlon is going to be interested in what we are doing, they're all the enemy." Rather . . . he looks for—and kind of waits for, I think—someone to step out of the group and say: "Well, I understand what you're saying."[5]

Without this attitude, when Roger Shelley came along ready to listen to what Henry wanted Revlon to do, the opportunity to change the company's approach could easily have been missed.

Not dividing the world into saints and sinners isn't just sound tactics, it is also the way Henry thinks. "People can change," he says. "I used to eat animals and I never considered myself a cannibal."[6]

6. Seek dialogue and attempt to work together to solve problems. Position issues as problems with solutions. This is best done by presenting realistic alternatives.

Because he doesn't think of his opponents as evil, Henry has no preconceptions about whether they will or will not work with him to reduce animal suffering. So he opens every campaign with a polite letter to the target organization— whether the American Museum of Natural History, Amnesty International, Revlon, Frank Perdue, or a meatpacker—inviting them to discuss the concerns he has. Sometimes Henry's invitations have been ignored, sometimes they have received an equally polite response from a person skilled in public relations who has no intention of doing anything, and sometimes they have led directly to the change he wanted without any public campaigning at all. But the fact that he suggests sitting down to talk about the problem before he does any public campaigning shows that he isn't just stirring up trouble for the fun of it, or as a way of raising funds for his organization.

Henry puts considerable thought into how the person or organization he is approaching could achieve its goals while eliminating or substantially reducing the suffering now being caused. The classic example of an imaginative solution was Henry's proposal to Revlon and other cosmetics manufacturers that they should fund research into alternatives to the Draize eye test. For more than a year before his campaign went public, Henry had been seeking a collaborative, rather than a confrontational, approach with Revlon. In the end, after the campaign finally did go public, Revlon accepted his proposal and, together with other companies, found that for a very small expenditure, relative to their income, they could develop an alternative that enabled them to have a more precise, cheaper form of product safety testing that did not involve animals at all.

Having a realistic solution to offer means that it is possible to accentuate the positive, instead of running a purely negative campaign. In interviews and leaflets about the Draize test, for example, Henry always emphasized that in vitro testing methods offered the prospect of quicker, cheaper, more reliable, and more elegant ways of testing the safety of new products.

It is always possible to find a positive side if you look hard enough, though it may not be one that will appeal to everyone involved on the other side. There was nothing Henry could propose that would appeal to the cat researcher Lester Aronson, who had spent decades mutilating animals and was too near the end of his career to try something different. But Aronson could not continue to experiment without the support of the American Museum of Natural History and the National Institutes of Health. The interests of the museum and of the NIH were not the same as Aronson's. Henry sought to split his adversaries by arguing that the pointless cruelty of the cat research was actually turning sensitive young people away from the life sciences. Closing Aronson's lab would be an opportunity to put the museum's research funds into something creative and respectful of life, which could inspire people to choose a career in biology. The problem was to convince the museum and the NIH that this really was a better outcome. To do so, Henry had to generate problems for them. For the museum, those turned out to be the prospect of continuing bad publicity and threats to its public funding. For the NIH, it was pressure from Congress that could have had an impact on its overall budget. With such negatives in the offing, the previously spurned positive solution of closing the lab and funding different kinds of research started to look more attractive.

In terms of offering a positive outcome, the difference between the campaigns against the cat experiments and those against the Draize test was one of degree, not kind. If your tube of toothpaste is blocked, whether you will be able to get any toothpaste out of it will depend on how badly blocked the tube is and on how much pressure is exerted on it. So, too, whether an institution or corporation will adopt an alternative will depend on how negatively it views the alternative and how much pressure it is under. The more realistic the alternative is, the less pressure will be needed to see it adopted.

7. Be ready for confrontation if your target remains unresponsive. If accepted channels don't work, prepare an escalating public awareness campaign to place your adversary on the defensive.

If point 6 is about making it easy for the toothpaste to come out of the tube, point 7 is about increasing the pressure if it still won't come. A public awareness campaign may take various forms. At the American Museum of Natural History, it started with an article in a local newspaper, then it was kept up by pickets and demonstrations, and finally it spread through the national media and specialist journals like *Science*. The Revlon campaign went public with a dramatic full-page advertisement in the *New York Times,* which itself generated more publicity. The campaign continued with demonstrations outside Revlon's offices. The Perdue and face-branding campaigns relied much more heavily on advertising and the use of the media. Advertising takes money, on which, see point 8.

8. Avoid bureaucracy.

Anyone who has been frustrated by lengthy committee mee tings that absorb time and energy will sympathize with Henry's desire to get things done rather than spend time on organizational tangles. Worse still, bureaucratic structures all too often divert energy into making the organization grow, rather than getting results for the cause. Then when the organization grows, it needs staff and an office. So you get a situation in which people who want to make a difference for animals (or for street kids, or for rain forests, or for whatever cause) spend 80 percent of their time raising money just to keep the organization going. Most of the time is spent ensuring that everyone in the organization gets along with one another, feels appreciated, and is not upset because he or she expected to be promoted to a more responsible position or given an office with more windows.

Henry has been able to avoid such obstacles by working, essentially, on his own. That isn't a style that will suit everyone, but it has worked well for Henry. Animal Rights International has no members. It has a long list of advisers and its board consists of trusted close friends whom Henry can rely upon for support without hassles. Henry doesn't need a lot of money, but he does need some. He has been fortunate in finding two donors who support him regularly because they like to see their money making a difference.

When Henry needs more clout, he puts a coalition together—as he did on the repeal of the Metcalf-Hatch Act, in fighting against the Draize and LD50 tests, and now, to persuade McDonald's to take a leading role in improving the welfare of farm animals. Since his early success at the American Museum of Natural History, other organizations have been eager to join his coalitions. At their height, these coalitions have included hundreds of organizations, with memberships in the millions. Here, too, though, Henry keeps hassles to a minimum. Organizations are welcome to participate at whatever level they wish. Some get their supporters out to demonstrate or march, while others don't. Some pay for full-page advertisements, and others ask them to write letters to newspapers, where they may reach millions without spending a cent. What no organization can do is dictate policy. Henry consults widely, but in the end, he makes his own decisions, thus avoiding the time-consuming and sometimes divisive process of elections and committee meetings. Clearly, in the case of major disagreements, organizations have the option of leaving; but if the coalition is making progress, organizations will generally swallow the disagreements in order to be part of a successful team.

9. Don't assume that only legislation or legal action can solve the problem.

Henry has used elected representatives in his campaigns to put pressure on government agencies and to gain publicity. But the only campaign in which he achieved his aim through legislation was the repeal of the Metcalf-Hatch Act. Here, since bad legislation was the target of the campaign, he had no choice. Otherwise, as far as he can, Henry stays out of conventional political processes and keeps away from the courts: "No congressional bill, no legal gimmickry, by itself, will save the animals." No doubt there are other situations, and other issues, on which legislation will make a difference. But on the whole, Henry sees laws as maintaining the status quo. They will be changed only in order to keep disturbance at a minimum. The danger of getting deeply involved in the political process is that it often deflects struggles into what Henry calls "political gabbery." There is a lot of talk, but nothing happens. Political lobbying or legal maneuvering becomes a substitute for action.

10. Ask yourself "Will it work?"

All of the preceding points are directed toward this last one. Before you launch a campaign, or continue with a campaign already begun, ask yourself if it will work. If you can't give a realistic account of the ways in which your plans will achieve your objectives, you need to change your plans. Keeping in touch with what the public is thinking, selecting a target, setting an achievable goal, getting accurate information, maintaining credibility, suggesting alternative solutions, being ready to talk to adversaries or to confront them if they will not talk—all of these are directed toward creating a campaign that is a practical means of making a difference. The overriding question is always: *Will it work?*

A MEANINGFUL LIFE

To say that life is essentially meaningless is to express an attitude, not to state a fact. For that reason—and unlike the assumption that an individual cannot make a difference to the world—it is not an assertion that can be refuted simply by pointing to facts about Henry's life. But if, when we face the end of our life, we can look back on it with the satisfaction and fulfillment that come from believing that we have spent our life doing something that was both worthwhile and interesting to do, then perhaps that is enough to show that we have found a way to make life meaningful. That has been Henry's experience.

The best way in which I can describe how Henry has found his life meaningful is to explain how this book came to be written. I can't recall exactly when I first told Henry that I would like to write a book about him, but the idea had been with me for many years. One sunny October day in 1992, we walked into Central Park, found a lawn with a view of the midtown skyline, and made ourselves comfortable on the grass. I pulled out a tape recorder and for an hour or two asked Henry questions about his life. I left him with the tape, which he said he would get typed up. Then I returned home to Melbourne, and my time was immediately swallowed up by other work. Something similar must have happened to Henry, because for a long time no typescript of the interview arrived. Given my other commitments, I was relieved that Henry, instead of urging me to get on with the promised biography, had himself apparently let it sink down his priority list.

The typescript finally arrived in 1994, but I was still too busy with other work to do anything with it. In 1995, I was selected by the Australian Greens to lead their Senate ticket for my home state, Victoria, in the next federal election. When I saw Henry that year, he must have been thinking about his own mortality—he was sixty-seven then—because he asked me if I was still thinking of doing the book and, if so, what instructions I wanted put in his will about what should be done with the papers that, systematically filed and shelved, filled every room in his apartment from floor to ceiling. I said that in principle I was still interested, but if I were elected to the Senate, I wouldn't be able to do anything about it during my term of office, which would last six years. On the other hand, if I were not elected, I said, there was a good chance that I could find some time to work on the book rather soon.

The election was held in March 1996, and I was not elected. No doubt to remind myself that this disappointing result did have its positive side, I sketched out an itinerary for an overseas trip, built around invitations to speak in Europe in May and at a March for the Animals in Washington at the end of June. On April 21, I sent Henry a fax telling him that since I had not been elected, "I'm starting to think about what else to do with the rest of my life. The book about you is one possibility, some time in the next two or three years." Could I stay with him for a few days in June, before my Washington commitment, so that we could talk about it?

That evening I had a message on my answering machine. It was unmistakably Henry's voice, saying that he wanted to speak to me and would call again soon, but there was something very troubling about his tone. I reached for the phone to call him back, but before I could do so, it rang again.

"Peter?"

"Henry, how are you?" I asked.

"Lousy, actually."

"Why, what's the matter?"

'I've got an adenocarcinoma of the esophagus, grade three."

"What does that mean, in layman's terms?"

"Let me put it this way: If you could choose the kind of cancer you were going to have, you wouldn't choose this one."

I made some inadequate kind of response. Henry then said that while he'd really like me to do the book, he wasn't sure that he was still going to be around in late June.

I was in New York six days later. Over the next five days, I slept on the sofa bed in Henry's apartment, and we spent all our waking time together. Henry had lost a lot of weight and lacked the energy I was used to seeing in him. He had to be pushed hard to tell me about his illness, but eventually I learned that for years he had occasionally had to vomit after eating. In 1995, the problem had become worse. In September, he had had a barium examination. It revealed a suspicious obstruction in his esophagus. Henry had never concerned himself much with his own health, and for a time he tried to put off doing anything about it. By February, he finally had to accept that he could put it off no longer. On March 4, he was admitted to New York University Medical Center and was operated upon. The operation found a tumor in his esophagus. The surgeon cut out a large part of the esophagus and adjoining areas of his stomach. Henry spent the next ten days in the hospital before he was able to go home. Now, seven weeks after the operation, he was still weak and had trouble keeping any food down. The outlook was even worse: The cancer was invasive, and the pathology report showed that it had spread into some of his lymph nodes. His life expectancy was a matter of months. His doctor had recommended radiation and chemotherapy, but he was unable to give him any statistics to show that this would help. Henry checked out the literature himself and found that there was no evidence that radiation or chemotherapy offered any significant life-prolonging effect for the kind of cancer he had. What he did know was that it would make him feel very bad. He rejected his doctor's recommendation. That wasn't the only recommendation Henry rejected. His friends and acquaintances suggested an amazing number of unorthodox cures for cancer, ranging from special diets to having all his fillings removed. He didn't try any of them. Instead, he began looking for a doctor who would help him die when he had had enough. Meanwhile, there was work to do.

During my time in New York, Henry and I worked hard on making this book possible. Before leaving Melbourne, I had reasoned that if Henry wasn't going to be around much longer, it would be a good idea to record some interviews on videotape. I didn't have any specific idea about what I might do with the tapes, but I wanted as much as possible of the Henry I knew to be preserved for posterity—not just the words he said, but the way he said them. So at my suggestion, Henry phoned Julie Akeret, an independent filmmaker who had once made a short film about me called *In Defense of Animals*. Julie came over with a cameraman she knew, and despite Henry's weak condition, we taped several hours of interviews, which provided the outline for this book and many of the quotations used in it.[7]

Henry gave me the contact details for many people who had been important in his life. I called some of them from his apartment. Many—including his sister Renee, who lived only an hour away, on Long Island—had not been in touch with Henry for some time and had no idea how ill he was. Henry had not tried to hide the news, but he hadn't felt like phoning and saying, "Hey, I've got cancer and will probably die in a month or two."

The most remarkable thing about Henry during this period was the total absence of any sign of depression. Life had been good, he said, he had done what he wanted to do and had enjoyed it a lot. Why should he be depressed? The thing that really worried him about the cancer was that he would die a slow, lingering death. He was looking for a doctor who would help him to die sooner rather than later, and at home rather than in a hospital, where he feared losing control over his own life. While I was staying with him, he went to a doctor and came back to the apartment with a bottle of pills that the doctor had given him—officially for pain relief. Together we looked up the drug in a pharmacopoeia that Henry had. The bottle contained about four times the lethal dose. Henry's relief was palpable. With that worry taken care of, he seemed remarkably untroubled by the fact that he was expecting to die soon.

Henry did not die in the time his doctors predicted. When I returned to New York in June, on my way back from Europe for the March for the Animals, he was markedly stronger than he had been at the end of April. He set up interviews for me with many of the people quoted in this book, including Berta Green Langston, Dolores McCullough, Roger Shelley, Myron Mehlman, Susan Fowler, Elinor Molbegott, and Mark Graham. He even went to Washington and spoke at the march, though he had always been a bit cynical about the value of spending too much energy on activities that lacked a specific goal. As this book goes to press, in March 1998, Henry is still very much alive and working hard on farm animal issues, targeting the fast food chains McDonald's, KFC, and Burger King. He is also watching the development of the Center for a Livable Future. I can't help wondering if his strong sense that the biggest gains for animals still lie ahead has kept him going far longer than the nature of his cancer gave him any right to expect.

One mark of living well is to live so that you can accept death and feel satisfied with what you have done with your life. Henry's life has lacked many of the things that most of us take for granted as essential to a good life. He has never married or had a long-term, live-in relationship. He has no children. His father and one of his sisters committed suicide, and his mother was mentally ill for much of her life. His relationship with Renee, the sole surviving member of his immediate family, is not close. His rent-controlled apartment, while spacious and well situated, is spartan. He doesn't go to movies, to concerts, to the theater, or to fine restaurants. He hasn't taken a holiday for twenty years. Yet at the age of sixty-eight he was able to contemplate his own imminent death with no major regrets about the way he had lived. What makes up for the absence of so much that, for most people, are the essentials of a good life? In our 1992 interview, I tried to locate the source of Henry's satisfaction:

Peter: So, looking back on what you've been doing for the last twenty to thirty years, what do you feel about it? What sort of a life has it been?

Henry: Well, I think for one thing, I've totally enjoyed it. And I think that if I had a choice of what it is that I wanted to do, that's what I would have wanted to do. And looking back, I think it was worth the effort, it was worth the energy, and I think that I pushed things along, as best I could.

Peter: Some people might say that you've sacrificed a lot of time and effort, while not doing very much for yourself.

Henry: I've never felt that I've sacrificed for others. I just felt that I'm doing what I really want to do and what I want to do most. And I feel most alive when I'm doing it.

Peter: Is that a matter of personal temperament? What's the secret of why you enjoy it?

Henry: I don't know why I enjoy it, but I think one can be a lot more effective if one really feels good about doing it, if one gets up in the morning just raring to pick up where one left off the night before—as opposed to doing it for others, doing it because it should be done, doing it because it's the right thing to do.

Peter: What if someone said that you get your kicks out of sticking it into other people, like Frank Perdue?

Henry: I don't think I've ever stuck it into others just for the sake of sticking it in. I think we try to dialogue. I think the pleasure you really get is out of conceptualizing a campaign and moving it along. And you want to move it along the fastest way possible. The fastest way possible is to move it along with cooperation and collaboration. It's only when you get forced into an adversarial position that you then try to do the best you can in that direction.

Peter: You couldn't say that you really minded being in an adversarial position, could you?

Henry: No, I think once you're in it, one sort of thrives on it. But it's basically that one is forced into it to begin with. I think I'm comfortable working either way; but I think the thing that you really get your satisfaction out

of is conceptualizing a campaign that you know is absolutely going to work,
and then seeing it work.

The real satisfaction, Henry told me on another occasion, is "not the fact that
you made somebody else feel like gone-over garbage," but the "creative high"
that comes from getting all the pieces of the puzzle together, which gives him
a sense that "lightning has struck."

The idea that no matter how serious the cause for which you are working,
you should still enjoy what you are doing, is one that Henry has held for a long
time. Among the radical thinkers he had read in his youth was the American
anarchist Emma Goldman. Goldman liked dancing, a pastime that her more
puritanical anarchist friends regarded as frivolous. It was not, they told her, an
activity fit for a revolutionary. Goldman responded: "If I can't dance, I don't
want your revolution." It was a line that had always struck a chord with Henry:

> The point [Goldman] is making is, you've got to enjoy what you're do-
> ing to be effective. What you're doing is what you've absolutely got to be
> doing, not because you feel you've got to do it but, rather, because this
> is what your life is about. You feel good when you're doing it. . . . I feel
> best when I'm doing something that's going to make a difference. When
> I go, I want to look back and say, "I made this a better place for others."
> But it's not a sense of duty, rather this is what I want to do. . . . I feel best
> when I'm doing it well.

As for the more common idea that you enjoy yourself best by earning a lot
of money and living it up, Henry rejects that position: "When I was working
on the ships I had so much money I didn't know where to put it. I stayed in
some of the best places . . . it was interesting for the experience, but I didn't
want the lifestyle. It didn't give me a high."

Although Henry emphasizes that he has chosen his life because he feels
good about what he does, rather than because some sense of duty makes him
feel that it is the right thing to do, there is no doubt that he is motivated by a
strong sense of doing something worthwhile:

> I guess basically one wants to feel that one's life has amounted to more than
> just consuming products and generating garbage. I think that one likes to
> look back and say that one's done the best one can to make this a better
> place for others. You can look at it from this point of view: What greater
> motivation can there be than doing whatever one possibly can to reduce
> pain and suffering?

While others may feel the same motivation, few manage to keep it going
throughout an entire life. In a magazine interview in 1995, Henry was asked

whether, in view of the size of the problems he is tackling, he ever gets tired of trying. He replied:

> It's crucial to have a long-term perspective. Looking back over the past 20 years, I see progress that we've helped achieve. And when a particular initiative causes much frustration, I keep looking at the big picture while pushing obstacles out of the way. And there's nothing more energizing than making a difference.[8]

During my April 1996 visit, when Henry and I thought his life nearly over, I asked him to sum up what he thought he had achieved. He said:

> I've pushed the idea that activism has to be results-oriented, that you can win victories, that you can fight city hall, and that if you don't like to be pushed around and you don't like to see others pushed around, you can have an impact. . . . It's like this guy from the *New York Times* asked me what I'd like my epitaph to be. I said, "He pushed the peanut forward." I try to move things on a little.[9]

I asked if he was satisfied with having achieved that.

> I might have done some things differently, but on the whole, I've given it the best shot that I've got. . . . Looking back on my life, it's been satisfying. I've done a lot of things I wanted to do. I've had an enormous amount of fun doing it, and if I were going to do it over again, I'd do it very similar to the way I have done it.

Notes

NOTES TO CHAPTER 1

1. This quote and all subsequent quotes in this chapter from Margit Spira are from a long letter she wrote to Henry on March 5, 1954.

2. Renee Landau, Henry's cousin, is the source of the story about Maurice being the victim of a con artist.

3. Nachum Meyers, letter to author, September 10, 1996.

4. Ibid.

5. Gaston Firmin-Guyon, videotaped interview with Julie Akeret, New York, 1996.

6. Henry Gitano [Henry Spira, pseud.], "Bosses I Have Known," *The Militant,* November 4, 1957.

7. Auto Worker [Henry Spira], "Bosses I Have Known," *The Militant,* August 5, 1957.

8. Henry Gitano, "National Guard Opens Plant to Scabs in Indiana Strike," *The Militant,* October 17, 1955.

9. Henry Gitano, "Bus Boycott Solid in Florida; Six-Month Alabama Fight Firm," *The Militant,* June 11, 1956.

10. Henry Gitano, "The Walkers of Tallahassee," *The Militant,* December 3, 1956; also published as "'I'll Work, but I Won't Ride': Chronicle of the South's 'New Negro,'" *Los Angeles Tribune,* December 12, 1956.

11. Henry Gitano, "March on Washington Showed Determination to Win Equal Rights," *The Militant,* May 27, 1957.

12. Henry Gitano, "The American Way of Life in Mississippi," *The Gazette and Daily* (York, PA), June 28, 1963.

13. Henry Gitano, "Ain't Gonna Let Nobody Turn Me Around," *The Independent and the Californian* (New York), January 1964.

14. Ibid.

15. Henry Gitano, "The Battle of St. Augustine," *The Militant,* July 27, 1964.

16. Ibid.

17. *New York Post,* May 20, 1958.

18. Henry Gitano,"What the FBI Shows the Public on Guided Tours in Washington," *The Militant,* January 12, 1959.

19. FBI memo, December 17, 1958, obtained by Henry Spira in 1976 under freedom of information legislation.

20. Ibid.

21. *Columbia,* vol. 39, no. 5 (May 1959): 9–11, 46.

22. *Congressional Record,* May 5, 1959, appendix, pp. A3743-3745; see also *Firing Line* (a publication of the American Legion), vol. 8, no. 6 (March 15, 1959).

23. Berta Langston (formerly Berta Green), videotaped interview with author, New York, December 1996.

24. Henry Gitano, "I Saw a Cuba Where the People Are Running the Show!" *Young Socialist,* April 1960.

25. Henry Gitano, "First Year of the Cuban Revolution," *International Socialist Review* (Spring 1960), 38–42.

26. Langston, interview. Also, an article in *Problems of the Fourth International* (n.d.), refers to Henry as the one who "started the ball rolling" in terms of the left taking notice of what was happening in Cuba.

27. See, for example, Henry Gitano, "Case History of Guantanamo," *International Socialist Review* (Winter 1963): 9–12, 22.

28. Berta Langston, videotaped interview with author, April 30, 1996.

29. Robert McG. Thomas Jr., "Myra T. Weiss, 80: Radical Who Ran Quixotic Campaigns," *New York Times,* September 20, 1997, p. A11.

30. Langston, interview, April 30, 1996.

31. Henry Spira, "Rebel Voices in the NMU," in Burton Hall, ed., *Autocracy and Insurgency in Organized Labor* (New Brunswick, NJ: Transaction Books, 1972), pp. 47–48. For details of seamen's wages, see various issues of *The Call for Union Democracy,* for example, July 1969.

32. A. H. Raskin, from *Atlantic,* November 1964; quoted in "How the Curran Machine Operates," *The Call for Union Democracy,* March 1967.

33. Henry Spira, "Fighting to Win," in Peter Singer, ed., *In Defence of Animals* (Oxford: Blackwell, 1985), p. 195.

34. *New York Times,* May 21, 1966; quoted in *The Call for Union Democracy,* March 1967, and in Henry Spira, "Rebel in the NMU," p. 48.

35. See Lincoln Steffens, *The Dying Boss,* to which Henry refers in an anonymous letter in the *Village Voice,* "Open House at the NMU but Not for Seamen," June 4, 1964.

36. Anonymous, "Open House at the NMU," ibid.

37. "Jobs That Never Hit the Board," *The Call for Union Democracy,* July 1970.

38. "Curran Ignores an ACLU Request," *The Militant,* March 1967, p. 1; citing an ACLU letter from John Pemberton Jr., Executive Director, ACLU, and Aryeh Neier, Executive Director, New York Civil Liberties Union, dated October 3, 1966.

39. Firmin-Guyon, interview.

40. "Seaman Threatened on Ship in New York Union Fight," *The Sun* (Baltimore), September 6, 1969.

41. Mary Wilbert, interview with author, April 30, 1996.

42. James Wechsler, "In a Notebook," *New York Post,* November 21, 1969; reprinted in *The Call for Union Democracy,* January 1970.

43. "Notice to All Members of the National Maritime Union and to All Unlicensed Seamen," *The Pilot,* January–February 1971, p. 47.

44. Comment by Alejandre Care, "Haaren," *Like It Is* 2 (June 1969).

45. Student comment in *The Liberator* (Haaren High School newspaper), November 14, 1975.

46. Dolores McCullough, videotaped interview with author, May 1996.

47. Ibid.

NOTES TO CHAPTER 2

1. Irwin Silber,"... Fan the Flames," *National Guardian,* April 18, 1973, p. 9.

2. Peter Singer, "Animal Liberation," *New York Review of Books,* April 5, 1973.

3. Henry Spira, "Fighting to Win," in Peter Singer, ed., *In Defence of Animals* (Oxford: Blackwell, 1985), pp. 195–196.

4. Peter Singer, *Animal Liberation* (New York: New York Review, 1975).

5. Spira, "Fighting to Win," p. 196.

6. Ibid.

7. Ibid., p. 197.

8. Ibid., pp. 196–197.

9. Ibid., p. 196.

10. Kevin Morrissey, "Henry Spira: An Animal Activist Who Gets Things Done," *Animal Crackers* (newsletter of the Society for the Prevention of Cruelty to Animals of Illinois), vol. 5, no. 3 (Fall 1979): 5.

11. Spira, "Fighting to Win," pp. 197–198.

12. John F. Burns, "American Museum Pinched for Funds," *New York Times,* February 16, 1976, p. 23.

13. Henry Spira, "Animals Suffer for Science," *Our Town,* July 23, 1976.

14. Roger Simon, "Cutting Up Cats to Study Sex—What Fun!" *Chicago Sun-Times,* July 25, 1976; quoted in James Jasper and Dorothy Nelkin, *The Animal Rights Crusade* (New York: Free Press, 1992), p. 28.

15. Ann Brown, memo to Tom Nicholson, September 8, 1976.

16. Thomas Nicholson, "Report of the Director," in American Museum of Natural History, *108th Annual Report, July 1976 Through June 1977* (New York: American Museum of Natural History, 1977).

17. Quoted in Spira, "Animals Suffer for Science."

18. Quoted in Spira, "Fighting to Win," p. 199.

19. Storm Whaley, Associate Director for Communications, NIH, letter to Henry Spira, August 22, 1977.

20. Nathaniel Sheppard Jr., "U.S. Agency Will Review Tests on Cats at American Museum," *New York Times,* July 28, 1976.

21. Diana Loercher, "Anti-vivisection Battle Shifts to New York Museum," *Christian Science Monitor,* September 20, 1976.

22. Nicholas Wade, "Animal Rights: NIH Cat Sex Study Brings Grief to New York Museum," *Science,* October 8, 1976.

23. Ibid.

24. Nicholas Wade, videotaped interview with John Swindells, December 1996.

25. Wade, "Animal Rights."

26. Ibid.

27. Lester Aronson, letter to William Prokasy, March 14, 1977.

28. Ibid.

29. Wade, interview.

30. Lester Aronson, letter to Donald Clark, February 3, 1977.

31. *New York Times,* May 3, 1977.

32. Donald Clark, letter to Lester Aronson, May 6, 1977.

33. Whaley, letter to Spira.

34. "Antivivisectionists Escalate Activities," *National Society for Medical Research Bulletin,* vol. 28, no. 10 (October 1977): 1.

35. Nicholson, "Report of the Director."

36. Wade, "Animal Rights."

37. Elinor Molbegott, videotaped interview with author, New York, June 1996.

38. Quoted in Henry Spira, "Museum Victory for Animal Rights," *Our Town,* February 26, 1978.

39. Ibid.

NOTES TO CHAPTER 3

1. Henry Spira, "Amnesty International Scandal," *Our Town,* October 28, 1977.

2. David Hawk, "A.I. Responds," *Our Town,* November 11, 1977.

3. *National Society for Medical Research Bulletin,* August 1977 and September 1978.

4. For a sample article, see Henry Spira, "Metcalf-Hatch Repeal Means Lab Accountability," *Our Town,* April 29, 1979.

5. Michael Connor, "Henry Spira Advocates Animal Rights in Albany," *Sunday Record,* May 6, 1979, p. A9.

6. "Law on Strays May Die," *Times Record,* May 8, 1979.

7. Henry Spira, *Strategies for Activists: From the Campaign Files of Henry Spira* (New York: Animal Rights International, privately circulated in 1996), p. 152.

8. Henry Spira, letter to members of the Coalition to Abolish Metcalf-Hatch, June 25, 1979.

9. *Guardian,* February 8, 1978; cited in Richard Ryder, *Victims of Science,* 2nd ed. (London: National Anti-vivisection Society, 1983), p. 151.

10. David Paterson and Richard Ryder, eds., *Animals' Rights: A Symposium* (Fontwell, Sussex: Centaur Press, 1979).

11. Henry Spira, "Fighting for Animal Rights: Issues and Strategies," in Harlan B. Miller and William H. Williams, eds., *Ethics and Animals* (Clifton, NJ: Humana Press, 1983), pp. 373–377. Seventeen years later, a portion of this quote from Frederick Douglass was to be used by Gary Francione for the title of a book in which he attacked Henry for taking a "welfarist," rather than an "animal rights," stance. See Gary Francione, *Rain Without Thunder* (Philadelphia: Temple University Press, 1996); see also chapter 4.

12. Henry Spira, "Towards Animal Rights," *Agenda,* no. 2 (March 1980).

13. Peter Singer, *Animal Liberation* (New York: New York Review, 1975), pp. 50–51; this is a slightly edited quote from my book, for the material presented in the class was a draft version.

14. David Smyth, *Alternatives to Animal Experiments* (London: Scalar Press, 1978).

15. Ibid., p. 68.

16. C. S. Weil and R. A. Scala, "Study of Intra- and Inter-laboratory Variability in the Results of Rabbit Eye and Skin Irritation Test," *Toxicology and Applied Pharmacology,* vol. 19 (1971): 276–360.

17. Lynne Harriton, "Conversation with Henry Spira: Draize Test Activist," *Lab Animal,* vol. 10, no. 1 (January–February 1981): 16.

18. Henry Spira, "Fighting to Win," in Peter Singer, ed., *In Defence of Animals* (Oxford: Blackwell, 1985), p. 202.

19. Quoted in "Animals in Testing," *Chemical Week,* December 5, 1984, p. 38.

20. "Cosmetics: Kiss and Sell," *Time,* December 11, 1978, pp. 86–88.

21. Barnaby Feder, videotaped interview with John Swindells, Chicago, December 1996.

22. Henry Spira, "An Open Letter to Revlon," *Our Town,* June 8, 1980.

23. "Revlon Chief to Propose Biggest Annual Dividend Increase," *Women's Wear Daily,* May 4, 1979.

24. Henry Spira, letter to Michel Bergerac, July 23, 1979.

25. Henry Spira, "Abolishing the Draize Rabbit Blinding Test," August 23, 1979; privately circulated by ARI.

26. Spira, *Strategies for Activists,* p. 165.

27. Andrew Rowan, videotaped interview with John Swindells, Boston, December 1996.

28. Jane Gregory, "We're Being Beastly to Animals," *Chicago Sun-Times,* November 27, 1979; Jane Gregory, "Science and Research: Doing unto Animals," *Los Angeles Times,* December 9, 1979.

29. Feder, interview.

30. According to an article in *Chemical Week* ("Cosmetics Firms Feel Heat over the Draize Test," September 10, 1979, pp. 18–19), the coalition spent $78,000 on newspaper advertising.

31. "Revlon: Formal Statement" (n.d.); this statement is virtually identical to an interoffice memorandum from Frank Johnson to Officers, Executives, General Managers, and Domestic Department Heads, April 17, 1980.

32. "The Need for Animal Testing," *Chemical Week,* September 10, 1980, p. 5; see also James Gorman, "Burden of the Beasts," *Discover,* February 1981, p. 24; and Constance Holden, "New Focus on Replacing Animals in the Lab," *Science,* vol. 215 (January 1, 1982): 37.

33. *Congressional Record,* September 30, 1980, S14128.

34. "Draize Test Campaign Update," *International Journal for the Study of Animal Problems,* vol. 1, no. 4 (1980): 213.

35. Harriton, "Conversation with Henry Spira," p. 21.

36. Susan Fowler, videotaped interview with author, New York, December 1996.

37. Roger Shelley, videotaped interview with author, New York, June 1996.

38. Ibid.

39. Michael Marten, "Revlon Campaign Hots Up," *The Beast,* no. 7 (Autumn 1980): 1.

40. "Cosmetics Firms Feel Heat over the Draize Test," 18–19.

41. Michael Marten, "Anti-Revlon Campaign Goes International," *The Beast,* no. 8 (Winter 1980-81): 6; Michael Marten, "Revlon Buckle: Avon Calling?!" *The Beast,* no. 9 (Spring 1981): 4.

42. Shelley, interview.

43. Henry Spira, letter to Roger Shelley, November 5, 1980.

44. Feder, interview.

45. Shelley, interview.

46. Spira, "Fighting to Win," p. 203.

47. "Remarks of M. C. Bergerac, Chairman and Chief Executive, Revlon, Inc., at the Revlon-Rockefeller University Press Conference, the Plaza Hotel, December 23, 1980," typescript distributed at the conference; Shelley, interview.

48. "Eyes New Tests for Makeup," *Daily News* (New York), December 24, 1980.

49. "Remarks of M. C. Bergerac."

50. Shelley, interview.

51. Coalition to Stop Draize Rabbit Blinding Tests, "News Release: Revlon-Rockefeller: More Than a Cosmetic Venture," December 23, 1980.

52. Quoted in "Revlon's Eyeful," *Financial Times* (London), December 31, 1980.

53. Henry Spira, letter to David W. Mitchell, February 27, 1981.

54. Henry Spira, letter to Richard Gelb, August 21, 1981.

55. Bristol-Myers, "News: For Immediate Release," November 16, 1981.

56. Consumer Product Safety Commission, "Log of Meeting," May 11, 1981; and Carlos Perez, letter to Henry Spira, January 8, 1982, quoted in FDC Reports, *The Rose Sheet,* vol. 3, no. 5 (February 1, 1982). The full text of the letter was read into the *Congressional Record* (vol. 128, no. 12) by Senator Durenberger (February 11, 1982). See also Coalition to Stop Draize Rabbit Blinding Tests, "Coordinator's 1981 Report to the Coalition," p. 3.

57. Cited by Senator Durenberger, *Congressional Record: The Senate,* vol. 128, no. 109, August 11, 1982; "Anesthetics for Draize: Follow-Up," *International Journal for the Study of Animal Problems,* vol. 2, no. 4 (1981): 174.

58. Henry Spira, draft letter to Alan Goldberg, April 14, 1982.

59. Quoted in Teresa Carpenter, *Missing Beauty* (New York: Norton, 1988), p. 51.

60. William Douglas, *In Touch,* vol. 1, no. 1 (May 1982): 1–2.

61. Information on Douglas's crime is drawn from Carpenter, *Missing Beauty,* and from Henry Spira.

NOTES TO CHAPTER 4

1. For the determination of the LD50 of distilled water (469 ml/kg of body weight), see E. M. Boyd and I. L. Codi, "Acute Oral Toxicity of Distilled Water in Albino Rats," *Industrial Medicine and Surgery,* vol. 36: 609–613; cited in Andrew Rowan, *Of Mice, Models, and Men* (Albany: State University of New York Press, 1984), p. 204.

2. G. Zbinden, "A Look at the World from Inside the Toxicologist's Cage," *European Journal of Clinical Pharmacology,* vol. 9: 333; quoted in Rowan, *Of Mice, Models, and Men,* p. 207.

3. Henry Spira, "Coordinator's 1981 Report to the Coalition," January 1982.

4. Helaine Lerner and Barbara Clapp, videotaped interviews with author, July 1996.

5. Michael Marten, "International Coalition to Abolish LD-50," *The Beast,* no. 10 (Summer 1981): 10; "Animal Welfare's Tribute to Henry Spira," *Animal Welfare,* June–August 1981, p. 14.

6. "U.S. Drugs Firms May End Lethal Dose Test," *New Scientist,* October 14, 1982, p. 19.

7. "Smith Kline Beckman Demonstration Called Off," *The Unicorn* (Reading, PA), vol. 2, no. 13 (November 1982): 1.

8. "Smith Kline & French Laboratories Supports Animal Use Reduction," *In Touch* vol. 1, no. 2 (November 1982): 1; "Animals in Testing," *Chemical Week,* December 5, 1984, pp. 36, 38. I am grateful to Sue Leary, formerly of the Pennsylvania Animal Rights Coalition, for supplying copies of letters and other information.

9. Pharmaceutical Manufacturers Association, "News Release: PMA Board Acts on LD-50 Test," Washington, DC, October 21, 1982.

10. "NSMR Adopts Policy on LD50 Testing," *National Society for Medical Research Bulletin,* vol. 33, no. 10 (December 1982): 1; FDC Reports, *The Rose Sheet,* vol. 4, no. 22 (May 30, 1983): 5; Leonard Rack and Henry Spira, "Animal Rights and Modern Toxicology," *Toxicology and Industrial Health,* vol. 5, no. 1 (1989): 138.

11. David Rall, letter to Henry Spira, March 3, 1983.

12. Marjorie Sun, "Lots of Talk About LD50," *Science,* vol. 222 (December 9, 1983): 1106.

13. "Committee Wants Lethal Test Abolished," *New Scientist,* August 4, 1983.

14. Nancy Heneson, "American Agencies Denounce LD50 Test," *New Scientist,* November 17, 1983, p. 475; "FDA Establishing Animal Testing Task Force to Perform Agency-Wide Policy Review," *The Rose Sheet,* vol. 4, no. 45 (November 14, 1983): 5.

15. Sun, "Lots of Talk About LD50," p. 1106.

16. Consumer Product Safety Commission, "Animal Testing Policy," *Federal Register,* vol. 49, no. 105 (May 30, 1984): 22522–22523; Food and Drug Administration, "Talk Paper: Animals Used for Research," September 5, 1984.

17. United States Environmental Protection Agency, "EPA Announces Revised Testing in Acute Toxicity Testing," *News Release,* August 29, 1984.

18. Henry Spira, "Fighting to Win," in Peter Singer, ed., *In Defence of Animals* (Oxford: Blackwell, 1985), pp. 203–204.

19. Henry Spira, letter to Owen B. Butler, October 13, 1982.

20. Marion Steinmann, "Taking Animals Out of the Laboratory," *Moonbeams* (Cincinnati, OH), September 1983, p. 8.

21. See Alex Pacheco with Anna Francione, "The Silver Spring Monkeys," in Singer, ed., *In Defence of Animals,* pp. 135–147.

22. See Lori Gruen, Peter Singer, and David Hine, *Animal Liberation: A Graphic Guide* (London: Camden Press, 1987), pp. 9–23.

23. *New York Times,* June 15, 1984.

24. Sharon Begley, "Liberation in the Labs," *Newsweek,* August 27, 1984, p. 66.

25. Jim Mason, "Animal Rights: Out of the Closet, into the Mainstream," *Animals' Agenda,* vol. 5, no. 1 (January–February 1985): 1, 8–9.

26. *The Sciences,* March–April 1983; cited in Coalition to Abolish the LD50, "Coordinator's Report '83," p. 1.

27. "Unnecessary Animal Research on Wane, Researchers Say," *American Medical News,* May 25, 1994; Drug Research Reports, *The Blue Sheet,* vol. 27, no. 23 (June 6, 1984); "Looking for Alternatives to Animal Tests," *Chemical Week,* May 23, 1984, p. 35.

28. William Powell, Senior Executive Vice President, Colgate-Palmolive, letter to Henry Spira, March 28, 1984; "Unnecessary Animal Research on Wane"; Drug Research Reports, *The Blue Sheet;* Colgate-Palmolive, *1986 First Quarter and Annual Meeting Report,* p. 11.

29. Bristol-Myers Company, *Second Quarter Report, 1982,* p. 5; John F. Corbett, Chairman, Corporate Toxicology Committee, Bristol-Myers Company, letter to Henry Spira, August 28, 1984.

30. Bristol-Myers, New York, newsletter, October 1984.

31. "Cosmetic Industry Halts Use of LD50," *CTFA News Release,* June 11, 1985.

32. Rack and Spira, "Animal Rights and Modern Toxicology," p. 139.

33. "Letters," *Animals' Agenda,* April 1986, p. 35.

34. Animal Rights International, "News Release," October 13, 1987; Barnaby Feder, "Beyond White Rats and Rabbits," *New York Times,* February 28, 1988, sec. 3, p. 8; Patricia Gallagher, "Variety Spices P&G Meeting," *Cincinnati Enquirer,* October 14, 1987.

35. Ingrid Newkirk, letter to Coalition to Abolish the LD50 advisers, November 10, 1987.

36. See above, p. 68–70.

37. "No Support from Spira for End to Product Tests on Animals," *International Society for Animal Rights Report,* November–December 1987. After Henry threatened to take legal action over the implication that he did not support an end to product testing on animals, Jones agreed to publish his news release on this issue in its entirety

(Henry Spira, letter to Helen Jones, January 26, 1988, and Helen Jones, letter to Henry Spira, February 8, 1988).

38. *Animals' Agenda,* November–December 1997, p. 22.

39. "Animal Research," Procter & Gamble Fact Sheet, 1997; "Remarks by Mr. John E. Pepper on Animal Research," P&G Annual Shareholders Meeting, October 14, 1997, typescript provided by P&G; Katherine Stitzel, letter to the author, March 5, 1998; *Animal People* (Clinton, WA), November 1997, p. 13.

40. Barnaby Feder, "Pressuring Perdue," *New York Times Magazine,* November 26, 1989, p. 34.

41. Ian Harvey, "Animal Rights: Them or Us?" *Toronto Sun,* November 1, 1987.

42. Feder, "Pressuring Perdue," p. 60.

43. Barnaby Feder, "Noxell Replaces Rabbits in Tests of Cosmetics," *New York Times,* January 10, 1989.

44. Constance Holden, "Cosmetics Firms Drop Draize Test," *Science,* vol. 245 (July 14, 1989): 125.

45. "Pulling Rabbits Out of the Lab," *Chemical Week,* August 9, 1989, p. 20; see also Feder, "Beyond White Rats and Rabbits."

46. The firm in question was Perceptions Press, an imprint of Perceptions International, on which see pp. 144–146.

47. "Effective Boycott?" *Animal Rights Reporter,* vol. 1, no. 5 (March 1989).

48. Alston Chase, interview with Jim Preston for *Life* magazine, June 13, 1989; the interview was never published.

49. Deborah Rudacille, "CAAT Marks Anniversary with Scientific Program, Ceremony," *Newsletter of the School of Hygiene and Public Health, Johns Hopkins University,* vol. 10, no. 1 (Summer 1992): 8.

50. Henry Spira, letter to Kathy Guillermo, PETA, January 14, 1992; see also Henry Spira, letter to Irwin Bloom, Doris Duke Foundation, November 6, 1991.

51. "A Deceptive Victory over L'Oréal?" *Vegetarian Times,* August 1994, p. 17.

52. "Final Report of the EC/HO [European Commission/Home Office] Study," *Frame News,* May 1996, p. 5, reporting on a study published in *Toxicology in Vitro,* vol. 9 (1995): 871–929.

53. Paul Cotton, "Animals and Science Benefit from 'Replace, Reduce, Refine' Effort," *Journal of th e American Medical Association,* vol. 270, no. 24 (December 22–29, 1993): 2905–2907.

54. "Interview: Henry Spira," *Newsletter of the Foundation for Biomedical Research,* vol. 10, no. 1 (January–February 1993): 4–5.

NOTES TO CHAPTER 5

1. Henry Spira, "Less Meat, Less Misery: Reforming Factory Farms," *Forum for Applied Research and Public Policy,* vol. 11, no. 1 (Spring 1996): 39.

2. "LD50 Meeting Draws 40 of the Movement Leaders," *Animals' Agenda,* vol. 5, no. 2 (March–April 1985): 18.

3. William Severini Kowinski, "One Man's Beef," *Daily News Magazine* (New York), April 14, 1985, p. 12.

4. *New York Times,* May 18, 1977, p. C13.

5. Henry Spira, letter to Frank Perdue, April 28, 1987.

6. *New York Times,* October 20, 1989, p. A17.

7. Elaine Barnes, Executive Assistant to the Chairman, Perdue Farms, Inc., letter to Henry Spira, December 20, 1989.

8. Phil McCombs, "Cheap Ads Skewer Perdue," *Washington Post,* December 27, 1991; see also Jill Brandt, "Animal Rights Group Protests Perdue's UM Board Seat," *Prince George's Sentinel,* December 19, 1991, and Alan Farnham, "Skewering Perdue," *Fortune,* February 24, 1992, p. 111.

9. Mark Graham, videotaped interview with author, New York, May 1996.

10. *Washington Times,* September 9, 1992, p. A5. The ad ran in the same paper on September 16, 23, 30 and October 15, and in the *City Paper* (Baltimore), September 11, 1992; *Columbia Journalism Review,* September–October 1992; *New York Press,* September 23, 1992; *City Paper* (Washington, DC), October 2; and *The Flyer* (student newspaper of Salisbury State University, which had links with Perdue), September 29 and October 6 and 13, 1992.

11. *Catholic Review,* September 23, 1992, p. A10.

12. *Her New York,* October 14, 1993; the same ad also appeared in the *New York Observer,* March 28, 1994, p. 7.

13. Henry Spira, "Forum," *Animals' Agenda,* vol. 9, no. 7 (September 1989).

14. David Hershkovits, "Animal Liberation Strikes NYU," *Soho Weekly News,* March 22, 1979.

15. "An Open Letter," *Animals' Agenda,* vol. 5, no. 3 (May 1985): 3. At our invitation, the letter was also signed by three other prominent activists, Michael W. Fox, Holly Jensen, and Patty Mark.

16. Kieran Crowley, "Bomb Suspect Gets No Cut in Bail," *New York Post,* November 15, 1988.

17. Leslie Pardue, "Who Is Fran Trutt?" *Fairfield County Advocate,* November 21, 1988; see also Crowley, "Bomb Suspect Gets No Cut in Bail."

18. Pardue, "Who Is Fran Trutt?"

19. John Capsis, "Police, U.S. Surgical Implicated in Bomb Plot," *Westport News,* January 11, 1989.

20. John Capsis, "Trutt: Mead Gave Me $1200 to Buy the Bomb," *Westport News,* January 18, 1989; Editorial, "Clarifying U.S. Surgical Case," *Westport News,* January 19, 1989.

21. John Capsis, "'Trust Mead,' Trutt Told by Second Operative," *Westport News,* January 25, 1989; Denise Buffa, "Second Informant Revealed in U.S. Surgical Bomb Plot," *The Advocate,* January 27, 1989; Merritt Clifton, "Hello Mary Lou, Goodbye Trutt," *Animals' Agenda,* vol. 9, no. 4 (April 1989): 28.

22. Spira, "Forum."

23. Barclay Palmer, "Trutt OKs Plea Agreement," *The Advocate,* April 17, 1990.

24. Andrew Rowan, "Action and Reaction," *Animal Policy Report,* vol. 7, no. 2 (August 1993): 1.

25. *Washington Times,* September 25, 1991.

26. Temple Grandin, "Shackling, Hoisting Live Animals Is Cruel," *Meat and Poultry,* September 1987, p. 142.

27. See Temple Grandin's autobiography, *Emergence: Labeled Autistic* (Tunbridge Wells, Costello, 1986); Oliver Sacks, *An Anthropologist on Mars* (New York: Knopf, 1995). Sacks's essay on Grandin first appeared in the *New Yorker,* December 27, 1993, pp. 106–125.

28. Henry Spira, letter to Bruce Ingersoll, *Wall Street Journal,* August 17, 1994; "Memo of Conversation," USDA Inspector General's Office, August 10, 1994, obtained under Freedom of Information Act.

29. Henry Spira, letter to Shelby Yastrow, February 6, 1993.

30. Shelby Yastrow, letter to Simon Billenness, Franklin Research & Development, February 16, 1994; a shortened version of the statement appears in McDonald's 1993 annual report.

31. Karin Horgan, "Big Mac Takes a Big Step," *Vegetarian Times,* July 1994, p. 17.

32. "Big Step for the Big Mac," *Investing for a Better World,* April 15, 1994; Spira, "Less Meat, Less Misery," p. 42.

33. Henry Spira, "McDonald's and the Push for Standards," in *Strategies for Activists: From the Campaign Files of Henry Spira* (New York: Animal Rights International, privately circulated in 1996).

34. *McDonald's Corporation and McDonald's Restaurants Limited v. Steel and Morris,* quoted from the McLibel Trial Web Page: http://www.mcspotlight.org.

35. Robert Lawrence, videotaped interview with John Swindells, Baltimore, November 1996.

NOTES TO CHAPTER 6

1. Barnaby Feder, videotaped interview with John Swindells, Chicago, November 1996.

2. The ten points that follow draw on Henry Spira, "Fighting for Animal Rights: Issues and Strategies," in Harlan B. Miller and William H. Williams, eds., *Ethics and Animals* (Clifton, NJ: Humana Press, 1983), pp. 373–377, and Henry Spira, *Strategies for Activists: From the Campaign Files of Henry Spira* (New York: Animal Rights International, privately circulated in 1996), esp. p. 3.

3. "Singer Speaks with Spira," *Animal Liberation,* January–March 1989, p. 5.

4. Ibid., p. 6.

5. Susan Fowler, videotaped interview with author, New York, December 1996.

6. "Singer Speaks with Spira," p. 5.

7. With a lot of help from others, especially John Swindells, who became co-producer and director, the video was eventually transformed into *Henry: One Man's Way,* a documentary shown on SBS-TV, Australia, on August 22, 1997. The video is available in the United States through Bullfrog Films, Oley, PA (1-8 00-543-3674).

8. Joan Zacharias, "The Satya Interview: Making a Difference: An Interview with Henry Spira," *Satya,* July 1995, p. 9.

9. Henry is referring to the following passage from Barnaby Feder, "Pressuring Perdue," *New York Times Magazine,* November 26, 1989, p. 72: "When asked what his epitaph should be, he ponders and suggests, 'He pushed the peanut forward.'"

Index

About the Author

Peter Singer is the author of *Animal Liberation,* the book often credited with starting the modern animal rights movement. His other books include *Democracy and Disobedience, Practical Ethics, The Expanding Circle, How Are We to Live?* and *Rethinking Life and Death.* He was born in Melbourne, Australia, in 1946, and studied history and philosophy at the University of Melbourne and philosophy at the University of Oxford. Currently a professor in the Centre for Human Bioethics at Monash University in Australia, he has also taught at Oxford University, New York University, University of Colorado, and La Trobe University. In 1999 he will take up the DeCamp Professorship of Bioethics at Princeton University. Professor Singer has been involved in the animal liberation movement since 1971, and is now president of The Great Ape Project and of Animals Australia, as well as being coordinator (with Henry Spira) of the International Coalition for Farm Animals. He is married and has three daughters.